Hartford Public Library
500 Main Street
Hartford, CT 06103-3075

RAISE more MONEY

THE BEST OF THE GRASSROOTS FUNDRAISING JOURNAL

D1308663

Edited by Kim Klein and Stephanie Roth

GFJ Publications
Oakland, CA

SHELLS AND MONEY

The image on our cover is of a sand dollar, an ocean animal related to the star fish. Its dried skeleton, often found on the beach after high tide, looks like a large, white coin.

The cowrie — the shell of a mollusk that was widely available in the shallow waters of the Pacific and Indian oceans — was one of the most widely used forms of early money, beginning around 1200 BCE. Large numbers of money cowries, often tied together in strings, were found in early Chinese tomb sites. The Chinese character for "money" originally represented a cowrie shell, and the first coins included cast bronze imitations of cowries. In parts of Africa cowries were used as money as recently as the middle of the 20th century.

Money was originally used both for non-economic purposes — as tribute, for ceremonial and religious rites, and for ostentatious ornamentation — as well as for barter, trade, and as a form of reparation as in blood-money and bride-money (to compensate a family for the loss of a daughter's services).

Among Native Americans, the best known form of money was wampum, made out of the shells of a type of clam that was popular for ornamentation. Wampum came to be used extensively for trade by the colonists as well as the natives. Some tribes, such as the Narragansetts, specialized in manufacturing wampum by drilling holes in the shells so that the beads could be strung together. When the spread of steel drills enabled unskilled workers, including the colonists themselves, to increase the supply of wampum a hundredfold, its value massively decreased.

Copyright 2001 by Kim Klein and Stephanie Roth

All rights reserved. No part of this book may be reproduced or transmitted in any form or by any means, electronic or mechanical, including photocopying, recording or by any information storage and retrieval system, without permission in writing from the publisher.

Library of Congress Catalog Card Number: 2001091805

ISBN 1-890759-10-4

Cover and book design by Cici Kinsman, C² Graphics, Oakland, CA
Editing by Nancy Adess
Illustrations by Lisa Krieshok
Printed in the United States of America
Printed on recycled paper with soy ink

GFJ Publications, an imprint of Chardon Press
3781 Broadway
Oakland, California 94611
www.chardonpress.com

10 9 8 7 6 5 4 3 2 1

Contents

Organizational and Board Development

Fundraising as a Profession

About the Authors

Index

Preface

Fellow fundraiser Lisa Honig and I started publishing the *Grassroots Fundraising Journal* in 1981 to help grassroots organizations raise more money. Since then, the *Journal* has been in continuous publication, now reaching more than 10,000 readers with six issues each year. Several years ago Lisa left fundraising to become a public interest lawyer. In 1993, Stephanie Roth joined as co-publisher. In celebration of the *Journal*'s 20th anniversary, we have compiled this anthology of 56 articles that we feel reflect some of the best articles that have appeared in the magazine.

This anthology has been both the most fun and the most difficult book I have ever worked on. It was fun because I reconnected with many people I hadn't been in touch with for years, because I was reminded of ways fundraising has changed and ways it has stayed the same over twenty years, and because so many great people were involved in putting this anthology together.

It was difficult because it is hard to take some 300 articles and narrow them down to the 56 you see here. We had to define what we meant by "BEST." Some articles that were the best for the time they were written are now hopelessly out of date. Others still had helpful information but would not be useful without extensive rewriting. Should we publish material that might be nostalgic or quaint but not too helpful? Some articles had already been published in the *Grassroots Fundraising Journal* collections, *Getting Major Gifts* and *The Board of Directors*. Should we include those because they are good, even though a lot of readers already have those reprints? We couldn't track down two of the authors of articles we wanted to use. Should we use their articles anyway and hope the authors would be pleased if they found out? How should we balance all the topics we needed to include?

In the end, we dropped everything that would not be useful to a fundraiser today, authors brought their articles up to date with some serious rewriting, we did not use the articles from authors we could not find, we used only a couple of articles that had appeared in our other reprints because we really felt they were the BEST of the *Journal,* and we strove for balance among a variety of topics.

To begin the process, we asked readers for their favorite articles. Quite a few people responded and all of those articles are all included. Then Stephanie and I re-read all 300 articles and narrowed that group down to 110 for possible inclusion in this compendium. We then asked two colleagues who represent our target audience to name, from the 110, their top 50. These two people, Mike Perez and Priscilla Hung, have worked for both grassroots organizations and larger institutions, and they are full-time development professionals and social justice activists. Both are becoming fundraising trainers as well as practitioners. Mike Perez is the Development Associate for the Oblate School of Theology in San Antonio, TX. Priscilla Hung is co-editor of *Reversing the Flow: A Guide to Corporate Grantmaking in the Bay Area* (Chardon Press), and the Development Associate for the DataCenter. Both are graduates of the Intern and Training for Trainers Programs of the Grassroots Institute for Fundraising Training (GIFT). Between them, Mike and Priscilla narrowed our 110 to 60 articles. Stephanie and I made the final choices.

Nancy Adess, who has edited every article as it appeared in the *Journal,* reedited the articles for the anthology and put the collection into a manageable order. Nan Jessup did a superb job of shepherding the process through dozens of details without ever losing her composure. Cici Kinsman once again brought her excellent design skills to the project, and Stephanie oversaw the whole process.

We thank the 19 authors whose work appears here and the many authors whose work does not, but who have contributed so much to the *Journal* over all these years.

We hope you find this anthology useful. If you would like to appear in Volume II, which will be published in 2020, start writing now!

—KIM KLEIN

Principles &
Philosophy

Reflections on the Purpose, History, and Future of Philanthropy

By KIM KLEIN

Kim Klein gave the following plenary speech to the Institute on Philanthropy on November 11, 1999, as part of the Creating Change Conference sponsored by the National Gay and Lesbian Task Force.

The most important thing I have learned from 23 years of fundraising is to think big. "Imagination is more important than knowledge," said Einstein. I think all of us who work for justice stay in this work not because of what we know, but because of what we can imagine. We know we are oppressed, but we imagine that we could not be. In fact, I think the driving philosophy of most of us who have worked for social justice for many years was succinctly expressed by Che Guevara: "Be realistic. Do the impossible."

In this speech, I am going to be realistic. I am going to look at what our society should look like; then I will present a little about the history of philanthropy and close by telling you what I think this has to do with you and me today.

When I am asked to help a group with their fundraising, I start by asking what they intend to do and how much it is going to cost. We start with a goal: "We need to raise $100,000 in six months in order to do our organizing campaign or continue our outreach program or staff our hotline or whatever." After the goal, we specify a time frame, and we look at what fundraising strategies we are going to use, who our prospects are, and who is willing to help.

Likewise, I start here by reminding us of our overall goals. We are working for a particular kind of society. We have been so beleaguered since the election of Ronald Reagan in 1980 that we sometimes lose sight of what we are, what our goals are. I will be 46 next week. According to the actuarial tables, I am slated to live to be 92. I am going to describe the kind of society I want when I am 92. I would remind everyone that the society I outline exists in various ways in countries around the world, and some parts of it even existed in our country at one time.

It is a society in which the following things are universal, which means free and of high quality to anyone who wants them: health care; elementary, secondary, and college education; child care; public transportation, parks, swimming pools, libraries, and community centers. All of these are accessible to people with disabilities. When I am 92, clean air and clean water are the norm and the idea of polluting water is unthinkable. We have long since abandoned the notion that people are superior to animals and animals to plants, and instead we value wilderness and understand ourselves to be part of a larger ecosystem. We know from our past, but not our present, that the loss of any part of the ecosystem is a loss to the whole.

We have basic income levels: first, a guaranteed annual income to all adults, which is the minimum wage. The minimum wage is high enough to keep people out of poverty, so the percentage of people living in poverty is zero. This is a vast improvement from the 25% of people who live in poverty now. Second, each community has figured out an amount called the living wage, and the living wage is the minimum that employers are required to pay to employees. Finally, there is a maximum wage, which is never more than 20 times what the lowest-paid person earns. This is the most dramatic change from today, where CEOs of large corporations earn, on average, 491 times as much as their workers. (I am indebted to United for a Fair Economy for many of these ideas.)

The book of Exodus in the *Torah* describes this society this way: "The person who had much did not have too much and the person who had little did not have too little."

The society we work toward is characterized by a sincere affirmation that difference is good, and that one's gender, sexual orientation, or race is a source of pride, but not superiority. Children are safe and well fed. We are measured and valued by how well we love each other and how kind we are to one another, not by how much money we earn or how much money we have raised or how many votes we can influence.

Our military is small. Largely it consists of the National Guard, which is brought out during hurricanes and earthquakes. There is no market for weapons, and missiles are displayed in museums — the leftover products of a more primitive age.

There are many other components to this society — it respects age, people are involved in governing themselves, the nation as a whole tries to do what is best for each person and values each person as an individual. Every individual considers what they do in terms of what is good for the whole.

I spend time outlining this society because I believe that you must know where you are going in order to make plans to get there. If you don't have goals, then all your plans, your organizing, your advocating, your litigating, your fundraising have no real purpose.

WHERE PHILANTHROPY BEGAN

Now, I am going to step back from the society I want us to have by the time I am 92, and go back about 90 years to the period of 1900–1920. As is happening now at the turn of the 21st century, the turn of the 20th century saw vast amounts of wealth being accumulated by a few people. The number of millionaires in the United States increased from 100 in 1880 to 40,000 by 1916. I want to discuss three of these wealthy people: John D. Rockefeller, Andrew Carnegie, and Henry Ford.

I find these men remarkable. I hope most of us are familiar enough with history to know that they were also remarkably ruthless. Many of their actions can only be described as evil. However, they were also complicated men and the institutions they endowed have had a profound influence on all of us. I think knowing a little more about what they had in mind when they set up their foundations and charities might help us in conceptualizing the future of foundation philanthropy.

Let's start with John D. Rockefeller, Sr. In 1913, he was the wealthiest man in the world, with a personal fortune of some $900 million. He was a close friend of the man who has probably exerted the most influence on the structure of foundations of anyone — a man named Frederick Gates. Frederick Gates was a Baptist minister, a close friend of Rockefeller since 1889, when Rockefeller had committed $600,000 to the University of Chicago, which was founded as a Baptist college. Gates became Rockefeller's personal giving adviser.

Rockefeller wanted a more planned method for giving away money, and Gates conceptualized what was called "scientific benevolence." This marked a change for Rockefeller from giving to individuals who had needs to giving entirely to institutions and, over time, to institutions that he created. The Rockefeller Foundation, the earliest of the private foundations, was created in part because, while touring some of the mining towns he owned, Rockefeller felt the degree of poverty the miners lived in was so extreme that it could lead to revolution. To avoid a full-scale revolt would require ameliorating poverty. To do so, Gates and Rockefeller began what would become the Rockefeller Foundation. The desire to avoid revolution subconsciously informs much philanthropy today.

Rockefeller's contemporary, Andrew Carnegie, was also a self-made millionaire who held very different beliefs about wealth than did Rockefeller. ("Self-made," as my friend Naomi Brussel points out, is a misleading term, since he made the money from his workers. What we mean by "self-made" is that he didn't inherit money that someone else made off the workers.) Carnegie believed that wealthy people should give away all their money before they die, and that a hefty estate tax was the wisest tax. He said, "By taxing estates heavily at death, the state marks its condemnation of the selfish millionaire's unworthy life." He further says in his famous essay, "The Gospel of Wealth," "I would as soon leave my son a curse as the almighty dollar."

Beginning in 1881, Carnegie provided funds to establish libraries; by 1907 he had contributed more than $40 million toward more than 1,600 of them. In 1902, he sold his steel enterprises to J. P. Morgan for $300 million and started a series of foundations, some of which still exist.

Henry Ford, on the other hand, abhorred both charity and philanthropy. In 1914, he attempted to deal with his large wealth by creating an innovative profit-sharing plan for Ford Motor Company employees. He believed that everyone who worked for him should earn enough to be able to afford a Ford. Late in his life, he set up the Ford Foundation but didn't specify what the money would be used for. When he was asked what he thought about the ability of private philanthropy to adequately address social problems, he said, "They may do some good. Of course they are not adequate. But my idea is justice, not charity. I have little use for charity or philanthropy as such."

As you can see, these were complex individuals, but the most important thing to remember is that they reflected their time. They represented solid business thinking of their day.

As these and other less wealthy people began establishing foundations, people started asking whether private individuals should have so much influence on the way social services were provided, in effect controlling the destiny of the poor. This controversy came to a head with the Ludlow Massacre of 1914. United Mine Workers trying to unionize the workers at Rockefeller's Colorado Fuel and Iron Company were met with violent confrontation. A number of strikers were killed, the National Guard and federal troops were called in, and Rockefeller was strongly denounced by the UMW.

In response to the rising influence of wealthy industrialists, Congress created the Commission on Industrial Relations in 1915. Under the leadership of Congressman Frank Walsh, this citizens' commission took on the task of hearing testimony on the topic of "Centralization of Industrial Control and Operation of Philanthropic Foundations." The title of the investigation gives us an idea that Congress had questions about the relationship of the concentration of industrial power to the establishment of these new foundations. There was testimony both in favor and against the creation of foundations. The hearings resulted in an 11-volume, 11,000-page document. Its majority view was that foundations were a problem, but little could be done about them.

Barbara Howe, who has written widely about the early history of foundations, comments on the Walsh Commission, "Because of congressional ambivalence toward millionaires' foundations — which on the one hand fit well into popular models of rational social planning, but on the other hand were seen as symbols of continued paternalism on the part of exploitive capitalists — the creators of the American philanthropic foundation were unable to gain either explicit credibility or open praise for their new institution."

The outbreak of World War I overshadowed the public debate about the role of foundations and the problem they pose remains unresolved to this day. Anyone who is interested can read about how foundations have shaped higher education, research, the direction of social movements, health care, and so on. But it is important to note, as Robert Arnove says, that "Foundations and their staff represent neither retrograde reactionaries nor subversive radicals. Rather they represent a sophisticated conservatism, supporting changes that help maintain and make more efficient an international system of power and privilege. Their watchwords are efficiency, control, and planning."

WHERE PROGRESSIVE PHILANTHROPY FITS

What is the role of progressive philanthropy in all this? Starting in the mid-1970s, people who agreed with the criticisms leveled at traditional foundations asked a question of imagination: Can we do it differently? In response, they started their own foundations, beginning with the Bread and Roses Community Fund in Philadelphia, the now-defunct Youth Project in Washington, D.C., and in the late 1970s and early 1980s, the Funding Exchange and its member funds, the Astraea Foundation, the Peace Development Fund, and others.

These were people deeply troubled by our nation's involvement in Vietnam and not about to recommend that the government be in charge of anything. The slogan of the Funding Exchange could really describe the whole movement: "Change, Not Charity." These were people who believed that foundations could address the root causes of social problems. They sought to democratize private philanthropy. Their gains are extraordinary.

Community control of grantmaking — the extremely radical and previously unthinkable idea that grantees and activists would control how money was distributed — has become completely acceptable. Site visits by foundation staff and board are now common. The availability of published annual reports, grant guidelines, access to foundation staff and even to foundation donors are taken for granted. Some of us have forgotten to tell others of us who are too young to know, that these are profound, extraordinary cultural shifts in foundation philanthropy. The mid-1980s and the 1990s saw another major development in organized philanthropy, the creation of identity funds — women's foundations and queer foundations. Many of these share a progressive world view with their leftist counterparts; others do not.

Progressive and queer philanthropy have proven that foundations can be vehicles for serious, lasting social change. Can they stay that way? I believe they can only through relentless and constant self-examination, by the constant application of imagination, asking, "What is the cutting edge of philanthropy now? What is the next innovation that will make philanthropy a vehicle for lasting social change?"

CREATING THE FUTURE

I explored this lengthy history of foundations because most of us don't know it, and because it is important to remind ourselves that foundations have always caused people uneasiness. If they cease to make us uneasy — whether we are donors to them, as I am, recipients of grants from them, as I am, creators of them or staff for them, as I have been — the minute we feel good and peaceful about our progressive foundations is the minute we lose that very edge that made our progressive foundations important in the first place. I encourage all of you to learn more about the history of giving and receiving from the Bible, from the creation of our country, and from the excellent books written about it. Rooted in history, we may be able to create a new history and a new society.

When you look deeply into philanthropy, you see another hidden history in a story in the Christian testament. Jesus is standing in a synagogue and watching the people go in and out. Jesus watched rich people put large sums into the treasury. And then a poor widow came and put in two copper coins, the equivalent of a penny. Jesus commented on this, saying, "This widow put in more than all those who contributed because they contributed out of their abundance, but she, out of her poverty, put in everything she had."

The backdrop to all philanthropy is the philanthropy of the middle class, working class, and poor. Here in the United States, 82% of all the money given away comes from families with incomes of $60,000 and less. Seventy-one percent of taxpayers file a short form, meaning, among other things, that they receive no tax benefit for their giving. Yet seven out of ten adults give away money — in fact, more people give money than vote.

Who are these people? Some of them have public faces: Bill Gates, Ted Turner, the Packard Foundation. But the majority of them, contributing the majority of the money, are people who give because it is the right thing to do. They do not have disposable income. They give because they are asked. If their financial situation worsens and they must decrease their giving, as soon as their situation improves, they increase their giving.

It is for the sake of these people, the majority of givers, that I return to the society I wish to see in 40-some years. The world we desire to create cannot be brought about by private philanthropy alone. We who believe in the possibility of progressive social change must form an uneasy alliance with the government. For our own personal voluntary giving to have real impact, we must insist that our mandatory giving — our taxes — be used properly and collected fairly, and that the tax system itself be constructed progressively.

Warren Buffett, head of Berkshire Hathaway, Inc. and certainly one of the most successful men of our time, says that he finds it absurd that capital gains taxes are lower than income tax. When he sells a share of stock, he says, he pays a smaller percent in tax on his profit from that sale than a social worker helping someone stay off drugs pays on his income from his job.

Capital gains tax, estate tax and income tax are methods of redistribution of wealth. They are part of the solution to poverty. It is therefore ironic that few activists work for tax revision. Taxes offer an extraordinary organizing opportunity that we have largely ignored.

I want to suggest the following as necessary for moving from where we are to where we need to be:

1. Look at the word philanthropist. Either reclaim it, so that everyone who gives away money thinks of themselves as a philanthropist, or abandon it and stop using it at all to describe anything progressive or queer.

2. Focus on the subtext of my talk. All social justice requires an understanding of money — how it works, who has it, how it is taxed, how it is given away. Therefore, fundraising is central to program work, not ancillary, not supportive of, central to. Get rid of the barriers between program and fundraising.

3. Whatever your work is — hospice, litigation, teaching, writing, giving money, raising money — be clear about the context. Why are you doing this work? What do you hope to accomplish? We must walk a fine line between Reinhold Neibuhr's belief, "Nothing worth doing can be accomplished in our lifetime, therefore we must be saved by hope," and Rabbi Hillel's questions, "If not me, who? If not now, when?"

Sources:

Robert Arnove, ed. *Philanthropy and Cultural Imperialism.* Bloomington, IN: Indiana University Press, 1982.

Teresa Odendahl. *Charity Begins at Home: Generosity and Self-Interest among the Philanthropic Elite.* New York: Basic Books, 1990.

2000

Organizing and Fundraising:
Sisters in the Struggle

By VICKI QUATMANN

After 14 years of fundraising for a community organization in the mountains of east Tennessee, I have some observations to share about the ways that fundraising and organizing need to work more closely together to build people power.

From 1979 until 1993 I was the fundraiser for an Appalachian community organization called Save Our Cumberland Mountains, better known as SOCM (pronounced SOCK-EM). I had initially been hired to answer the phone and be available in the office as backup to six organizers who were busy outside the office, but fundraising tasks kept coming my way. Since I had come to SOCM because I wanted to be an organizer, I watched the work of the organizers closely.

Slowly, I learned the meaning of the word "organizing" and the intricacies of the strip mining and surface rights issues that SOCM was already famous for addressing during its short seven-year history. I learned that the job of an organizer is to make it possible for people to work together for what they believe in. It is about gaining control over decisions about new industries, jobs, landfills, strip mines, water, taxes, and schools that can make a life-and-death difference to the future of small rural communities. It is about making elected officials accountable to us, the taxpayers who pay their salaries.

Understanding organizing was intoxicating. It made sense to me — more sense than all my past years of summer volunteer work doing service to needy people through youth camps, cheese lines, and free day care.

I learned that a good organizer never does *for* the people she is working with; rather, she shows them how to do for themselves. A good organizer doesn't speak at the public hearing; rather, she helps those upset about the incoming strip mine to prepare their own testimony and practice their own speech. A good organizer is never found quoted in the press but rather sees to it that the press contacts the local people concerned about the strip mine and helps them prepare their own words for the media.

I learned that a good organizer lays out possibilities and challenges the people to try all the strategies that have been successful elsewhere in similar fights, and before the final strategies are chosen, backs away and lets those people directly affected by the promised strip mine decide how much they are willing to risk in their fight to stop it. Organizers don't tell people, they ask.

I saw organizers push people into taking action by refusing to do it themselves. I worked with organizers who knew that if they did it themselves, they would erode the very foundation of the people-power they were trying to build. I learned that an organizer has done a first-rate job when he is forgotten at the end of a successful legislative campaign and the members are proudly owning the victory, claiming they did it themselves.

Good organizing is about ownership. It's about providing people with the opportunity to become aware of their own capabilities and potential. In fact, a good organizer, if successful, turns each person she meets into a temporary organizer. Cesar Chavez, one of the great organizers of this century, said that people are infinitely more appreciative of what they do for you than what you do for them.

I saw that good organizers must be astute people-readers. They recognize the person who can "spare a little time" who is actually ready to give it all if only someone would ask them. They recognize when the moment is right to put someone to work, knowing that if they don't, they'll lose them for the cause. They are always looking for commitment. They want to grab that first spark of interest and give it a job. Then they move that person to more steady involvement — regular meetings, phone tree, help with research. Eventually, they move the person to the kind of commitment that can only be made with risk and total awareness, the kind that moves a person to speak out publicly on issues dividing their local community or take responsibility as chair of the local chapter or a position on the board.

When an organizer position came available on a campaign opposing the Department of Energy's irresponsible disposal of hazardous waste in the ground and streams surrounding Oak Ridge, Tennessee, I applied for it. As I worked on the campaign over the next two years, I learned an even deeper respect for what it takes to be a good organizer — strong commitment, sharp intelligence, bulldog persistence, an ability to work with people, and a sense of humor that keeps it all in balance.

Two years into my organizing job, the person who replaced me as fundraiser left on two weeks' notice, throwing my old job back into my lap along with the organizing. Our search for a new fundraiser dragged on and on. Though good organizing is every bit as difficult as good fundraising, there are hundreds of people who believe they can do the one and not the other. I chose to return to my old fundraising job with a renewed sense of purpose and insight into what I was supporting and SOCM hired another organizer.

TWO SIDES OF THE COIN

Along with the organizers, my job as the fundraiser was to be out there asking, asking, and asking some more — challenging the membership to greater commitment through their financial gifts; showing them how true ownership and control begin with owning the resources that power their own organization. I became excited about my part in the work. For the first time I proudly identified myself as a fundraiser.

One of my favorite sources of inspiration during my years of fundraising for SOCM was a little booklet titled *Axioms for Organizers* by Fred Ross, Sr. I read it often and simply substituted the word "fundraiser" for "organizer." Try it yourself. Substitute "fundraiser" for "organizer" in the section above where I speak about what I learned about good organizing.

As my years at SOCM fled by, SOCM celebrated it 10th, then its 15th and then its 20th anniversary. Each anniversary became the occasion for making stronger demands for support on SOCM's constituency. At the 10th, pledges per mile on an 1,800-mile canoe trip by one

of the senior staff set the occasion for the first serious big-dollar asks. At the 15th, we built a small "Can Do It Fund" to pay for corner-turner opportunities in the midst of rough campaigns. For our 20th, we established our first endowment, a "Year 2000 Fund," and solicited three-year pledges from every member of the organization.

As a fundraiser my job was to get a donor's first gift. We call it an impulse gift. Often the organizers got it in the form of the annual $10 dues. Then I set up opportunities that encouraged giving at other times during the year so that the new member donor might become a habitual giver. Finally, someone from the organization (myself or another staff member or another SOCM member) asked the member donor to give a significant gift, one that required risk and a serious level of commitment. (Does this sound like organizing?)

I dreamed of a whole army of member volunteers who might join in asking other members to make that step toward serious ownership through a significant gift to SOCM. The staff and I weren't a big enough asking force. Besides, a friend or a neighbor in the community who has made the same commitment is better heard, more respected.

I wanted people to give at a level that moved them away from saying, "You people at SOCM ought to…" to "We ought to…" I wanted them to feel, through their donations, that they were in charge, they owned and had real say over their organization. I dreamed of the day that the greatest part of SOCM's support would come from this membership and supporters, not from foundations.

I have taught fundraising to future organizers at the Southern Empowerment Project where I use an exercise describing a major paper company about to locate in an area that has been primarily dependent on tourism. The weak local chapter of an existing community organization has decided to fight location of the plant. I lay out, in detail, the geography, sociology, and politics and economics of the specific area that will be affected. Then I split the group into two. One half is to be organizers and plan the strategy for how to address this devastating intruder; the other half is to be fundraisers and decide how to raise the $20,000 that the first year's campaign efforts will cost.

Both times I've tried this exercise the organizer group has been amazed at the powerful potential that the fundraising plan has for broadening the constituency committed to the campaign. In fact, it has been generally true that the fundraising plan, more than the organizing plan, has incorporated the greater effort to broaden the commitment to a greater number of people. The organizing strategies tend to quickly become heavily focused on research and similar strategies that depend on a few skilled leaders.

All the skills used by good organizers are the very same skills used by good fundraisers. Both organizers and fundraisers must be sensitive people-observers. Both must be intensely aware of the potential activist's/donor's self-interests and how those interests mesh with the overall group's goals. Both must be willing to ask the potential activist/donor to make a commitment — of time and/or money — and to take a risk in trusting the integrity of the organization. Both must know how to inspire confidence, convey to the activists/donors that their contribution is extremely important and show regularly how that contribution is making an important difference.

INTEGRATING FUNDRAISING AND ORGANIZING

If good organizing is about deepening commitment, no aspect of the campaigns our organizations address will be more effectively served than by our good work to pay the costs. A strong base of constituent support that is giving at its capacity and helping to increase that support in an organized annual campaign is the most important ingredient in assuring our organizations' financial stability and long-term future. A big pool of donors is like a major savings account and organizational pension plan rolled into one — and far more reliable and predictable than any single foundation grant. The effort to build such a pool contributes more to the organizing mission of our organizations than a million-dollar grant from a foundation.

Why not have an equal number of fundraisers as we have organizers? Maybe we could partner each fundraiser with an organizer. Or, why not agree to train all organizers to be effective fundraisers and that there is no longer a distinction? The latter may be the tougher road. Changing old ways isn't easy. That leads me to another "why." Why do we let our organizers get away with claiming that they have no time to raise money in the midst of an intensely hot issue? We know we are kidding ourselves! There is always time for one more sentence with each person we are working with. "Will you give $___ to support this effort?" "This effort for this year will cost $___; how will you be helping to pay for it?" No time is better for raising the money that will cover the cost of a campaign than during the hottest moments of the fight! Organizers know that the time when an issue is most deeply felt is when they will get the greatest time commitments. It should be no surprise that the same holds true for fundraising.

It is time for our organizer training schools to teach organizers everything about fundraising and fundraisers everything about organizing, recognizing that the two are equally critical to the health and future of our grassroots social justice groups. It is time for all of us to stop departmentalizing and make fundraising an integral part of the everyday organizing work of each employee and leader of our organizations.

1994

Prospect Identification:

You Already Know All the People You Need to Know To Raise All the Money You Want to Raise

By KIM KLEIN

The title of this article is taken from a phrase I often use in my fundraising trainings. It meets with skepticism, denial, laughter, incredulity, and occasionally two reactions that mark people who might actually go somewhere in fundraising: horror and relief. It is obvious why relief would be a great reaction to have to the idea that you already know the people you need to know, but why horror? People who are horrified by this notion realize that their best prop has just been knocked down; the excuse that worked when all others failed has just failed. If they already know who they need to know, what is stopping them? How can they not raise money? Their horror is that they have been found out. But many of them recover from horror and go on to raise money.

What does it mean that you know who you need to know in order to raise the money you want to raise? Simply this: As we point out every year, and sometimes more often, the most money given away in the U. S. comes from middle-income, working-class, and poor families. This happens to be most people. Most people give away most money. This is good news. Imagine if most money were given away by corporations — we would have even more elite universities, a handful of well-funded arts groups, and a lot of funding going to research, scholarships, and cause-related themes. If, similarly, most money were given away by foundations, we would again have a much smaller landscape of nonprofits, with a much greater focus on large organizations. The concept of grassroots fundraising and, consequently, grassroots groups would not exist.

We have a diverse, creative, and extraordinary group of nonprofits because we have a diverse, creative, and wonderful population of people who give away money.

In 1995, however, an ominous trend in grassroots giving was tracked and analyzed by the research wing of Independent Sector, a coalition of nonprofit organizations that provides research and advocacy on behalf of the nonprofit sector. Virginia Hodgkinson, vice president of research at Independent Sector, reported that the 68 million households that had made donations in 1995 was 4 million fewer households than had given in 1993, a drop of nearly 5%. Part of this loss was attributed to who was asked for money. The survey reported that only 60% of Americans were asked to contribute to nonprofit organizations in 1995, down 17% from 1994. Clearly, millions of people who would give are not being asked!

WHY AREN'T PEOPLE BEING ASKED TO GIVE?

Nonprofits have themselves caused the problem of people not being asked to give: They focus on the wealthiest potential donors and often pass over lower-income or middle-income households. "If they are targeting more affluent households, they are losing other participants in society," commented Hodgkinson.

Now, one of my own areas of promotion as a fundraiser and trainer is major gifts — how to find them and how to get them. As a consequence, I feel some responsibility when I read a study like this. But perhaps my full message has not been heeded, as I always stress that even your biggest gifts may not come from your wealthiest donors. Giving and having are often unrelated. Havers have. That's why we call them "the haves." Even some very poor people are "haves." What little they have, they hang onto. Some very wealthy people are also "haves." They hang onto the great deal that they have, and they try to have more.

In fundraising, we must focus on givers. Since most people give when asked and, as corollary studies show, do not give when not asked, we must increase the number of people we are asking.

This brings us to the logical question: Who are we missing? One answer is suggested by Independent Sector's research. They identify the "underasked" as young people and people of color. Furthermore, they find that when these "underasked" are asked, 78% respond. This is a higher percentage than the percentage of givers thought to be in the population at large (about 70%). Since giving and volunteering are habits often developed when young, if we continue to underask young people, we can expect a continuing decline in contributions in the future.

REVERSING THE TREND

How can we make sure to reverse this trend of focusing our asking on affluent households and not asking millions of people who might give?

First, start your fundraising with people you know. Don't focus on posh neighborhoods or major donors to other groups, or act from rumors about how many millionaires are setting up family foundations.

I was recently with a wonderful organization in Oregon that had been grappling with this issue for more than a year. A member of the fundraising committee had carefully researched and compiled a list of business people in town who gave money to various causes. It numbered about 200. Here's an example of her excellent research (with names changed):

- Joe Smith, owner of three hardware franchises, chair of Rotary and active in the Chamber of Commerce. Gifts include $300 to his child's school foundation, $250 plus hardware to a homeless shelter in town, $500 to his alma mater.
- Mary Jones, vice president of a local bank, active in her church and in Rotary, $500 to a battered women's program, $500 to the local symphony orchestra, and a large amount (exact amount unobtainable) to Habitat for Humanity's building program through her church.

And so on, for all 200 names.

All this research had taken about a year to complete. The volunteer who had done it had pored over program books, newsletters, social pages of the newspaper. All of the information was derived from public sources. Once the research was completed, the committee had decided to approach each person on the list individually and divided up the names among themselves. Of the 200

names, 25 were people known to one or more committee members, and those people were asked. Half gave and half declined to give. Those who had given had been asked for introductions to others on the list, yielding introductions to about 20 more on the list.

The remaining people, whom no one on the committee knew personally, did not get asked, despite the committee's intentions and various deadlines set for themselves. In fact, five committee meetings had transpired at which the names were divided up and assigned or reassigned, only to be followed by another meeting at which members reported that for the most part these prospects weren't being approached. This process went on for a full year, so that two years had been devoted to this project — one for the research and one for the follow-up, or lack of it.

In frustration, the group asked me what they should do to motivate themselves to approach the rest of the names on the list. The volunteer who had done the research was understandably peeved that so little had been done with her efforts, although she too admitted that she had not approached any of her designated prospects.

I told the committee something they probably knew in their hearts already: They should give up approaching people they don't know. Nevertheless, the research will be helpful as they are bound eventually to meet some of these people through their known contacts. In the meantime, I suggested, each committee member should make a list of 15 people they know and ask these people for donations. I saw looks of relief on many faces: "It would be a lot faster for me to ask people I know," said one young woman. And another added, "If I ask ten friends and only get $20 each, I'll still have more than I was able to raise from one of these contacts." Then the horror chorus started: "But these are the most prestigious people in town. These are the movers and shakers. We can't ignore them." I pointed out that I wasn't suggesting ignoring them. "I am suggesting that you start with who you know; these are much more likely to be the movers and shakers for your group. Then you can see who these people know."

Finally, the chair suggested a compromise. All those who wanted to ask people they knew should compile a list of those people and bring it to the next meeting so that the group could ensure that no one was being asked more than once. Those who wanted to keep working from the list of 200 could do so. Of 13 committee members, 11 decided to ask people they knew and 2 decided to work the list. Ironically, the volunteer who did the original research was one of the 11 who decided to ask people she knew.

Six months later, 8 of the 11 people who agreed to ask people they knew had done so, resulting in 70 new gifts and $1,900 raised. The two who were plugging away on the original list had asked three more people and raised $750 from two of them. The other three members of the committee had compiled their lists but not quite gotten around to asking.

This is excellent progress.

STARTING WITH WHO YOU KNOW

When you start with people you know, start with the person you know best — yourself. Make a gift that feels good to you and then ask your friends for a gift in that range. Much time is lost trying to determine how much to ask people for. The most important thing is to have them feel good about their gift, should they choose to give. A person will feel good about the size of his or her gift if the gift is comparable to the gift given by their friend. Some people may give more and some may give less. You may feel comfortable asking people with considerably more resources for a gift larger than the one you gave, and you probably want to scale back your request when approaching people who have considerably less than you do. Using yourself as a benchmark will save a lot of time. Once a person has given, their gift becomes their own benchmark to start the process of asking for more.

If all of us involved in fundraising ask people we know, we probably won't leave out the millions of households that went unasked in 1995. However, if our circles of acquaintances are not diverse, we may have a large segment of potential supporters whom no one in our group knows and who don't get asked by us. Therefore, it behooves us to make sure that our boards of directors and our staff and volunteers represent the broadest range of demographic possibilities of our communities.

EXPANDING THE FUNDRAISING COMMITTEE

A final point: Make sure everyone in the organization knows how to raise money — staff, volunteers, board, everyone. Any time you notice the faintest enthusiasm about fundraising from a client, a staff person, the janitor of your building, or whomever, bring them on your fundraising committee.

Here is an example: A group was planning its 20th anniversary celebration. The committee was meeting at the home of a board member, whose 16-year-old daughter was eavesdropping on the committee meeting. At one point she piped up, "I have an idea for how you can raise even more money." Committee members smiled and her mother said, "Good — why don't you tell me later." Looking puzzled, the girl left the room. A few minutes later, one of the committee members passed the girl's bedroom on her way back from the bathroom. On a whim, she said, "What's your idea of how we can make more money?" The teenager said, "A lot of people coming to your event will have to hire baby-sitters. I can organize a group of my friends and offer free baby-sitting at the event, and people can contribute what they would have paid for sitters to the organization. It will be much more fun for the little kids and will let me and my friends help." This was a good idea that resulted in an extra $600 being given to the event, and a bunch of 16-year-olds whose ideas will not so easily be overlooked next time.

We have too much money to raise to be able to afford to lose even one household's giving, particularly over something so correctable as that they just needed to be asked.

1997

Common Mistakes in Building Relationships with Donors and How to Avoid Them

By STEPHANIE ROTH

The single biggest mistake people make in fundraising is not asking for money. As Millard Fuller, founder of Habitat for Humanity, says, "I have tried raising money by asking for it and by not asking for it, and I always got more by asking for it."

This article is about the next biggest mistake people make in fundraising: failure to understand that the process of building a base of loyal donors involves much more than asking for money. Because fundraising is all about building relationships, completing a successful ask is only the beginning. Let's look at five examples.

FIVE EXAMPLES

Did You Say Thank You?

An environmental organization has been successfully building a donor base through direct mail. Two years ago, they instituted an upgrade process with some of their most loyal donors. Those who had given by direct mail for three or more years were identified and board members contacted them by phone or visited them in person and asked them to increase their gift.

About half of the donors approached with a phone call or visit doubled their gifts. In addition, there was a much higher than average renewal rate from the donors who were approached with a personal letter.

This campaign failed, however, on the back end. Some people never received a thank-you note, and those that did received form letters, badly photocopied, stating, "Thank you for your recent gift of $ _____ . As required by the IRS, this letter verifies that you did not receive any goods or services for your gift, and therefore it is fully tax-deductible." The amount of the gift was written in, but no other personal note was added, and there was no acknowledgment of the relationship this donor had with the organization. Nothing indicated how much the gift was appreciated by the organization, or what it would mean for the organization's work.

The following year, the methods this group used to appeal to major donors were inconsistent — some were personal but many were not. Not surprisingly, the group found that many of the folks who had increased their gifts in the previous year did not renew at all.

WHAT SHOULD HAVE HAPPENED

Here a group organized itself to ask its current donors for bigger gifts, but then failed to respond adequately to the gifts it received. Any contribution that is made as a result of a personal approach, such as a phone call from someone the donor knows, a face-to-face meeting, or an ask at a house party where the donors are known to the host, needs to be acknowledged in writing soon after the gift comes in and in a personal way.

The acknowledgment could be done with a form letter if a handwritten note is added at the bottom of the letter; or it could be a handwritten letter from the person who conducted the solicitation. It could be a phone call from the person who made the ask in addition to a form thank-you letter from the office.

The acknowledgment process needs to be part of the whole concept of a major donor campaign. The message you want to communicate to the donor is not only that you appreciate their support, but that your relationship with them continues after they say yes and send in their money. Not only is this a far more respectful way to treat your donors, but they will be more likely to renew their gift in the years to come.

Hot and Cold

A community theater has worked carefully with its board of directors to increase board members' involvement in personal solicitations. As a measure of its success, three-quarters of the board members participate in the group's annual major donor campaign. Three years ago, one of the board members did all the right things in approaching an acquaintance for a major gift. She wrote a personal letter asking for a meeting, called to set up the meeting, and then made the request in person. She asked for $250; the donor agreed to give $200.

That was the first and last time this donor was ever approached personally for a gift. The board member who had gotten the gift left the board shortly after this solicitation was made. No one else in the organization knew this donor, and because a gift of $200 was not considered a major gift by others in the organization, they simply added the donor to the mailing list and sent her regular mailings. She now receives newsletters, invitations to buy tickets to their plays, and an annual fundraising appeal. She has only given one other gift to the organization, $100 in response to an end-of-year appeal.

WHAT SHOULD HAVE HAPPENED

When this board member left the organization, she should have been asked by the board chair or chair of the fundraising committee if she would be willing to continue asking the donors she knew for renewals once a year. Alternatively, she could have been invited to sit down with the executive director, development director, or another board member to review the list of people she had solicited over the time she had served. Those donors could have then been assigned to someone else who could call and begin to develop their own relationship.

If your major donor list gets so large that you don't have enough board members, staff members, or volunteers to keep up with personal contacts, consider holding a small reception once a year where major donors have an opportunity to meet in an intimate setting with board members and the executive and development directors. Don't begin a major donor program without the infrastructure in place to continue it.

I Don't Know You, But...

Joe, a staff member of a legal rights organization, also belongs to a pro-choice group, where he has met a donor who has been giving the group $1,000 annually for several years. Joe recommends to his executive director that this donor might be a prospect for their legal rights organization too. With this information, the executive director (who does not know the pro-choice donor) writes her a letter introducing the legal rights organization, then calls her to ask for a meeting to discuss a $1,000 donation. The prospect gives $100, and turns down the request for a meeting.

WHAT SHOULD HAVE HAPPENED

It never ceases to amaze me that, when it comes to questions of fundraising and money, any common sense a person might have in almost any other situation goes out the window. What makes us think we can approach someone we do not know (even on the recommendation of someone who does know them) and who has never given to our organization and ask them for a very large gift as their first-time gift? There might be situations where a new prospect could be asked for $1,000 the very first time. But too often, a decision about how much to ask is not based on any prior history or knowledge of how best to approach the prospect. Just because someone gives $1,000 to Organization A does not mean they are a prospect at that level for Organization B. Their gift amount to Organization A is not enough information on which to base a decision about how much Organization B should ask them for.

As you do prospect research, think about not just how much the person can give, but where they are in relation to your group. Even very wealthy people rarely start by giving $1,000. A starting gift for a person who can give $1,000 is usually closer to $100, and that is what this prospect should have been asked for.

I Give You My Word

The Children's Rights Network in a midsized city has developed a strong individual donor base over the past 12 years. They have grown from having fewer than 100 donors in 1988 to a donor list of 930, from raising approximately $6,000 in 1988 to a goal of $125,000 in 2000. They have upgraded many donors over the years through a combination of personal contact, handwritten and personalized thank-you notes, and annual requests for renewal gifts or upgrades.

Despite all this success, they are frustrated with one aspect — collecting the money promised by several of their major donors. One donor, for example, has pledged $1,000 each year for the past three years, but only paid $500 of the pledge the first year and $750 each of the second and third years. Every year, a board member who is a colleague of the donor asks again for $1,000, hoping that, one year, the donor will finally pay the amount promised.

WHAT SHOULD HAVE HAPPENED

When a donor pledges $1,000 to be paid out over the course of the year, instead of leaving the payment schedule up to chance, the organization should ask the donor to be more specific about when he would be able to make the payments — will there be two payments, one every six months, quarterly payments, or monthly? Does he want reminders? By phone, mail, or e-mail? If the donor agrees to a payment plan and still does not send in the money as promised, contact them by the method they prefer and ask if there is a problem and any way you can be of help. If they still do not send in the money, or send in less than promised, the following year you can ask them to renew at the level they actually contributed — not what they said they would do — the previous year.

Some donors do not keep track of their giving and need to be reminded, sometimes more than once. Others would like to be more generous than they can afford to be, so they agree to a pledge that they won't be able to fulfill. There will always be a percentage of donors (usually less than 5%) who can't bring themselves to say no, but because their answer really is no, they will commit to something they won't, in fact, ever do.

Love 'Em and Leave 'Em

A board member left after serving his term of three years. Although during that time he had donated $500 a year to the organization, once he left he was never approached personally for a gift. He remained on the mailing list and continued to receive direct mail appeals and newsletters, but no one bothered to call him and ask him to renew his gift personally. As a result, he did not give at all and, after two years, was dropped from the mailing list altogether.

WHAT SHOULD HAVE HAPPENED

Former board members and volunteers who have given their most precious resource — their time — and often significant gifts of their money, need to be treated like major donors and dealt with personally. This man should have been called by the chair of the board or someone from the fundraising committee and asked to renew his gift. He should have been invited to a reception or board get-together and shown that his contribution was appreciated.

FACELESS FONTS OF FUNDS

All of these scenarios point to symptoms of a common problem: treating donors as nameless, faceless numbers that add up to a line item on your budget or a projected outcome in your fundraising plan. These stories also reveal an inconsistent approach to developing relationships with donors, where one day a prospect is approached with the utmost care and respect and then, after making a gift, never hears from anyone in the organization again in a personal way. Shortchanging this constituency of your organization translates into losses on three levels — personal contact, public relations, and advocacy.

- **Personal Contact:** Donors may begin to feel less connected to your organization, losing a sense of how they fit into the work you do beyond providing financial support. Even if providing financial support is all they expect to do, going from being more personal to less personal in your approaches to them over time will leave them wondering how much you need their gifts.

- **Public Relations:** In addition to financial support, donors serve a public relations purpose for your work. They talk to their friends, family, and colleagues about you. They may join advocacy efforts you engage in. If they feel excited about what you do and connected to it in some way, they can play an important role in spreading the word about your work. They may even bring in new donors. Conversely, if they bad-mouth you because they don't feel they've been treated respectfully, they may discourage other donors or potential donors to your organization.

- **Advocacy:** As much as members, clients, consumers, board members, or volunteers, donors are a part of an organization's constituency. By keeping them completely separate from the rest of your work, you lose a group of people who could possibly be mobilized to take action on an issue requiring evidence of community concern and involvement. This is where the connection between fundraising and program activities is most commonly lost.

Organizations certainly face many challenges in their fundraising efforts, including lack of adequate resources and experienced fundraising staff, along with the frequent reluctance of board members to participate in fundraising. However, many problems, including those described in the scenarios above, have fairly simple and straightforward remedies. What may seem like insignificant details or time-consuming steps that you can't afford often make the difference between a thriving and growing fundraising program and one that stays at the same level year after year, or even declines.

Your donors are people who have the potential to give far more than money. They can give their time as volunteers or board members, they can encourage others to become donors, and they give credibility to your work as part of a growing group of people who support you. However, like any other relationship, they require some attention, some thought, and some common sense to help make the relationship as strong and meaningful as possible.

Ten Mistakes You Can Avoid

By KIM KLEIN

I was recently asked to give a talk at the annual conference of the Women's Funding Network. I decided to share with the group the ten biggest mistakes I have made during my seventeen years of fundraising. This article is taken from that talk.

One of the most important lessons to remember in teaching is that people learn as much (and sometimes more) from your mistakes as from your successes. In my workshops I have always tried to share mistakes that I have made or that I have been a party to, but this is the first time I have tried to prioritize them into the top ten.

My challenge to you is to avoid these mistakes — of course, you will make mistakes, but try to make new mistakes. Invent whole new categories and themes of mistakes. There is something sad and banal about making mistakes that someone else has already made.

THE TOP TEN

When I say these are the top ten mistakes I have made, I don't mean that they are the worst mistakes I have made or the most disastrous, but the ones I made the most frequently and the ones that are the most avoidable by others.

So, in no particular order, here they are.

1. Looking for money in all the wrong places

By now I hope you know that 90% of all the money given away in the United States comes from individuals, and that 82% of that money comes from families that have incomes of $60,000 or less. Even knowing these facts, I spent the first few years of my fundraising life trying to raise money from foundations, corporations, and people who were rumored to "have money." Once I finally realized the obvious implication of the fact that if the majority of money is given by middle-class people, the majority of my efforts should be focused on this group, I began to really raise money.

2. Asking people for gifts of $500 and more who had not been properly qualified as "prospects"

For many years after ceasing to repeat mistake #1, I adopted this mistake. I would hear or read that someone gave $500 to the symphony and immediately think the person was a prospect for a group working on rent control or a civil rights initiative. After all, I knew they gave money, so I wasn't falling into the trap of looking for people who "have" money. I knew how much they gave, and I knew their name.

But this is not enough. To be a prospect for a major gift, a person has to have demonstrated *ability* to give money. They also must have demonstrated a *belief* in the cause for which you are fundraising or in a similar cause. Even though people who give money to symphonies might be sympathetic to rent control, there is no inherent reason to think that will be so.

Finally, someone in the group needs to know about the prospect or know someone who knows them. Once you have positive verifiable information that someone you know or know of gives money and *cares* about your cause or a similar cause, you have a prospect. If you are missing any of those things, you don't have a prospect.

If you ask someone for money who is not properly qualified as a prospect, you greatly increase your chances of getting turned down, and you can give the prospect the impression that your organization really doesn't know what it is doing.

In learning to overcome this mistake, I was most helped by the Buddhist saying, "We have so little time, we must proceed very slowly." Take the time necessary to qualify people, to find out what you need to know to be confident of their interest in the cause, and to assign the solicitation to someone who has enough of a relationship with the prospect to be able to set up a meeting.

3. Seeing donors as water faucets: turning them on when I want money, and leaving them off otherwise

In the last ten years, many of the organizations I have worked with have had "building an endowment" as part of their long-range dream. An endowment is a good idea: a glorified savings account that yields a certain amount of money year in and year out.

However, keep in mind that your donors are already an endowment: a group of people who, if treated properly, will also yield a certain amount of money year in and year out.

In this light, you can see why building relationships

with donors becomes of paramount importance. Some of these relationships will happen naturally. You and the donor will like each other and become friends. Some of these relationships already exist among board members, volunteers, and people on the donor list. Others take more work. Ask yourself if the donor would make a good board candidate or a good committee member.

If neither of these options works out, at least write or call each major donor two or three times a year without asking them for money. Send them information you think they would find interesting or call to invite them to an event the group is putting on or just to tell them something about your group. Call to thank them for their gift and chat briefly. The relationship does not have to have a great deal of depth, but my mistake early on was focusing only on my need to raise money and only seeing the donor as a vehicle to meet that need.

If you have hundreds or thousands of donors, you can't possibly know them all, but you can make sure that your most loyal donors are contacted occasionally.

4. Not asking for money

A classic mistake is to do everything right — identify the prospect, set up the meeting, have an interesting conversation, and know that the prospect is very enthusiastic about your group — and then lose your nerve. I sometimes ended solicitations with "Well, thanks for your time and we'll be in touch," or even the more pitiful, "Whatever you can do, we will be most grateful." I am sure the prospects felt as frustrated as I did by my lack of direction.

A variation on this mistake is to strike up a conversation, learn that the person is very interested in your group, offer to send more information and be in touch, and then not do it. You might lose the address, or decide on reflection that the person was just being polite, or that a pressing grant deadline takes priority. By the time you can get to following up, you decide it is too late.

Dozens and dozens of gifts vaporized for me during the years I made this mistake (which I occasionally still make).

Avoiding this mistake requires a daily commitment to introduce money into as many conversations as possible. It requires keeping in mind that people are paying groups I work for to do work they want to see happen: ending racism, stopping pollution, reforming health care, or whatever. People want to help; my job is to facilitate that desire and suggest that making a donation is a concrete and very helpful thing to do.

It is also critical to remember that people who are interested in your group are puzzled when you don't bring up money; they are left feeling you must not need it or you would have mentioned it.

5. Using war-like language to describe asking for money

We constantly hear phrases such as "hitting up donors," "twisting their arms," "sitting on them," making them "cough up," "going for the jugular," "twisting the knife," getting the donor to "pop," and so on.

This kind of language dehumanizes both the solicitor and the donor. It puts the solicitor into an aggressive mode and makes getting the gift an act of winning or losing. I've made a lot more friends and had a lot more fun and, not coincidentally, raised a lot more money since abandoning that language (and, therefore, that attitude).

6. Exaggerating the importance of any one interaction

I have spent thousands of pointless hours, often in the middle of the night, replaying an interaction with a prospect or a donor in which I felt I made a monumental faux pas, irreparably damaging our relationship and destroying the organization's chances of ever getting money again. With each replay in my mind, my bungle becomes more embarrassing.

These incredible gaffes would be something like the following: I see the donor at an event with her new baby and say, "What a cute baby." Later at home I deride myself with, "How true, how stupid. 'Cute.' What a vapid word. Couldn't I have said something more meaningful about the child?" Or I say to a donor, "Could you double your gift?" and when the donor says, "I don't think so…possibly. Let me think about it," I respond, "It would be really great if you could. You don't have to give it all at once, but you can pay it out in a pledge." I end the conversation agreeing to talk in a few days, but later at home I scold myself with, "I shouldn't have been so pushy. Now she thinks our group is greedy," or "I should have pushed harder. Now she thinks our group is wimpy." Torturing myself with both scenarios could keep me awake for several hours.

The worst was when a donor actually complained about something. "Kim, there were three typos in the newsletter — it looks sloppy." I apologized and later believed absolutely that this person would never give another donation.

Obviously all of this self-rebuke reflected a lack of confidence in myself, but it also reflected the fact that I was giving way too much importance to interactions that were in themselves not important. Certainly the donors were not staying awake playing our conversations over and over and looking for hidden meanings in my comments. People who complained were usually trying to be helpful.

I got over this mistake by lowering my sense of my own importance.

7. Being afraid to disagree with donors

Similar to #6 was an idea I carried that donors should not be contradicted or they may not give again. In fact, donors, like the rest of us, are interested in issues and learn by debating, discussing, and being presented with new information.

Mistakes #5 through #7 were all part of a large mistake of seeing the donor as separate from me. However, I am always a donor myself to the groups I work for and believe in, and all my friends are people who give away some money to some groups. The distinctions I was drawing were false and misleading. Would I feel free to disagree with a friend or a colleague? Certainly. Would I tell a volunteer or board member if I thought their idea might not work? Of course. Real relationships are built on the ability to have honest dialogue among all the parties.

8. Knowing it was easier to do it myself and being certain I could do it better

This perception is often not a mistake. Most often I did know best how to get a fundraising task done. But when I was the only one who knew how to do something, I always had to do it whether I wanted to or not or whether I had the time to do it or not. Not only did I make myself indispensable, a liability to my group (what if I got hit by a truck?), but I also kept my group from growing and advancing by not empowering others with fundraising skills and knowledge.

So, I learned to be a trainer and to train others to raise money. The training, writing, and consulting I have done have been my most important contribution to the non-profit sector, with far more lasting results than the money I have raised myself.

I have avoided the "do it myself" trap for many years by adapting the first rule of organizing to fundraising, "Never do anything for someone that they can do for themselves." Good fundraising involves a lot of people doing the asking and feeling comfortable with the process, and a critical piece of fundraising is training others.

9. Not holding people to the commitments they made

I used to think that if someone said they would do something, they would do it. If they didn't do it, I saw it as a sign that they were not serious about the work. In fact, this is not true even of me. I commit to things, then forget to do them, or keep moving them from one to-do list to another and never get around to doing them until someone calls me.

My friend Sharon Delugach, who is a fundraiser and organizer in Los Angeles, always says, "Fundraising is 10% perspiration and 90% follow-up. When people say they will do something, assume they will; if they don't, assume they just forgot." Now I follow up with people on what they said they'd do, and most people honor their commitments most of the time.

10. Letting lack of knowledge stop me from trying new things

Many people have asked me questions over the years about grassroots organizations' ability to fundraise. Can a small group have a planned giving program? How do you raise money from a constituency that consists in large part of people on welfare? How can gay and lesbian groups raise money from straight people? What, if anything, is different about raising money if you are a person using a wheelchair?

I didn't know the answers to these questions, and I would venture to say that no one did. People had their own ideas and their own experiences, but a lot of work in raising money for grassroots organizations was speculative.

If we had waited for articles to be published or studies to be done, we would be long out of business. How do you find out if a small group can do a planned giving program? By setting one up, or preferably by setting up several and monitoring them.

The Center for Third World Organizing has this motto, "We will find a path, or make one." If knowledge doesn't exist now, create it. Experiment. Value your own experience, and know that your experience is knowledge: not all knowledge, but it adds to the existing information.

WHAT I DID RIGHT

Of all the many mistakes I made, I did always do something right, which has helped me in learning from my mistakes and avoiding many others I might have made. That was always to give money myself and come back to my own experience of being a donor. Even when my biggest gift was $100 or $50, I still knew the feeling of sitting down and deciding how much I could afford to give.

I have always given away 10% of my income, and in some high-income years, more than that. This has probably helped me more than anything else to ask others to give. I am always asking people to join me in making a commitment, and any issues I need to think through before making a gift were useful in anticipating what other people might say.

The final thing about mistakes is to feel fine about making them. They add to the body of knowledge about fundraising. Don't be careless and thoughtless, but when you do make a mistake, move on. Learn from it and decide not to make it again.

1994

The Thank-You Note

By KIM KLEIN

In 1977 a woman sent $25 to an advocacy group working on women's health issues. The organization was run collectively by 2 utterly overworked and underpaid staff and 40 volunteers. They had won recognition for their work exposing the dangers of the Dalkon Shield IUD and championing reproductive rights issues. The donor did not receive a thank-you note for her gift. However, she did receive the group's newsletter and heard about the group from time to time.

A year after her gift, when she received a letter requesting a renewal, she threw it away. Some time later, she learned that a friend of hers was in the group. "That group sounds good," she told her friend, "but they don't even have it together enough to send thank-you notes for gifts. I can't imagine that they are really fiscally sound or that they use money properly."

Her friend defended the group, saying, "They do really good work. Maybe they should take time to thank people, but saying they don't use their money wisely is an unfair conclusion." The one-time donor replied, "It is fair. It is my only contact with them. They claim to want a broad base of support, yet they show no regard for their supporters. But since you are in the group, I'll give them something." She sent $15.

During the year between the donor's $25 gift and her $15 one, the group had hired me to be their fundraiser. I sent the donor a scrawled, three-line thank-you note:

> "Thanks for your gift of $15. It's a help financially and also a great morale boost. We'll keep in touch."

Two weeks later, the woman sent $1,500.

VALUING ALL GIFTS

Although I had been drilled from childhood about the propriety of sending thank-you notes, I never really believed they were worth much one way or the other until that lesson. After I met that donor, she told me she often sent relatively small gifts to groups she liked to see what they would do. If she sent $100 or more (a lot of money in 1977) most groups would thank her. But that would not tell her how much regard they had for smaller donors. "Most grassroots groups talk a good line about class and everyone being welcomed," she said, "but the only people they really care about are the program officers of foundations and wealthy donors."

As it turned out, this woman was very wealthy, but she wanted to give money only to groups that had proved they valued all gifts. I was flabbergasted that a sign of proof could be a three-line thank-you note, but for her it was better proof than a longer form letter with her name typed in.

Since then I have seen over and over that a simple, handwritten note or typed thank-you letter with a personal note as a postscript can do more to build donor loyalty than almost any other form of recognition. Unfortunately, thank-you notes tend to be the one thing that organizations are sloppy or even thoughtless about. They either don't send them, send them weeks too late, or, now endowed with computers, send form thank yous with the person's name inserted every few lines. These practices are unjustifiable. Sending thank-you notes too easily falls too low on people's work priority lists. They have to be placed at the top.

WHY PEOPLE LIKE THEM

It is not clear to me why people like thank-you notes so much, particularly when there is usually very little content in the note. Probably reasons vary. Like our wealthy, testing donor, some see them as a sign that the group knows what it is doing. Others may just like the attention. While psychologists may be able to figure out why people like to be appreciated, for fundraisers it is enough to know that it is true. Doing what donors like — as long as we stay inside the mission and goals of the organization — builds donor loyalty. A loyal donor is a giving donor, giving more and more every year.

DON'T DO AS I SAY

What about the donor who claims not to want a thank-you note, or the one who even more strongly states that thank yous are a waste of time and money?

The first type of donor, who claims not to want a thank-you, but doesn't seem emotional about it, should get one anyway. These are generally people who are genuinely trying to save groups time. You will have greater loyalty if you send a thank-you note anyway. When these donors say, "You really shouldn't have done that," or "That's really not necessary," they often mean, "Thank you for taking the time. I can't believe someone would be bothered to notice me."

The second style of donor, who actually resents thank-you notes, probably should be thanked in some way, but without using a thank-you note. Try calling to thank her or him instead of writing. If the person is close to the group, you can combine your call with another function, such as to remind them of a meeting: "I called to remind you about the meeting Wednesday at 7 P.M. at Marge's. By the way, thanks for your gift — we can really use it."

Overall, experience shows that, all else being equal, when you thank donors you keep them and when you don't you lose them. Of course, there will be exceptions to this rule, but it is almost impossible to figure out who really is an exception and who is just pretending to be, so thank everyone and save yourself the time you would have spent worrying about it.

DO IT NOW

How can you most efficiently thank your donors, and who should do it? Perhaps the most important rule about thanking donors is that no matter who is doing it — from the board chair to an office volunteer — gifts should be acknowledged *within two days of receipt,* a week at the outside. If possible, a person who knows the donor should sign the thank-you note.

If you are fundraising properly, you will have dozens of donations coming in from people you don't know. Volunteers and board members can send thank yous. It is actually a good way to get board members who are resistant to fundraising to do some, because the thank-you note is a part of fundraising.

Buy some nice note cards, or have some made with your logo on the front. Small cards have only a small amount of space on the inside, so you can take up the whole space with a few short sentences. That is much better than a lonely three-line thank you on a full sheet of stationary.

People should come to the office to write the notes; only the most loyal and trustworthy people should ever be allowed to write the notes at home. It is just too tempting to put them aside at home. Also, information about a person's gift, while not secret, is also not something you want sitting around someone's living room.

The only requirement for handwritten thank yous is legible handwriting. The format is simple:

> Thank you for your gift of $_____. We will put it right to work on (name your program or most recent issue). Gifts like yours are critical to our success, and we thank you very much.
>
> Sincerely,
> (Your name)
> Board member

If you know the person, follow the same format, but add something more personal: "Hope your cat, Fluffy, has recovered from her spaying." So that the donor can use the thank you as a tax receipt, add, "No goods or services were exchanged for your donation."

It may be that handwriting thank yous or handwriting all of them is impossible, especially when you get a lot of contributions, such as at year end, and volunteers aren't as available, or after a successful direct-mail appeal when you are swamped for a few days with responses.

Then you go to the next step, which is a word-processed letter. Put this on stationery and make it a little longer. Start the thank you several lines down the page, and use wide margins.

> Dear Freda,
> Thank you for your gift of $100. We have put it right to work on our shelter. As it turned out, your gift came at a particularly crucial moment, as our boiler had just given its last gasp. We were able to buy a refitted, good-as-new boiler for cash (saving us $), which we wouldn't have been able to do without your gift.
> I am hoping you will be able to come to our art auction next month. We have the works of some well-known local artists and will be featuring paintings and sculptures by some of the residents of the shelter. I enclose two complimentary tickets.
> Again, thank you so much! I look forward to staying in touch.

You will notice that the letter refers to a recent event (the boiler). This gives a sense of immediacy to the gift. If the organization had not used the money for the boiler, they could have still used the story, as follows:

> Your gift came the same day our boiler broke for the last time. I would have been really discouraged, but your contribution cheered me up. Fortunately, we were able to get a refitted, good-as-new boiler for much less than a new one would have cost.

The letter also invited the donor to an event. You do

not need to provide free tickets, nor do you need to be having an event. The point is to refer to things happening in your office every day. Give your donors some sense of your daily work. Even things that seem routine to you can be made to sound interesting.

For example:

Dear Ricardo,

We got a pile of mail today — bills, flyers, newsletters, and then, your gift of $50! Thank you! $50 goes a long way in this organization, and we are grateful for your support.

I just finished talking to a woman who used our educational flyer with her son. She said she had expected a miracle, and though of course that didn't happen, maybe something more long lasting did. Her son called the HelpLine. It's a start, and that's what we provide for people.

I hope you will feel free to drop by sometime. Though we are usually busy, we can always take a few minutes to say hello and show you around. I'll keep you posted on our progress.

Or,

Dear Annie Mae,

I just came in from an eviction hearing of one of our clients. I feel really good because we won, and we got some damages to boot! Then, going through the mail, I came to your gift of $25. Thanks! I feel like you are a part of this victory.

Or,

You wouldn't believe how many people came to our community meeting last night — more than 50! People are hopping mad about this incinerator proposal, and I am feeling confident that we may be able to defeat it and finally get the recycling bill passed. Your gift of $50 is going to go a long way in helping us with flyers and phone calls. Thanks for thinking of us at this time. You don't know what a great morale boost it is to receive gifts from supporters like you.

If you have a matching campaign or a goal for an annual campaign, then include that:

Your gift of $100 will be matched dollar for dollar. Your gift brought us to just under $2,000 raised in just two months!

Or,

Your gift of $75 took us over the $1,000 mark in our goal of $3,000. Thanks!

If you are a volunteer, mention that in your thank you:

Giving time to this organization is one of the high points of my week. I know we are making a difference, and I want you to know that your gift helps make that difference too.

THE FRIENDLY FORM LETTER

The least effective option for thank-you notes, but one you sometimes have to resort to, is the form letter. If you use a form letter, acknowledge that it is impersonal, but give some sense of the excitement that would lead you to use such a method.

Thank you for the recent gift. Please excuse the impersonal nature of this thank you — we are no less enthusiastic about your gift for not being able to write to each of our donors. The response to our call for help with sending medical supplies to El Salvador was both gratifying and overwhelming. We will send you a full report about this effort in a few weeks. Right now, we are packing up boxes of supplies — supplies you helped pay for. Thanks again!

CALL THEM WHAT YOU WILL, BUT THANK THEM

There are two common questions remaining about thank yous. One is, how do you address people you don't know? The choices are by first name only, by first and last names (Dear John Smith) or by title (Dear Mr. Smith). There is no clear right or wrong practice on this point and no way to avoid possibly offending someone. In general, you will probably offend the least amount of people by using titles, "Dear Mr." or "Dear Ms." Certainly, you could write to the person according to how they write to you. A letter signed, "Mrs. Alphonse Primavera" should be answered in kind. If there is ambiguity about whether a donor is a man or a woman, write "Dear Friend." If you live in a fairly laid back or not terribly formal place, you can use a first name, "Dear Terry" or "Dear Lynn."

Don't waste a lot of time worrying about this. Having received many thank yous that say, "Dear Mr. Klein," I know how offputting that can be, but it does not cause me to stop giving to that group. Anyone who will stop giving just because you (or anyone else) cannot tell from their name whether they are a male or a female, or whether they prefer to be called by their first name, last name, Mr., Ms., or Mrs. doesn't have much loyalty to your group.

The second question is, do all donors get a thank you? Yes. You have no idea how much a gift of $25 or $5 or $500 means to someone. You need to act as if you would like to get that amount or more again. You also don't know how people use getting a thank-you note to judge whether to continue giving to your organization, as with the donor at the beginning of this article. Why take a chance?

Do all donors get the same thank you? No, because the notes, if possible, are personalized. But people giving bigger gifts don't get bigger thank yous. If you have thousands of donors, you will not be able to write to them all personally, so sort out the ones you know and write to them. But make sure each donor gets something.

Keep up with thank-you notes as gifts come in. Each thank you is a link to the donor and you should see it as paving the way for the next gift.

1992

The Perennial Question of Clean and Dirty Money

By KIM KLEIN

I have received several phone calls and e-mails recently asking about a problem that surfaces at some point in the life of almost every organization. The problem was nicely laid out in the following e-mail:

> Dear Kim:
>
> My group is struggling with what I understand to be a perennial problem: dirty money. The questions are, Should we take dirty money and how do we decide? A corporation has offered us a large grant for operating expenses, but several people in our group have problems with this corporation because of the way they treat their workers (badly). On the other hand, we need the money and not many places give you money for operating expenses. What shall we do?

I thought *Journal* readers might be interested in my answer, which follows.

Dear Reader,

Your group has indeed stumbled upon the subject that has probably taken up more time in progressive groups than almost any other topic you could name. In fact, had some groups held a "dirty money discussion-a-thon" and sought pledges for each minute they spent discussing the very questions you raise, they would be handsomely endowed by now and could change their discussion to dirty and clean investment policies. However, you raise serious questions that are not easy to answer, which is why this debate is perennial.

I would like to divide your question into two parts and look at them both. The first part deals with the definitions of clean and dirty money; the second part deals with perceptions about the donor.

I don't subscribe to the idea that there is dirty money and clean money. Money is a tool. Similarly, a hammer is a tool. A hammer can be used to help build a house or to bludgeon someone to death, but we never talk about dirty and clean hammers. Because we don't credit hammers with power they don't have, we are able to see just what a hammer is and to separate the hammer itself from what it might be used to do. We need to get that kind of perspective on money. Money can be used wisely or squandered. It can be raised honestly or dishonestly. It can be earned, inherited, stolen, given, received, lost, found, and many combinations of all of these. It is not in itself dirty or clean.

If you let go of the idea of dirty and clean money, you can focus on the real questions in accepting money: How does it make you feel to accept money from a corporation whose labor practices you find appalling? And how does it make you look to others to accept this money? What will be the cost in goodwill, faith in your organization, or even actual money given to your organization, if you accept this money?

I have seen organizations answer these questions in various ways. The most sensible one was adopted by San Francisco's Coalition for the Medical Rights of Women in 1980 during a marathon discussion about accepting an offer of free printing from the Playboy Corporation. As many readers will remember, the Playboy Corporation has always been a strong supporter of civil liberties and reproductive rights groups, and used to offer to print stationery, envelopes, invitations, newsletters, and the like for nonprofit groups working for those causes. The group simply had to put "Printing donated by the Playboy Corporation" somewhere on the printed piece.

The Coalition (the first place I worked as a development director) had occasionally used Playboy for some of its printing, which was a big help financially, but many in the group had always felt greatly uneasy with the practice.

Because of this, and because we operated as a collective, we scheduled a discussion of whether to continue taking the free printing. We argued back and forth, with those in favor saying, "Playboy made their money off of women and we should get some." Those against argued that Playboy exploited women and promoted sexism and we would help them in their sex-for-money pursuit by taking their free printing. Late that night, after we had made and remade every argument several times, one person finally said, "I don't know whether it is right or wrong to take this money. All I know is that the idea of taking Playboy's money or their free printing makes me want to vomit." That was enough to end the discussion.

From then on, in questions about taking money, we applied the Vomit Test. If a person who was important to the organization — staff, board, volunteer, longtime friend — said, "Taking money from such-and-such place makes me want to vomit," then we wouldn't take it because that person and her continuing contributions to our group were more important than any money.

I have never found a more rational answer to the question, "How does it make us feel to accept money from a source whose practices we do not condone?"

The second question, "How does it make us look to the outside world to take this money?" is a more practical one. Sometimes a source of money will pass the Vomit Test, but fail this second test. For example, a board member of a tiny health center in rural New Mexico had a fraternity brother who was the vice-president of a large uranium mining operation. The mine is polluting the entire area around it with radioactive uranium tailings. Through his contact, the board member secured a grant from this mining corporation, which so outraged several major donors to this group that they stopped giving. The ensuing bad publicity and loss of donations was a major factor in the demise of that group the following year.

When an organization accepts money from a source that is controversial, it needs to think about how its other sources of money might react. Of course, others' reactions are sometimes hard to judge, but generally, people will be shocked or offended if an organization accepts money from a place or person whose work or reputation is perceived to be in conflict with the goals of the organization. So when a mining corporation whose irresponsible practices are causing serious health problems donates to a health center, it can be predicted to cause outrage. Had the donation gone to the public library, there might have been less outcry.

The other factor in accepting money from a controversial source is the amount of money relative to the budget of the organization, and what kind of recognition the source wants for their gift. Though this may have happened, I have never heard of an organization spending hours debating whether to accept a $25 donation from even the most foul corporation or from one of that corporation's employees, because that amount of money cannot buy any influence. Similarly, I rarely hear of an organization refusing to accept even a large gift from an individual who may have made their money from a horrible corporation, because the corporation will not receive any glory for that gift.

Sometimes an organization will accept money from a corporation if they do not have to publicize that gift, but refuse to accept it if they do. The hypocrisy of that position can be helpful to groups sorting out whether to take money or not. Ask yourself, "If this gift from this source were to be headline news in our local paper tomorrow, would we be happy or would we be nervous about the consequences?" If happy, take the money. If you would rather people didn't know about the gift, then don't.

The issue of clean and dirty money generally comes up in relation to corporations. Since corporations are only responsible for about 5% of all the money given away in the private sector, and only 11% of corporations give away any money at all, I think organizations are better off focusing their fundraising efforts on building a broad base of individual donors. Seeking corporate funds may not be a winning prospect, no matter how you look at it.

2000

Clean Up Your Language

By KIM KLEIN

A few weeks ago I was talking with the development director of a medium-sized organization with a budget of $500,000. He is reputed to be competent and efficient at his job. He is warm and friendly and I believe he probably is good at many parts of his work. However, he used language that I found offensive and degrading to the process of fundraising. Had he been the only person ever to use such language, I would not take the time to write an editorial about it. But I find that the language he used has crept into the vocabularies of a lot of fundraising professionals and even into the vocabulary of board members, activists, and grassroots staff people.

The offensive words and phrases are the following:

"We could hit him up for $1,000."

"Sure, she's got the money. Just stick the knife in a little further. Tell her some sob story. She'll cough up big time."

"I just kept pounding him with the facts until he surrendered. I got $200 out of him."

"We're in the foreplay phase; I'm working her up slowly and I hope she'll give big."

I am sure you get the idea. Fundraising is borrowing phrases from boxing, football, war, and, sometimes, seduction. But donors are not enemies or objects. They are not to be tricked out of their money or coerced or "seduced" into giving.

Some of these phrases are in common usage, such as,

"Hit her up for a gift." Some are more obviously offensive, such as, "Twist the knife." All reflect a hostile mentality that is demeaning for both the donors and the solicitors.

Asking for money for a worthy cause ought to be a dignified interaction between the parties involved. One party — the solicitor — presents the cause, answers questions, and asks for money. The other party — the prospect — gives or doesn't give. But no one is physically hurt or defeated or rejected by the outcome. No one else is "victorious" or "scoring." One person says what he or she wants and the other says what he or she is willing to do. It is simple and straightforward and, in the scheme of things, no big deal.

When I have challenged people on their language, many have said, "It's just a saying, it doesn't mean anything." I disagree. Language reflects how a person thinks and how they relate to other people. Hostile language in common usage, even if it "doesn't mean anything" at first, can create a hostile attitude where none previously existed.

So let's resolve to clean up our language. In doing so, we will return to the values that motivate us to do this work in the first place — compassion, respect for the rights and well-being of all living things, and the firm belief that the world can be a better place because of our work.

1993

Raising Money for Progressive Arts and Culture Organizations

By KIM KLEIN

I generally avoid discussions about what kind of issues are harder to raise money for than others because they go nowhere and they are usually started by people who feel sorry for themselves. What makes it harder or easier to raise money for an organization will depend on a host of factors besides the issue the organization is addressing. Location, age, being a program of a much larger group, whether the people involved have fundraising experience or not — these factors can all work for you or against you.

Nevertheless, there are challenges in being a progressive arts and culture organization that will drive the most optimistic person to the self-pity well from time to time. In this article we will look at what some of those challenges are and how to turn them to your advantage.

The first challenge is defining what a progressive arts and culture organization is. I believe it is an organization with one or more of the following attributes:

- It provides a venue and encouragement for the artistic expression of people outside the mainstream: prisoners, gang members, people with disabilities, students (especially in poor school districts), and the like. The artistic expression can be through music, literature, theater, dance, film, the visual arts, or various combinations of these.

- It promotes the art and culture of groups or types of people who are usually not represented in the mainstream or are represented inaccurately.

- It explores or seeks to expand the boundaries of art with experimental expression.

- It uses the arts to promote political analysis, through street theater, some kinds of graffiti, murals, political posters, or other artistic means.

- It brings artists and musicians into venues where people generally don't have access to art, such as prisons, mental hospitals, nursing homes, and home-less shelters. This can be done to entertain, politicize, educate, or empower.

Organizations that fit these descriptions have trouble raising money for a variety of reasons, chief among them their own failure to claim their importance. The saddest statements come from board members who say, "It's not like we save lives or really change things. I enjoy it, but sometimes it seems fluffy compared to other kinds of issues." A slight upgrade is the attempt to justify working in the arts like this: "When kids learn to read music, their math scores go up. Kids that get to act in plays will often learn to read better." Others see arts as a marketing mechanism: "Having people act out their experiences with landlords/the welfare office/the police helps them feel more powerful and makes organizing easier."

All of these justifications miss the message that arts and culture groups need to put forward: "Art is central to any kind of decent society. In the kind of society we are working toward, art will be accessible to everyone, whether as audience or creator or both." The fact that arts can be shown to raise test scores or improve self-esteem or bring people together in a unified movement is ancillary to the central tenet that art, in itself, by itself, is important. The fact that art can be used in a variety of settings and with almost any kind of people speaks to its extraordinary flexibility and the universality of its language.

The second difficulty arts and culture groups face is the image of arts as either the elitist purview of wealthy socialites or boring, stodgy, and irrelevant. Large mainstream arts groups and the media have unwittingly collaborated to promote this image. For example, in an article about the opening of the last symphony season, the *San Francisco Chronicle* spent three columns on the food and dress of members of the audience and one paragraph on the music. A literature teacher in a poor high school invited the curator of a large art museum to share slides of great art with his sophomore class. The curator talked for 40 minutes and showed ten slides. When the lights came up, all but one student was asleep. As the curator left, he told the teacher, "I didn't expect these students to be so well behaved."

CHANGING THE PICTURE

Between low self-image and vapid public image, it is no wonder that many arts and culture organizations have trouble raising money. What are the solutions? Here are six approaches to consider.

1. Veteran organizer Gary Delgado often counsels organizations to "reframe the debate." Ask the questions that you want to answer and answer them. For example, a group that teaches writing and theater to high school dropouts and young homeless people compiled their own list of the 100 greatest authors of the last two centuries. Rather than include the usual canon, they chose those authors they thought had something to say to their constituency. Then they asked each school in their district to compare this list to what their school was teaching. The list generated the media's interest, and the local paper published it as part of a story about the group. This organization had reframed the debate and provided its own answers.

2. Assume everyone who comes into your sphere is a potential donor. I have seen performance groups with one mailing list for people who attend performances but who have never been otherwise asked for money and a much smaller list of people who give money. If the organization has been supported by foundations, they may not have a list of donors at all. People who come to a performance, even if the performance is free, should be asked for money at intermission. They should be asked to sign up for the mailing list. Within a month of signing up on the mailing list, they should be asked for money by mail. If the performance is for children, the children should be sent home with an appeal. Once people have given, they should be asked to give again, then to give more, and then to give even more in a systematic and respectful way. Having an organized fundraising program is a big boost to actually raising money.

3. Practice cross-promotion. Small arts and culture groups should form alliances with each other so that a person can buy a season ticket that gives them admission to several different performances — music, theater, a lecture, a film. Every organization should have their own Web site but be linked to all similar groups and perhaps even share a secured area for receiving donations. They could also buy a full-page ad in the Sunday paper and advertise several different kinds of artistic and cultural experiences. This saves money and also begins the process of presenting a different definition of what the public generally thinks of as art.

4. Work with other organizations to promote the idea that new and emerging artists and cutting-edge art deserve government funding. This strategy, whose payoff will only be realized in the long term, is possibly the most important one. Taxpayers (almost everyone) need to understand more about how taxes work, how they should work, and what tax money goes to. For the arts to thrive and be accessible to the population at large will require subsidies from the government. The attacks on the National Endowment for the Arts in recent years and the failure of the public to defend this important cultural promoter reflect in part the lack of organizing arts and culture groups have done on issues of taxation. That the public can be organized around taxes is evident in right-wing organizing that convinces people that paying for a bloated military is good and paying for welfare is bad.

5. Help progressive foundations see the role that art and culture play in organizing and social justice work. When funders understand the relationship between art and organizing, then arts and culture will cease to be a sideline of other funding and become full-fledged programs. Progressive foundations can be helpful in promoting an overall agenda for arts and culture groups to more mainstream foundations that fund large, traditional arts organizations in part because they don't see enough examples of other kinds of art groups.

6. Build a broad base of individual donors who will carry your message and your definition of art and culture into the community at large. By redefining what is meant by art and culture, you will begin to attract donors from all walks of life and your donor base will reflect the kind of audience you are trying to create.

Arts and culture groups must be proactive in putting forward an inclusive picture of themselves, both as artists and audience. The images of the starving artist alone in a garret apartment, or the waitress who is really a writer, or the not-of-this-world-hate-to-think-about-money musician, though arguably romantic, are ultimately harmful to a lasting integration of arts and culture into a progressive agenda and a democratic society. Art is not simply the expression of an individual, nor will many talented people be drawn to careers in the arts so long as suffering seems to be a requirement. The equation of arts organizations and wealthy people is equally harmful because so many people do not see themselves reflected in that section of society.

By using the principles of good organizing and good fundraising, most of which are the same, progressive arts and culture groups can raise the money they need and take their rightful place in the panoply of organizations that make up a progressive movement.

2000

Planning

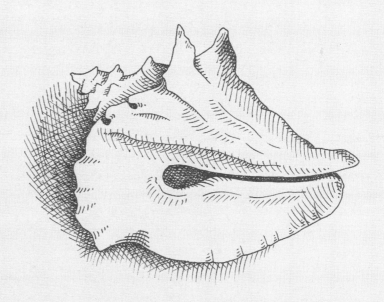

How to Plan Your Fundraising Strategy:

Keep Your Organization Financially on Track with a Year-Round Plan

By PAT MUNOZ and LIZ RAISBECK

Just as a bee makes honey to survive through the winter, so must every nonprofit raise money to accomplish its goals and to prosper. But nonprofits have an advantage over bees — we can (and must) raise money all year! This is often a hard truth for the board of a small nonprofit to internalize and act upon, but it is essential for an organization's survival. The organization that puts all its energy into issues but neglects to stock the financial honeycomb will surely starve in short order. And to ensure that our nonprofits make honey at every possible opportunity, every group needs to formulate an annual fundraising plan (see sample on page 31).

GETTING STARTED

When formulating a fundraising plan, it is important to get input from board, staff, and volunteers. Hold a special meeting of your organization to brainstorm and gather input. It is very important to get your board and staff involved in this process from the beginning so that they will take ownership. Some organizations delegate this function to a fundraising committee, but with small organizations, it is better to involve the entire board. Without board and volunteer involvement in fundraising, most organizations wither and die. Fundraising must be a shared responsibility. If you have board members who say that they just don't do fundraising, the board needs to consider whether those unwilling members' contributions are so important as to merit exemption from this important board obligation. Morale will be high if everyone pitches in, but if some don't, morale could suffer.

SETTING GOALS

There are two approaches to establishing an overall income goal for your fundraising plan. The first involves putting together an expense budget and using the total expense figure (plus a small additional amount to serve as a modest surplus) as your fundraising target. The second is to look at last year's income, analyze this figure to see if it includes any special income that might not be repeatable

(such as a special bequest), then increase this figure by a modest amount to allow for reasonable increases in most of your fundraising categories. You can do an even better job here if you look at income over the past several years.

As you compare numbers from one year to the next, you will see definite patterns emerge that will give you a good idea of how much of an increase it is feasible to project for the upcoming year. Later, once you have laid out the specific strategies and monetary goals for each fundraising activity, you may adjust this figure slightly. In the meantime, this figure-analyzing process will give you an overall number to shoot for.

CONSIDER YOUR ASSETS

Assets are not always monetary. In putting together your fundraising plan, you should consider any special fundraising assets that your board, staff, or volunteers have to offer. For example, perhaps someone on your board owns a whitewater rafting company, a restaurant, or a beautiful country home. Think about how you can use these special assets in your fundraising plan. Here's an example of how you would incorporate one of these assets into your plan:

Strategy: Hold a party at the riverside home of John Smith, board member

Action: Select a date and time; plan the event; compile invitation list; prepare and mail out invitations; hold event; do follow-up

Who: John Smith, with help from board and staff

When: November

Other examples of the kinds of fundraising assets to look for include:

- People with special talents (writers, artists, singers, etc.)
- People with access to good mailing lists that you might use in member recruiting
- Business owners who might donate items for a raffle or premium
- A strong corps of volunteers willing to sell tickets for a raffle, etc.

A good way to go about taking an inventory of these assets is to set aside some time at the initial brainstorming session specifically for this purpose. Get one board member who understands this concept to list a few assets she or he might be willing to contribute, then brainstorm or do a "round robin," asking each board member to list her or his own contributions.

INTEGRATE FUNDRAISING WITH OTHER ACTIVITIES

Your fundraising plan should fit together hand-in-glove with your annual action plan. Develop a fundraising plan that maximizes your project goals. For instance, if one of your projects is to develop a river greenway that will not only improve the quality of life in your town but will also attract tourism and make your river healthier, be sure to include in your fundraising plan a strategy to recruit business memberships. The business community will very much appreciate the benefits your organization's project will have for the town. Also, consider reaching out to civic associations. By connecting with them, you will be achieving your project goal of increasing stakeholders, plus you will be raising money at the same time.

If you are planning an annual meeting to inform the community about your organization, consider incorporating a fundraising event, such as a live (or silent) auction, a dinner, a raffle, or a concert, into that program activity. For almost any program activity you plan, you should be able to come up with a fundraising activity to complement it.

A FEW KEY STRATEGIES

But we are getting ahead of ourselves. Remember that you want to select a few fundraising strategies, not dozens! So sort through the ideas generated at your meeting, look over your list of fundraising assets and your annual program plan, and begin to select those fundraising strategies that will maximize your efforts, best accomplish your goals, and most complement your program.

Incorporate these fundraising strategies into your annual plan. If your organization is new, it is probably best to concentrate your efforts on building a base of individual members; finding a few key donors (businesses, individuals, foundations) who will make major gifts, organizing one event that will generate funds, involve the community, and perhaps provide media exposure for your group; and exploring local and state funding sources, such as the local chamber of commerce, the local United Way, area churches, or state and regional agencies.

As your organization grows, you can expand your strategies to include a major donor program, a series of special appeals, a workplace giving strategy, and other more demanding activities.

The key here is to break down your fundraising plan into bite-sized strategies that are attainable and realistic and then to detail the monetary subgoals, action steps, responsible person or persons, and timetable for each (don't forget your budget). For example, here's what one fundraising strategy for building membership might look like:

Strategy: Recruit new members through the mail.

Goals: Recruit 50 new members; raise $1,250.

Action: Research landowners in watershed and compile a mailing list of 500 names; mail out a letter explaining benefits of the project and asking them to join; thank those who respond.

Who: Staff and volunteers

When: January (research); February (prepare mailing); March 1 (mail)

INCREASING YOUR REVENUES

To increase your income, think about new activities you might undertake or new activities you might add to existing categories to generate additional income. For example:

- Is this the year to initiate a major donor program?
- If you're already doing an end-of-the-year appeal, should you add another appeal in the spring to take advantage of a program activity you will be carrying out then?
- Are there new foundations or corporations to which you can go this year to solicit grants?

Think also about asking your members to upgrade their gifts. Many organizations continue to ask their members for the same amount year after year. Once people have become "habitual" givers (a term used for someone who has given to an organization two or more years in a row), you should occasionally ask them to increase their gift to a higher giving level.

IDENTIFY YOUR PROSPECTS

In order to make your fundraising plan as realistic as possible, make a list of your fundraising prospects. If you are planning to recruit new members, list the prospective mailing lists you will use and the number of individuals on each list. If you have targeted a certain amount of money from corporations, list those corporations and how much you plan to request from each. If you are budgeting foundation income, list each foundation you think might fund your organization.

To be even more precise in your forecasting, make a chart showing the names of each funding prospect, followed by the amount you think you can request and a rating (we use a percentage) to indicate your best estimate of what your chances are of getting a gift.

Next, multiply the amount requested by the rating. It may take a little time to develop your skill at rating your prospects, but with practice your forecasts will become uncannily accurate. Our own system is to give foundations that have given before a 75–80% rating; those that are new and where we have no contact receive a 10–20% rating. If you have done your estimates well, the resulting figures will give you the total amount of money you can expect to receive from that particular funding source. For example, your foundation forecast chart might look like this:

Sample Foundation Forecast

FOUNDATION	AMOUNT	PROJECT	%CHANCE	FORECAST
ABC Fund	$10,000	Lawsuit	50%	$ 5,000
River Foundation	$ 4,000	Membership drive	25%	$ 1,000
Watershed Trust	$15,000	General Operations	50%	$ 7,500
Greene Family Fund	$25,000	Training Program	10%	$ 2,500
Total Forecast				**$16,000**

This procedure takes time and effort, but provides a reality check for your fundraising planning!

TIMING IS IMPORTANT: MAKE A FUNDRAISING CALENDAR

In creating a fundraising plan, it is important to spread out activities over the entire year for a number of reasons:

1. Scheduling at least one major income-producing activity per quarter (or better yet, per month) will ensure that you will have a steady stream of income rather than having funds arrive in big bursts or all at once at the end of the year.

2. By spacing out the fundraising work, you will do a better job in each activity and be more likely to accomplish the goals your group sets.

3. The organization will establish a "fundraising culture," which regards raising money as an ongoing, day-to-day part of activities. This puts you at an obvious advantage over groups with a "crisis mentality," who put fundraising off until there is no money, leaving themselves in the worst possible position to do effective fundraising.

Moreover, certain fundraising activities just naturally lend themselves better to certain times of year. Establishing an annual calendar for fundraising will allow you to carry out these activities at the optimal time of year and obtain the best possible results for your efforts.

For example, if you are planning a river festival or river trip, the spring or summer will probably be the best times of year; the best time to mail out a request to join is probably between January and March, or September and November; if you are looking for foundation support, you should start early in the year (or even at the end of the preceding year) because the whole process, from initial research to approved grant, can often take nine months; and putting together a good raffle should probably start in April or May to take advantage of the summer months for selling the tickets.

APPROVAL AND IMPLEMENTATION

After you have refined and polished your plan, take it back to your board or committee for approval. Remember, their buy-in is crucial.

Once it is approved, you must implement the fundraising plan. The secret here lies in having one person coordinate and follow up on the various action steps. Usually the leader of the group, but sometimes the head of the fundraising committee, is the lead contact.

One nice thing about fundraising — the results are tangible and easy to measure. If the treasurer of your board reports each month on the income and expenses of the organization, this information will provide a direct measure of how well people are carrying out their parts of the fundraising plan.

REVISING YOUR FUNDRAISING PLAN

The fundraising plan should be a dynamic and ever-changing document, not one set in stone. It can be modified as results come in. However, it should be taken very seriously and referred to regularly to check progress and make sure that what needs to happen occurs in a timely fashion. With issue-oriented groups, most of the energy is usually focused on accomplishing project-oriented results, and this is as it should be. But this cannot be done at the expense of the fundraising activities or the organization will suddenly find itself without any fuel to power its engines. The fundraising plan, in conjunction with the budget, is a tool that the board and staff can use to monitor results and predict, and work to avert, crises before they happen.

RECRUITING VOLUNTEERS TO HELP

There is an old saying that making things happen is 10% work and 90% attitude. The staff and board will need to cultivate the right attitude toward fundraising in order to recruit others to help deliver the goods. If you market your fundraising program as achievable, simple, and actually fun, you will find it easy to gather those "many hands that make light work." Furthermore, if lots of people are recruited to do a small job that will fulfill a particular goal, you are less likely to burn out your star fundraisers. Remember, volunteer help won't just appear automatically. As part of your plan, ask your staff and board to take responsibility for recruiting others to help.

SAMPLE FUNDRAISING PLAN — ABC River Organization

STRATEGY	GOAL(S)	ACTION STEPS	WHO	WHEN	HOW MUCH
1. New Member Acquisition	500 new members $9,000	1. Do 2 direct mail campaigns to 10,000 prospects each (300) 2. Each board members recruits 1 member/month (120) 3. Participants in raft trips become members (50) 4. Buyers of books of raffle tickets become members (30)	Staff & consultant BD Staff Staff	May & Sept Monthly Summer Fall	$7,000 no cost no cost no cost
2. Renewals	100 out of 154 (65%) $2,000	1. Call last year's unrenewed members, asking them to renew 2. Do 3 mailings to current members, spaced 1 month apart 3. Call unrenewed members, asking them to renew	Staff/Vols Staff Staff/Vols	January Jan–March May	$50 $400 $50
3. Special Appeals	$2,000	1. Prepare a special appeal to all members on lawsuit 2. Prepare a follow-up request in six weeks	Staff Staff	Mid Oct Early Dec	$400 $100
4. Special Events	$10,000	Hold a raffle which will generate money, educate the public, and recruit members	BD Committee	June–Oct	$2,500
5. Major Donors	$5,000 30 Donors: 20 @ $100 8 @ $250 2 @ $500	1. Research names of potential major donors (120 names) 2. Create a special donor club with special benefits 3. Schedule personal visits with as many of these as possible to ask for money 4. Where visits not possible, call or write a personal letter	Staff/BD Staff Staff/BD Staff/BD	Ongoing	$500
6. Businesses	$2,000	1. Talk with local businesses and ask them to sign on as "Friends" with a gift of $100 2. Send proposals out to selected corporations	Staff/Vols BD Committee	Jun–Jul May	$100 $100
7. Foundations	$25,000 -0- (funds will come in next year)	1. Research & prepare a list of foundation prospects 2. Prepare & mail out proposals 3. Follow up	Intern Staff Staff	Jan Feb April	no cost $100 no cost
8. Workplace Giving	-0- (funds will come in next year)	Apply for admission to state environmental federation or local Combined Fed Campaign	Staff or BD member	Fall	no cost
9. Planned Giving		Put an ad about bequests in every other issue of newsletter	Staff	Ongoing	no cost
TOTAL INCOME	**$55,000**			**TOTAL EXPENSES**	**$11,300**

Key: BD = Board Members   Vols = Volunteers

REPRINTED WITH PERMISSION FROM RIVER NETWORK'S "RIVER FUNDRAISING ALERT." 1997

Choosing the Right Fundraising Strategy

By STEPHANIE ROTH and KIM KLEIN

The steering committee of the Coalition to Save Our Jobs is having a meeting. A local corporation is threatening to move out of town, claiming in a high-profile ad campaign that the labor union's demands are forcing them to move out of the community. The Coalition is trying to keep the corporation, and its jobs, in town. The Coalition has tried to publicize their side of the story, but without much luck. They need more money, both to get more publicity and to hire more organizers.

Each member of the steering committee has an idea of what fundraising strategy will be best. Joe says that they should put all their efforts into a golf tournament. They will get sponsorships from local businesses, churches, and sympathetic politicians, which will bring a lot of publicity. A golf tournament can raise a lot of money, he says, and, more important, will show that the religious and small business community is behind the Coalition.

Anne thinks a direct mail campaign will reach more people with one message and carry much less risk than a golf tournament. Once people read the Coalition's viewpoint, she says, they will want to join and help.

Barry thinks that a few people should simply ask a few of the current donors to the Coalition who can give bigger gifts to do so, and that the Coalition should keep their publicity efforts separate from their fundraising.

Who is right? The firmest answer we can provide is, "It depends." It depends on what else the Coalition wants besides money for the time it will put into a fundraising strategy, how fast they need money, and how many people can help with the fundraising. Once the Coalition has answered these question, it should then review the strategies that are available, discuss what each strategy can and can't do well, and choose the one that works best for their situation.

MATCH THE STRATEGY TO YOUR GOALS

There are thousands of groups like this coalition. Some are large and well established, and some are brand new, fresh from the grassroots. Many, unfortunately, have this in common: They tend to choose fundraising strategies badly and then to be disappointed with the results.

Fundraising strategies vary in what they can accomplish. Every fundraising strategy is good for some things and bad for others. For your fundraising activities to have successful outcomes, you need to know which strategies to use in which circumstances.

The following is a brief description of the most common strategies and what they are best used for, beyond or in addition to raising money, along with what response you can expect from each. In every case, we assume the organization knows how to identify donor prospects appropriate to the strategy. (For more on identifying prospects, see "You Already Know All the People You Need to Know to Raise All the Money You Want to Raise," by Kim Klein.)

As you consider which fundraising strategies to use, keep in mind what your goal is in approaching your donors or prospects:

- Are you trying to bring in new donors (acquisition)?
- Do you want to keep current donors giving regularly (retention)?
- Is your goal to get current donors to give larger amounts of money (upgrading)?

A healthy fundraising program will use a range of different strategies over the course of a year to accomplish all three of these objectives.

We have divided the range of strategies into those that require some personal knowledge of the prospect and those that can be used with people not known to the organization. Keep in mind that the closer someone is to your organization, the greater likelihood of them giving repeated and larger gifts, so we recommend concentrating first on those strategies that capitalize on donors or prospects who have an existing relationship with your group or someone in it.

STRATEGIES REQUIRING SOME PERSONAL KNOWLEDGE OF THE PROSPECT BY THE SOLICITOR

Personal face-to-face solicitation

What it is: This strategy, often associated with raising money from major donors, involves meeting with a prospective donor by prearranged appointment and asking them for a contribution to your organization. A prospect is defined as someone who 1) has the ability to give a gift of the size you're asking for, 2) believes in the work you are doing, and 3) knows either the organization or the person who is asking them for money.

Percent of response: 50% of prospects will say yes. Of that group, however, half will give less than the amount you asked for.

Best use: To upgrade donors, to bring in large gifts from qualified prospects, and to raise large amounts of money quickly.

Comments: Many grassroots organizations feel intimidated by this strategy, claiming they don't know anyone with enough money to justify setting up a face-to-face meeting, their board members are hesitant to ask, and other stumbling blocks. The important thing to remember with personal solicitations is to start with people you know, at whatever level of giving is appropriate for them.

Example: In 1992, the Center for Anti-Violence Education in Brooklyn decided to raise money from major donors (defined as gifts of $100 and up). Unable to reach their rather modest goal of $5,000 that first year, they were discouraged. They felt they didn't know enough people to ask and that the board members and volunteers who had agreed to participate in the campaign did not follow through in a consistent way. Nevertheless, the staff decided to keep trying. They arranged for more training for the board in asking for money, recruited board members more experienced in solicitation, and continued to ask their most loyal donors (numbering fewer than 50) to give larger and larger gifts and to suggest names of other people who might be interested in their work. Seven years after embarking on their first major donor campaign, they had 250 donors giving $100 or more, and were expecting to raise $45,000 from individual contributions.

Personal phone call

What it is: "Personal" is what distinguishes this strategy from phone-a-thons and telemarketing. Someone who knows a prospective donor calls them. Because the caller knows the prospect, they are more likely to get through than someone making a cold call, and because this is someone they have reason to believe would be supportive of the cause, they are more likely to get a gift.

Percent of response: 15–20% of those called will make a gift.

Best use: To upgrade donors, particularly moving people at the $50–$250 level to a higher gift; to work with thoughtful donors who live at a distance from the group and cannot reasonably be visited; to raise large amounts of money quickly.

Comments: Many groups have complained to us that it is difficult to get donors to agree to a face-to-face meeting. People are busy and they don't want to spend the little free time they do have in meetings about their contributions. While sometimes it is the solicitor who is not comfortable asking for a meeting, it does seem that more and more money is being raised without face-to-face meetings. This makes the phone call even more crucial as a way to continue to have contact with donors. Some groups have begun using e-mail in place of or addition to the personal phone call.

Personal Letter

What it is: While we usually recommend more personal contact with donors, either by phone or in a meeting following a personal letter, it is possible to generate large amounts of money from a well-written and personalized letter. It is the relationship between the person writing (or signing) the letter and the prospect that is key to the success of this strategy.

Percent of response: 10–20%.

Best use: A low-key way for board members, staff, or volunteers to ask friends and colleagues for gifts; useful for getting donors known to someone in the organization to renew their gift; occasionally useful for upgrading donors.

Example: The National Center for Youth Law in San Francisco increases its giving from individual donors every year through personalized letters. In 1992, they raised only $2,000 from individuals. Six years later, they raised $200,000, with one gift of $75,000 leading the way. One clue to this success is that the executive director attaches a personal note to every solicitation that goes to a donor who has given before — currently 500 donors — as well as to other people, not yet donors, whom he knows personally. The real key is the fact that this director is on a first-name basis with at least half of his organization's donors. Though he spends little time in direct fundraising with these donors, he is in contact with them throughout the year on the work of the organization. His note on their annual appeal is a reminder of this personal relationship, and they respond.

STRATEGIES NOT REQUIRING PERSONAL KNOWLEDGE OF THE PROSPECT

Door-to-Door Canvass

What it is: Volunteers or paid canvassers go door-to-door in designated neighborhoods, asking people to become members of an organization or simply to give a contribution. The solicitors don't usually know the people whose doors they are knocking on, which makes the rate of response relatively low. However, because a certain percentage of people will answer the door, the solicitors have an opportunity to engage people face-to-face in a way that is not possible with writing or phoning the same group of people.

Percent of response: 15%.

Best use: In combination with an organizing drive, so that people are asked to sign a petition or express an opinion as well as give money. Although you may get more gifts than from a phone-a-thon, the gifts received are often very small and usually not repeated.

Phone-a-thon

What it is: A group of people are recruited (or hired) to come together over several evenings to work through a list of prospective donors. The prospects are people who have not given before, but can be expected to be interested in the work your organization does. (These names are often gotten by exchanging mailing lists with groups doing similar, though not directly competing, work as yours, or by renting lists of people who, because of their affiliations or other giving history, would be expected to be interested in your work.) Usually an office with a large number of phones donates their space for these evenings, so that anywhere from 8 to 20 people can be calling at one time. The point of the calling is to reach people (not answering machines) who are willing to speak to you for a few minutes so that you can elicit their interest in your cause and ask them to make a pledge.

Percent of response: 5%.

Best use: Reaching large numbers of people with a message they can respond to immediately; good training in how to ask for money more personally; can raise a large number of small and medium-sized gifts quickly. Works best when the organization is set up to take gifts made with credit cards.

Direct Mail

What it is: This is an acquisition mailing, whose purpose is to get new people to become donors to your organization. People are targeted who have not given before but, as with the phone-a-thon, can be expected to be interested in the work your organization does. A standard letter is sent to a list of 200 or more people by bulk mail (200 is the minimum number of pieces you can send to qualify for bulk discount from the postal service), and the mailing includes a reply form and a return envelope.

Percent of response: 1–2%.

Best use: Acquisition of donors. Because direct mail often costs more or as much as it brings in, it is used as a way to reach hundreds or thousands of people with a consistent message and to convert some of those people into donors.

Comments: Because of the expense and risk of direct mail, we recommend that it be used after you have asked everyone you possibly can through the more personal strategies. When you have asked staff members, board members, volunteers, members, and current donors for names of people they think may be interested in giving, and have asked all of them for money, you may indeed run out of prospects. Direct mail is a way to reach people you have no other way to contact.

Special Event

What it is: A special event gathers a group of people to do something fun, entertaining, and/or educational, with the goal of building and strengthening your donor base. This is probably the best known, and most poorly used, of all grassroots fundraising strategies. Special events are an important strategy for meeting goals other than fundraising, including gaining publicity for your organization, getting people together to build a sense of community in the organization, introducing new people to your work, and raising money from sources you might not otherwise have access to.

Percent of response: Varies by event.

Best Use: To generate publicity and visibility for your organization. In addition, depending on the event, it can be used for acquisition, retention, or upgrading of donors. (See "The Correct Use of Special Events," by Kim Klein.)

Comments: The most successful events actually combine the strategies described above. Personal solicitation and personal phone calls are made to current and new donors and to local businesses to ask them to help sponsor the event with a donation. An invitation is mailed and follow-up calls are made to get the highest turnout possible. Because of the huge amount of time needed to produce an event and the risks involved of committing resources before money is raised, special events can be a risky strategy to choose, especially for organizations with small numbers of staff or volunteers.

One kind of special event that requires a lot less time and people-power than, say, a large concert or dance, is the tried-and-true house party. At a house party, the host invites friends, neighbors, and colleagues to their home to learn about the organization, have something to eat and drink, and be asked to make a contribution. There is generally no obligation to give, but people know in advance that they will be asked for money.

Example: Asian Immigrant Women's Advocates often asks its supporters to host house parties as a way to expand their donor base beyond their membership of low-income immigrant workers. One year, 35 people attending a house party in Berkeley in honor of the host's birthday contributed $1,200 in donations to AIWA in lieu of birthday gifts. The host sent all the invitations, provided all the food, and wrote all the thank-you notes for the donations. The staff of AIWA merely had to show up and give a short talk about their work. Three years later, one-third of those donors were still giving to AIWA in response to annual mail appeals. In this case, the house party was used as a way to acquire donors, who were then retained through a personalized mail appeal each year.

MAKING THE IMPERSONAL MORE PERSONAL

All of the impersonal strategies yield a greater response and larger gifts when they are used with people who have given to your organization before. Rates of response vary, but generally a phone-a-thon to people who are current givers will yield upwards of 15% response, direct mail to current donors will yield 10% response on any one mailing, and about 66% of your donors who give one year will give the next year.

The important thing to remember is this: No fundraising strategy will work if used exclusively. In planning for fundraising over the course of a year, all strategies should be considered and used appropriately. The purpose of acquiring donors is to be able to ask them again and get them to give year after year, and the purpose of doing that is both to have a large number of loyal donors and to identify a group of those loyal donors who will eventually be asked for very large gifts in person.

1999

Opportunistic Fundraising

By KIM KLEIN

Last Sunday when I came out of a church service, I saw two young women standing behind an ironing board with voter registration materials and information about an organization working to keep affirmative action in California. They were part of the move to defeat Proposition 209, called the "California Civil Rights Initiative" and nicknamed the "California Civil Wrongs Initiative," on the ballot in 1996. The two women called out to all of us as we came out of church, "Are you registered to vote?" I said I was and went over to their ironing board to see what materials they had. They told me about Prop. 209, and I agreed with them that it is an outrageous proposition and that their efforts to defeat it are very important. I had seen their materials before, and so I wished them luck and left.

These enthusiastic and committed women missed a chance with me and with everyone else coming out of church — the chance to raise some money. I have noticed this omission time and again, and want to point out here some ways in which fundraising needs to be one of the things people do in the midst of other organizing, speaking, marching, registering, or other activities.

A fundamental principle of fundraising is that people pay you to do work they cannot do by themselves. In this example, I cannot save affirmative action legislation by myself. I can vote against this proposition and urge my friends to do the same. I can talk about it and march about it, but all of these actions are useless unless I am part of an organized effort with lots of other people acting similarly. In many cases, I don't have time to march or organize, so I give money instead.

We miss hundreds of thousands of opportunities to involve people in our work when we do not ask them to do what is for many people the simplest thing they can do to improve the world: give money. The women registering people to vote needed to ask all of us who are already registered, "Would you like to make a donation to help us defeat Prop. 209? Any amount will help." They needed to ask anyone that they registered, "Can you also help with a donation today?" Sure, most people will say no or will not say anything, but some will give $1 or the change in their pockets and a few will give more in cash or write a check. When collecting signatures for a cause, there is a rule of thumb that you should get an average of a dime a signature. It is useful to incorporate this thinking into all organizing — every time you mention a group or a cause you are involved in, figure out a way to bring money into the conversation. Think of getting a dime for every mention of the group.

Here are some ways you can do that:

• **Wear a T-shirt from your group whenever possible.** When people comment on it, tell them they can have one too for a small donation of $25 (or whatever). I have five T-shirts in different colors from a group called SOCM (Save Our Cumberland Mountains). Somebody at my gym asked me if this was an important group to know about because she saw the T-shirt a lot. Since SOCM is in Tennessee and I am in Berkeley, I am fairly certain she is not seeing the T-shirt a lot, but is seeing me in several different colors of it. Nevertheless, I say (truthfully), "It is a very important group," and I tell her a little bit about it. I say, "If you would like to give, I can send you more information." "Okay," she says and gives me her address. She may or may not give, but I have done my part, which is that I have mentioned money.

• *At dinner parties, when you are asked what you are doing, tell people how great your group is and how important your work is.* Then you can casually mention that you are getting a lot more individual donors and that that kind of support really helps. You don't need to ask for money at the party — if you are like many of us, most of your friends are already giving, but just mentioning individual gifts reminds people about the importance of giving. You never know when someone will say, "I'm not a member of that group. How much does it cost to join?"

• *Consider turning your birthday, anniversary, Christmas/Hanukkah, etc. into a fundraiser.* Your invitations can say, "Instead of presents, please give a gift to Good Group." How much more stuff do you need? The funny thing is that people will often give more money to the group than they would have spent on a present. It is not always possible to tell people that you want them to give a donation in lieu of a gift, but let that be known about you. Tell people that a friend gave you a wonderful gift — a donation in your name to a group you like. Develop a reputation for that. You will have fewer dust catchers and your groups will be richer.

• *Always have brochures, newsletters, and return envelopes about your group with you in your briefcase, at your house, and in your car.* That way, you always have materials to hand someone if the topic of your group comes up, which it will because you are going to bring it up.

Remember when you first fall in love? You find ways to mention the name of your lover all the time and to turn the conversation to that person in various subtle and not-so-subtle ways. It does not require effort — in fact not talking about the person requires effort. You can see the same phenomenon when a person has a new grandchild or even a new kitten.

Although it will take more discipline and is probably less thrilling than talking about new love, fundraising needs to be incorporated into your daily conversations. No one will mind and your group will be the richer for it.

1996

Losing Foundation or Government Funding:
How to Cope

By KIM KLEIN

In 1988, an ad hoc coalition of social service providers in a large East Coast city proposed to create an umbrella organization that could advocate for their issues, conduct research, and generally coordinate work so that the agencies could eliminate duplication in these areas.

They approached four foundations to fund the umbrella organization. The foundations were so enthusiastic about the proposal that they agreed to provide start-up funding to create the organization and fund it for three years, and then to find other foundations to take over the funding. In this way the organization would not have to raise money from any sources other than foundations.

The foundations and the providers saw three advantages to this arrangement: The newly created organization would not compete with its member groups for individual or corporate donors; it would not have to seek or accept government funding, thereby enabling it to have an unfettered watchdog and advocacy role; and the staff of the organization would not have to spend time raising money.

The foundations provided the funding and for three years things went smoothly. The organization had an excellent staff and board and developed an impressive list of accomplishments. After three years, however, despite their earlier promises, the original funders tried only half-heartedly to find new funding; not surprisingly, they were not successful.

By 1992, this seemingly ideal situation was anything but ideal. The organization had to cut its budget; two of the original foundation founders told them not to request any further funding. A third foundation remained helpful in terms of advice about other funders but also could provide no further funding. The fourth foundation gave one more grant before announcing that they, too, could provide no further funding. By mid-1993 the group had been forced to eliminate the staff and the board was facing a debt of several thousand dollars that had accumulated in hopes of future foundation support.

This true story happened to a wonderful group that began with the best intentions and believed they had established sound financial footing. If they had been the only ones ever to be led down the rosy path of foundation or government funding, we would simply say, "Well, too bad; we hope they learn from that mistake." But their situation is all too common.

FACING THE LOSS OF FUNDING

What should a group do when its funding is about to dry up, or when it suddenly faces losing funding? If your group faces this situation, the following are steps that other groups have found to be useful.

Step One: Form a Recovery Team

The first step is to pull together a group of five to seven people made up of board members, staff (if there are any left, or if they are willing to work briefly on an unpaid basis), volunteers, clients, or friends of the organization who are willing to pitch in for a while. Some members of this team should come from the board, but it does not have to be made up entirely of board members. This group of people will need to devote seven to ten hours per month to planning and fundraising. The strategy team need not be skilled in fundraising, because they can learn fundraising techniques, but they must be enthusiastic and committed to the organization. And they must understand that their work will be entirely focused on fundraising.

Step Two: Train the Recovery Team in Fundraising

The initial stumbling block for the strategy team may be their lack of fundraising skills and, for many, their unwillingness to *ask for money*. Therefore, before any planning is undertaken, the strategy team should receive fundraising training at one of their early meetings. Although fundraising is hard work, the skills required for it are easy to learn. Therefore, a training session with enough information to create the fundraising plan can be relatively brief — from three hours to a full day.

If you hire a consultant, fees will range from $300 to $1,500 per day. Sometimes, excellent consultants will donate their time. In many cities, the United Way has a referral list of people willing to donate time, or you can check with any nonprofit management assistance organizations in your community. Be sure to ask for and check references of any consultant, whether paid or volunteer. Make sure the trainer is not only a skilled fundraiser, but also enthusiastic, flexible, and able to understand and respond to your organization's particular situation.

During the training and, if necessary, in addition to it, time should be set aside for people to talk about their fears about asking for money. Individual donor programs will need to be set up, and fears should not inhibit volunteers from getting donations. These fears can be brought under control by talking about them in a supportive setting.

Step Three: Put the Plan Together

After training and skill development, the team must plan two separate but related courses of action:

Cutting costs. Although we will not examine cost-cutting strategies here, exploring the following questions may help you design some cost-cutting measures: How long can you operate at your present level of service? Do you have any savings? What part of your organization's functioning (staff? program? office space? etc.) will need to end when your grant(s) runs out?

Raising money. At the same time, you need to determine where you can raise the money you are going to need. The rest of this article concerns itself with that question.

CREATE A BUDGET

With your financial picture in mind, create a budget projecting approximately how much money you will need each month to maintain a minimum level of service for the next four to six months. These monthly projections will vary, with temporary sharp cuts followed by projections of more revenue available in a few months. The staff may be willing or able to work on a half-time basis for up to three months (they should not be asked to do so for longer than that). Perhaps your landlord will give you one free month of rent or defer your rental payment rather than lose you as a tenant altogether. Ideally, you are aiming to have the lowest expenditures for the first three or four months of this plan, so that you can use what little money you have on hand to implement fundraising strategies, gambling that they will begin paying off.

DEVELOP YOUR FUNDRAISING PLAN

Once you have a cash flow budget for the next four to six months, you are ready to begin mapping out your fundraising plan. Use the list of sources and considerations detailed in Illustration 1 to begin identifying your most likely sources of income. You may want to compile this list into a chart (see Illustration 2) to make it easier to discuss.

Be conservative in estimating profit and liberal in estimating costs. Overestimate time and people needed. Be especially conservative in estimating how many corporate or foundation grants you can get.

Once you have listed all the income sources you can think of, examine each one critically to be sure you think it will work. When complete, your plan should look like the sample plan developed by Community Services in Illustration 3.

You may notice that some of your sources will raise larger amounts but will take a long time to realize the money. Other sources may have immediate payoff, even if the net gain is small. A good fundraising plan should have both long-term and short-term elements.

In the sample plan, note that Community Services identified funding strategies that will be fairly simple to implement. In some cases, they merely added a price tag to program work already underway. They also set low goals for each potential source of income. To be on the safe side, they arranged a line of credit from a bank. (A line of credit works on the same principle as a credit card: You borrow money as you need it, up to a limit, and pay interest on the money as you borrow it. There are many creative ways to borrow money, and you should consider them. Ask a bank or credit union for full information on their lending procedures.)

The ideal fundraising plan is as *diverse* as possible. Money should be projected from a variety of sources. This ensures that if one source fails, there will be others to draw on. Don't be tempted to seek all your funds from one or two sources, no matter how "sure" they may be.

Fundraising plans should always include seeking money from individual donors. There are many ways to solicit this money, including a membership drive, canvassing, major gifts campaign, subscriptions to a newsletter, and so on.

Step Four: Riding Out the Storm

The first few months of planning and fundraising will probably be the most frustrating for everyone. A lot of work will be put in, often without a clear or immediate payoff.

Further, an organization doing grassroots fundraising for the first time is like a brand-new organization, no matter how long it may have been in existence. Being brand new means that plans take more time than you think they should, people don't always do what they say they will, and you may estimate incorrectly how much work something will take or how much money it will bring in.

During the first six to twelve months of grassroots fundraising, while you are getting used to getting your money this way rather than from foundation or government sources, keep in mind certain clichés, such as perseverance furthers, success breeds success, form creates substance, nothing ventured–nothing gained, and the like. As much as possible, maintain an attitude of enthusiasm and momentum. Remind people who speak negatively that negative thoughts and negative speech do not raise money or build programs.

Many groups have discovered resources within their supporters that they were unaware of and a depth of creativity and willingness to work that mean the groups will not only survive, but grow.

The organization profiled in the beginning of this article formed a strategy team as described above. It committed itself to raise $1,000 a month for the first three months and $3,000 a month for the next three months, and to reevaluate their need and their capacity to meet the need at that time. They started with strategies designed to pay off quickly. Each of the team members wrote to ten friends asking for gifts of $50 to $500; within the first few weeks, $2,000 came in. They asked all board members and volunteers to do the same, and $2,500 was raised from those contacts. They planned two 2,000-piece direct mail appeals and three house parties. They submitted three proposals to foundations, but did not bank on money from that source.

They also made their first Tuesday evening of every month "Volunteer Night" at their office. For these evenings, the strategy team created a list of things for volunteers to do, including writing thank-you notes, entering donors' names and addresses into the computer, sending out mailings, calling to follow up on major gift solicitations, answering routine correspondence, paying bills, and so on. Each week more volunteers showed up, lending both talents and morale to the effort. The team created tremendous momentum.

WHEN TO CONSIDER MERGING

Merging with another organization can involve a variety of actions, from literally merging names, assets, and functions to creating an informal arrangement of sharing office space, computers, or conference rooms in order to lower overhead expenses. Any agreement you make along this continuum should be *in writing, in detail.*

In considering merging options, be creative. You don't need to merge with a group exactly like yours. For example, two organizations in the Midwest have merged their office space. One group operates from 9 A.M. to 5 P.M. and never uses the building in the evening. The other group runs a nighttime drop-in rap group and hotline counseling service, so uses the office and phones from 7 P.M. to 3 A.M. The groups split the rent and have worked out agreements about cleanup, phone bills, and desk space.

WHEN TO CONSIDER CLOSING

You should consider closing your organization if the following situations apply:

1. You need to raise more than $100,000 from grassroots funding sources the first year. The most ambitious, creative, and lucky organizations will probably not raise more than $100,000 from grassroots sources in the first year, and most groups should not count on more than $25,000 – $75,000 during this time.

2. There are other groups providing services similar to yours, and merging with them is not an option.

3. After training and planning, the strategy team does not carry out its tasks.

Just the act of considering closing can serve to renew commitment and determination among board, staff, and volunteers not to close. However, if you must close the organization, there is no shame in doing so. Closing does not reflect badly on your organization or the people involved. Further, although your group will be missed by the community you serve, no group is indispensable. A new group will form if the need is still great.

Illustration 1. Sources of Funds and Considerations About Them

☐ *Individual Donor Programs*
  Annual Giving Campaigns
  Membership drives
  Dues, subscriptions
  Pledging
  Direct mail, or small mail appeals
  Door-to-door canvassing
  Major gifts

All individual donor programs require an ever-expanding network of contacts. Each new donor leads to more new donors. All successful self-sufficient organizations have one and usually several forms of individual donor programs.

☐ *Special Events:* Usually planned in terms of the net income projected: small (net $1,000–$2,500), medium (net $2,501–$7,500) and large (more than $7,500). However, the size reflects not only the profit earned, but the amount of work, lead time, and front money required. In planning special events such as concerts, or any event that requires a "star" for a draw, start with who you know. A Sting concert might be a great moneymaker, but if no one knows anyone who knows Sting, it could take three to four years before you find a connection to the group and get on their schedule. You will probably want to start much smaller, such as with the high school glee club or a local band.

☐ *Fees for Service:* Seeking funds from clients as payment for services rendered. This can be set up on a sliding scale basis so you can serve all the people you want to, but those people who can will pay what they can afford.

☐ *Sale of Products:* T-shirts, bumper stickers, buttons, or developing more exotic products such as toys, games, stationery, etc., either related to your group or not (think school magazine sales) can bring in money. In the case of products, you need to research whether you will owe sales tax on the proceeds.

☐ *Sale of Information:* Most organizations have information that would be useful to people in written form. Developing booklets, pamphlets, and manuals and selling them for four to five times their cost can be a real moneymaker. The information is useful to the person buying it, and generally he/she gets it at a lower cost from you than any other source they would have to approach for it (such as an attorney, doctor, or bookstore).

☐ *Training/Education Programs:* Like the sale of information, offering classes that carry continuing education credit for doctors, nurses, lawyers, or other professionals, or a seminar for the general public, with a charge per participant, can both provide a needed service and make money for your program.

☐ *Honoraria:* Service clubs, guilds, professional organizations, and other groups seek speakers for their monthly or quarterly meetings. Up to now, your group may have spoken at these gatherings for free, but if you ask for a reasonable honorarium, you will probably get it.

☐ *Grants:* From other than the "usual suspects" might be available from local corporations, service clubs (Kiwanis, Rotary, Junior League), United Way, churches, synagogues, or unions.

☐ *Religious institutions:* Grants are often given through the local church parish structure and from national religious offices. Many churches are able to take a "second collection" for you on a Sunday. Many synagogues, churches, or other houses or worship will loan you the use of computers and phones, or give you office and conference space rent-free.

☐ *Loans:* Various types of loans, lines of credit, interest rates, etc., can be worked out through a bank, savings and loan, or credit union, or through an individual, foundation, or corporation. It often makes good business sense to seek a loan when you are first doing grassroots fundraising. Loans can be used for front money or for cash flow problems until your fundraising begins to pay off.

CONSIDERATIONS

For each source, ask yourself the following questions:

1. How much time will need to be spent researching and planning to seek money from this source (for example, foundation grants require research even before a proposal can be written)?

2. How much lead time is needed before money will be seen from this source, once the planning is underway?

3. How many people are needed to implement this strategy?

4. How much front money is required?

5. What special knowledge is required, and who has it?

6. Is the plan cost effective (counting staff salaries, overhead expenses, and volunteer time that could be used in different ways)?

7. Are there strings attached to this money if we do raise it?

8. How much money can we expect this source will bring in?

9. Is this a stable source of funding?

10. What is the worst thing that could happen by seeking money from this source?

11. What is the best we can hope for?

Illustration 2. Sources and Considerations Chart

	CONSIDERATIONS									
	TIME NEEDED	PEOPLE NEEDED	FRONT MONEY?	SPECIAL KNOWLEDGE?	COST ANALYSIS	STRINGS ATTACHED?	PROFIT?	STABILITY?	WORST THAT COULD HAPPEN	BEST TO HOPE FOR?
SOURCES										
Individual Donors										
Special Events										
Raffle										
Dance										
Phone-a-thon										
Fees for Service										
Sale of Products										
Honoraria										

Illustration 3. Community Services Fundraising Plan

For six months beginning January 1 ending June 30.

GOALS

1. Raise $30,000

2. New plan for rest of year developed and ready to implement

3. 10 new volunteers working primarily on fundraising tasks

SOURCES FOR $30,000

Mail appeals:

Our mailing list:
2,000 names, 3% response, median gift $25 .... $1,500

Friends of board, staff, volunteers:
200 names 10% response, median gift $35 .... $700

TOTAL MAIL $2,200

Major Gifts

1	@	$1,000	....	$1,000
1	@	$500	....	$500
4	@	$250	....	$1,000
5	@	$100	....	$500
10	@	$50	....	$500

TOTAL MAJOR GIFTS $3,500

Fees for Service
10 clients / week at $4/client × 24 weeks $960

Special Events (net income)
Donations at Unity Day Fair (2/3) $250
Dance (4/15) $2,000
Garage Sale (5/4) $1,500
Raffle (drawing 6/1) $2,500

Honoraria
5 speaking engagements @ $100 .... $500

Religious Discretionary Funds
Approach 10 faith institutions, hope for 3 @ $500 .... $1,500

Corporate Grants
2 @ $2,000 .... $4,000

Seminar (May)
75 participants @ $35 .... $2,625

Sale of "Tenants Rights" book
400 @ $10 .... $4,000

Loan
$5,000 line of credit $5,000

TOTAL .... $30,000+

Note that Community Services turned some of their program work into income-producing sources, such as their service to clients, a seminar originally planned to be given at no charge, and the distribution of a book, also originally planned to be given away. Although some people may object to charging for services or information, keep in mind that people often value things they pay for more than those they get for free. Also, charges can be kept nominal, or on a sliding scale, so that no one is deprived of service or information for lack of funds.

Looking Good:
Developing Effective Written Materials

By NANCY ADESS

An organization's written materials are a major, and often the only, link between its work and its many constituencies. Better-looking and better-written materials will improve your organization's visibility, broadcast its message more widely, and ultimately generate more supporters. This article discusses how to get the visual message right and how to work with production people to keep it that way, and concludes with a review of the basics of good writing.

THE LANGUAGE OF VISUAL IMPACT

Writing, editing and designing written materials to make them effective in a world overloaded with printed pages require a working familiarity with writing composition and editorial production. But without the benefit of training in these areas, most nonprofit staff are subject to an often frustrating trial-and-error learning process.

Based on my own learn-by-doing experience in nonprofit work and my subsequent professional training in editing and producing educational and information materials for nonprofits, I offer here a series of tips to help take some of the error out of the trial-and-error method.

The first part of this article focuses on graphic design tips that will enhance the visual appeal of projects you design in-house.

Written Materials Speak

Materials that have punch and style show respect for your audience and contribute to making people want to join with you, support your work, and donate to your cause.

Think about the enormous range of written materials going out of your office. You may be sending out newsletters, annual reports, press kits, educational pamphlets and booklets, grant proposals, membership appeals, information for volunteers, calendars, and invitations to events such as conferences, open houses, anniversary celebrations, educational forums, and fundraisers.

In fact, chances are that up to 90% of your interaction with your constituency and donors is through something you've written.

It's not the writing, however, that your reader first relates to, except for a headline or two — it's the visual impact of the piece. Your image as an organization is one of the primary messages of every piece you send out on those printed pages. Yet, if you're like most people, how that piece will look — what the first impression will be when your reader picks up the page — often gets short shrift in the rush to get it out. Here we look at your written materials in the reverse sequence to how you produce them, beginning with what they look like.

The Visual Message

The visual impact of each piece tells the reader who you are. The message may be negative or positive. A piece that has typos in it, that's crowded on a page, printed on dark paper, or poorly photocopied doesn't give a sense of respect for either the organization or the reader. While your materials don't need to look slick and high powered, they do need to look pleasant and easy to read. Your materials must invite the reader's attention in the first second or two, blocking out the distractions from all the other materials he or she could focus on at that moment.

The look of your materials should reflect something about the style of your organization. If you're a youth organization, for example, you probably don't want to choose layouts and typefaces that project a staid, conservative image. If you're an arts organization, you may want to include a number of visual examples.

Because your reader sees the page before he or she reads it, let's look at how you can make the most of the nonverbal language that speaks to the reader. If, as in many offices, you have computer programs that can turn out reasonably designed pieces (either by using templates that come with word processing programs or a professional design program, such as PageMaker or QuarkXPress), you may be designing a lot of your written materials in-house. The following tips on various aspects of basic design will help you create clean, good-looking materials that will capture your reader's interest.

1. COLOR

Color wakes up the eye and draws your reader's attention. It can be used sparingly, as an accent, such as a colored line along the top of a brochure, or to set off the name of a newsletter or the headlines and subheads of a pamphlet. Keep in mind that accent color counts as a second color at the printer; the black ink that is usually used for text is considered the first color.

The cost of adding a second color is usually around $40, depending on the printer. So, if you are printing a large number of pieces, such as a brochure you expect to use for a couple of years, the per-piece cost of adding a second color would be very small.

If you don't want the expense of a second ink color, consider using a light-colored paper instead, something other than the standard white, cream, or beige papers. A pale yellow or light blue for a brochure or an invitation can be very appealing.

2. ILLUSTRATION

Photographs, especially of people doing things, really are worth the proverbial 1,000 words. You don't need a professional photographer to get good action shots. All you need are black-and-white pictures taken from an interesting angle. A picture of people engaged in conversation or of a volunteer helping a client will have more appeal than a posed shot of a person or a group of people. Look in your local newspaper for examples of action shots. Then keep a camera handy at the office or at organizational gatherings and capture people in action.

Don't print a photo that depends on minute details, such as reading the writing on a proclamation or a check, to make the point; these details will blur out in reproduction.

Always caption a photo. Captions are read twice as frequently as story text. Use them to tell the story the picture illustrates. You can fit a lot of information into a few sentences under a picture. Instead of captioning a picture, "Dancers enjoying themselves at recent benefit," tell the story: "We raised $10,000 at our annual dance last month. Thanks to the dedicated leadership of _____, dancing here with chair of the board, _____ , our program to _____ is assured of a healthy future."

If photography is not available, use drawings to break up the text and illustrate your points. If you have a staff person or volunteer who likes to draw, ask them to come up with some simple line art. You can also take advantage of the hundreds of clip art pictures in standard computer fonts or on the Web that can be downloaded and incorporated into computer files. Or, you can find books of clip art images in an art supply store.

3. HEADLINES

To make sure your headlines and subheads are readable, put them in bigger type. They become part of the visual appeal and act as signposts for the reader. In a newsletter with several articles, easy-to-spot headlines keep the reader oriented and allow them to find quickly just what they want to read.

4. WHITE SPACE

Like illustrations, white space on the page rests the eye, giving the reader a short "breather" from text, pictures, and information. White space makes a piece look friendlier than a page covered with type. Concise writing, rather than a lot of words, will give your points more impact. If there's no relief on the page, your piece just won't get read. Incorporate white space between columns and between paragraphs, have extra space before and after headings and subheadings and around illustrations, and make sure the page has adequate margins.

5. LINE LENGTH

Another element that creates white space is line length — that is, the width of the lines of type on the page. An 8.5" × 11" page that has words clear from one side of the page to the other is difficult to read. Once you've gotten to the far right-hand side of that wide line, your eye has trouble holding its horizontal place on the page as it scans back to the left, so you end up reading the same line twice or skipping a line.

To avoid this problem, keep line lengths to five inches or less and put your text into columns. Be sure the columns aren't too narrow, though, so you don't end up with lots of hyphenated words; this also interferes with reading flow.

6. SUBHEADS

If your piece is long, you can give the reader needed breaks while keeping them interested in continuing. First, see if you can make your paragraphs shorter. Either shorten the sentences in each paragraph, or divide what may seem like a single idea into a couple of paragraphs of related ideas. Once something is set in four- or five-inch line lengths, even short paragraphs look long.

Another useful approach is to break the text into sections and give each section a title or subheading. These subheadings should be short descriptors of the material to come, in bold type either flush left or centered.

7. TYPE STYLES

Some typefaces are easier to read than others. For copy that is longer than a headline or a short piece (such as an invitation or announcement), a "serif" typeface is generally used. Serifs are the short strokes that "decorate" the letters, such as on the type you are reading now. These short strokes help carry the eye from letter to letter and therefore ease reading. Headlines, material in boxes, and shorter pieces will often be set in a "sans serif" typeface — as they are in the *Journal*. These create contrast and have a declamatory feel.

In general, it's best not to use more than two typefaces in a piece. Standard complementary typefaces often used in tandem are Helvetica (a sans serif face) for headlines and Times Roman (the typeface of the *London Times* — an authoritative typeface) for body copy. With the plethora of fonts now available on computers, it's fun and easy to play around with myriad typefaces. In the end, though, readability must come first, and matching serif and sans serif faces can be a hit-or-miss proposition unless you have some sophisticated knowledge of design principles.

Within each typeface, there are options for italic, bold, and other variations to lend emphasis to text. But not overdoing emphasis will keep a piece clean. Excessive use of underlining, bold, and italic tires the eye and makes the reader feel manipulated. Use these eye-catchers sparingly. And never use all caps to emphasize a word. In e-mail parlance, the use of all capital letters is called "flaming" because it makes the reader feel screamed at. Use italic for emphasis.

Many fundraising appeals arrive with handwritten notes in the margin, line after line underscored, dozens of exclamation points in the text, or whole phrases or sentences in all capital letters. These techniques will not stir your readers to action beyond wanting to dump the piece in the recycle bin as soon as possible. Lucid prose and a strong argument will make a much better case.

A final point about type: Be sure to make it large enough. If you have so much to say that your graphic designer or computer person is having to use a smaller type size (measured in "points"), decide where you can cut the piece rather than expect that people will strain to read smaller print. Most won't. Keep your pieces to no less than 12-point type with adequate white space between the lines and it's more likely to be read.

WORKING WITH PRODUCTION PROFESSIONALS

Working effectively with production people is key to getting the final printed product you want. Each person in the sphere of graphic design and production is a professional with a large body of knowledge and skills that can be useful to the final impact of your printed piece. However, in order to make maximum use of both their time and yours and to make sure you and they are on the same track, it's helpful to know the language they speak. The two production professionals you are most likely to deal with are graphic designers and printers or their representatives.

Even if you design much of your materials in-house, for pieces that need to have maximum impact, I recommend including some money for professional graphic design in your publications budget. If you factor in the time that paid staff spend fooling around with their computer to get materials to look good, you may find that going to a professional designer saves both time and money.

Here are some suggestions for working with designers and printers.

Graphic Designers

Graphic designers are skilled and experienced in placing text and artwork on the page to best effect. They know how different elements — text blocks, pull quotes, illustrations, photographs, headlines, subheads, etc. — should be balanced. They know what should be on the right-hand side of a page and what should be on the left-hand side, and they know how to keep the top and bottom halves of the page in balance and proportion so that the eye is drawn to each element without one or another getting more emphasis than it needs. Finally, they are familiar with design techniques to give your piece some flair.

However, a word of caution: To be sure your piece reflects your group, be very communicative in working with your designer. Even though graphic designers are professionals in presenting ideas effectively, they do not necessarily share your perception of your educational message. Not being as familiar with the content, they may be tempted to emphasize graphic elements at the expense of the educational message. In my very first experience working with a graphic designer, I was persuaded to let a photograph dominate a poster, subordinating the educational text to small type accompanied by obscure cartoon characters. The graphic designer and I had not "seen" the elements of the message in similar ways.

You can avoid such expensive and frustrating experiences by thoroughly discussing with your designer at the outset which elements you hold to be most important. This is as true for designing newsletters and brochures as for posters or public service ads.

Graphic designers have a host of fun things they can do to make a piece look spiffy and sophisticated, and they understandably want to try out their techniques when they can. Tints and screens, overlays, additional colors, special treatments of photographs, colors or photographs "bleeding" off the edges of the page, type reversed out of black or colored backgrounds — all of these can make a piece dramatic — and they all cost money when you get to the printer.

Because it's in the graphic designer's nature to expand their creative vocabulary and to produce visually interesting pieces, be sure you have some agreements at the start of every job specifying its cost limitations. These agreements should include an estimate of what the design job will cost, with an agreement to renegotiate if the designer begins to exceed the estimate by more than 10%; an understanding of the maximum you want to spend on printing (this will help determine how much you can invest in "special effects" at the design stage); and a time line. Beyond cost agreements, you should discuss with the designer at the outset the type of "look" or "feel" you want the piece to convey and what you see as its most important messages.

Proofreading

You are responsible for thoroughly proofreading material before it goes to print. Any errors are your responsibility to find and have corrected, not the designer's. This means that you have to allow enough time in your production schedule (usually a couple of extra days) for proofreading and for corrections to be made. When the corrections come back, these must be proofread as well.

Proofreading is a skill in itself, and people who are trained as professional proofreaders know how to look for the types of mistakes that occur most frequently. Do not count on your computer's spell-check function alone to proofread material you send to design. Spell-check programs will not question anything that is a word, even if it is the wrong word at that point. So, for example, if you type "and" when you meant "an," "he" when you meant "the," or "our" when you meant "your, " no spell-checker will alert you to those mistakes.

You can do an adequate job of proofreading your materials if you follow a few simple rules. First, two different people should proofread all materials. Regardless of how careful a reader one person is, they are likely to miss at least one or two errors. Second, if possible, at least one of the proofreaders should be someone who is not familiar with the text. Their mind will not race ahead of the type, knowing what's to come and skipping over what's actually on the page.

Third, the proofreaders should become familiar with proofreaders' symbols to indicate what's wrong in the type, taking the guesswork out for the person who is correcting errors. The most common symbols are the following:

℘	Delete one letter
℮	Delete entire word
∧	Insert
h̲	Make this letter capital
¶	Start new paragraph
∿	No new paragraph here (run on)
#	Insert space
∧	Period
=/	Hyphen
∧	Comma
italic	Italic
bold	Bold
∨	Apostrophe
∩∪	Transpose

Working effectively with production people is key to getting the final printed piece product you want. Each person in the sphere of graphic design and production is a professional with a large body of knowledge and skills that can be useful to the final impact of your printed piece. however, you need to know the language they speak in order to make maximum use of both their time and yours and to make sure you and they are on the same track. The two important production professionals you may deal with are graphic designers and printers or their representatives.

The illustration shows a piece of copy marked for corrections. You can find full listings of proofreading symbols in standard copyediting texts such as *Copyediting: A Practical Guide* by Karen Judd (Los Altos: Crisp Publications, 2001) and *The Chicago Manual of Style* (14th Edition, University of Chicago, 1993). Speaking the language of the designer by learning basic proofreading symbols will ensure that the corrections you want are the corrections you get.

Printers

As with choosing any professional, you need to get the right printer for the job. One criteria is how many pieces you are printing. According to one printer the *Journal* has worked with extensively, for jobs of less than 500 pieces, photocopying is often the best choice. Jobs of 500 to 2,000 pieces can be done by "quick printing" or "instant printing" shops (which use less durable paper printing plates). Larger jobs, up to 10,000 pieces, are best done by offset printing (which uses metal printing plates), and jobs even larger than that are usually run on a web press, which prints from large rolls of paper.

Printing prices vary widely, depending on many factors beyond the print run, including the type of machinery the printer uses, the number of colors on the job, the final size of the piece, whether folding, stapling, or gluing are involved, the turnaround time needed, and the type of deal the printer can get on paper (the cost of paper is a major, and constantly changing, variable). In addition, using a union shop may cost more; this is where your political decisions can affect costs. (For example, the *Journal* uses union printers on principle and willingly pays the extra cost to do so.)

Always get at least two bids on your print jobs and, where possible, visit printers to look at paper samples and samples of their work. The lowest bid doesn't necessarily come from the best printer, so let price be only one element in your choice.

As with the graphic designer, be very specific with the printer about what you want your finished product to be. When you deliver your job for printing, tell the printer in writing the following information:

- The number of pieces
- The direction of the fold — for example, if you have a legal-sized sheet being folded into four vertical panels, do you want it folded in half and then in half again, or do you want an accordion-style fold?
- The exact color(s) — most printers use colors from the Pantone Color Formula Guide (also called PMS)
- The specific paper — the printer should show you several weights and colors of paper and tell you the difference in price and quality
- The delivery date and address for delivery

Like the rest of us, busy printers are always juggling many projects, and some of them may go past the agreed-upon deadline; if your job can't wait a few days past its delivery date, make sure the printer knows that. Similarly, if there is some flexibility in when you need the job, the printer will be grateful to be able to build that into their press schedule, and may be particularly considerate in the future if you need something in a rush.

Production People: Where to Find Them

You find competent, efficient, and affordable production people the same way you find other consultants: Ask people in other organizations who they recommend; interview potential vendors, asking to see samples of their work and discussing their pricing policies; check their work style and reliability with their references.

Enough Time to Do the Job Right

The designer and printer are the last people in the flow of getting your printed materials out to your audience. As often as not, the development of the piece has taken longer than you anticipated: The annual report is now a month overdue, the newsletter has to get out in the next two weeks, and the fundraising letter really should have been in the mail already. As a result of our own delays, we often unwittingly end up saddling production people with the final urgency for getting a job completed. This puts them at a disadvantage in doing their best work, frazzles their nerves and yours, and can contribute to misunderstandings that will show up in the finished product.

If you've taken an extra week, or month, or more to get your work done, don't expect your production people to make up that time for you. Give them enough time to do their job right, and next time build more leeway into your planning so that everyone can accommodate those unexpected but inevitable delays.

JUST THE WORDS THAT MATTER

Once you've attracted your reader's attention with a good-looking, well-produced piece, you have to keep it with effective copy. Good writing, like most of the work we do, is the product of planning and style.

Just as with any project, written materials need to be planned. You wouldn't set out to have a dance or provide a new service without carefully thinking through all the details of the project, enlisting the people you need to help you, and going about it step by step. Producing written materials is much the same, although in a shorter time frame.

People often put off planning, thinking that action is more important — get that flyer written or that newsletter out. But unless you're an extremely clear-thinking person, you'd do well to give yourself the "luxury" of planning. This is more obvious when you're thinking about creating an annual report than producing an invitation to a conference or a letter to members, but the principle is the same. By planning well in advance, you can make a realistic timeline to include the elements that make your piece worth reading.

Four Key Planning Steps

First, decide your purpose: Why are you writing something anyway? What do people need to know? What is the primary message you want to get across? You may want to have others help you brainstorm this point. With a newsletter, for example, thinking ahead can help you avoid the last-minute rush to get articles, or help you know what to leave out if you have too much copy. If you plan ahead, you may be able to come up with themes or topics to build each newsletter around, and that means you could ask people for articles well in advance of the deadline.

If you are producing a major piece, such as an annual report, you may also want to develop a theme or pattern to unify the sections of the piece, such as a day in the life of your organization, profiles of people you've served, or case vignettes. A battered women's shelter, for example, could follow a woman as she comes into care and gains confidence and skills through the programs offered and the kinds of help she receives at the shelter. A hospital volunteer program could follow two (or more) volunteers through their days in the hospital showing the range of services the volunteer office provides.

Next, identify your audience so you can focus your writing to the intended reader. If your purpose is to tell city council members or legislators what you've accomplished, your approach will be different than if your goal is to inform potential clients about your services.

When thinking about your annual report, for example, decide whether it's meant to report on your program in a general way to donors, to educate your constituency about your services in a very specific way, or to impress your legislators or other decision makers with the importance of the services or advocacy your organization provides. You can see that purpose and audience go hand in hand.

Consider here how important statistics and financial data are to your purpose, so you know how to treat them in the text. If your financial information is not as important as your program reports, then tables of numbers and pie charts can take up less space than program information. If, on the other hand, your financial information is of primary importance to those reading the report, then by all means give it a lot of room and concentrate on making the graphic presentation as dynamic as possible.

Third, define your format: What will best meet your purpose, suit your audience, and possibly be new, stimulating, and exciting? For example, some years ago the Women's Foundation of San Francisco designed its annual report on one large sheet (11" × 17") that folded down to mailing size. They used a handsome paper and design to enhance the piece, and they fit all the basic information they wanted to give onto that one poster-sized page.

The ultimate "look" of the piece, as determined by format choices, may also influence how you write it. If, for example, you decide that a picture story might be a fresh and inviting way to present your material, you may limit your text to short but thorough explanatory captions rather than an essay.

Fourth, decide who can help you. Consider soliciting help in deciding what to say, such as with an educational brochure, or in actually writing drafts or sections of the piece, such as articles for a newsletter or segments of an annual report. If you have a standing editorial committee of your board (or other volunteers) that helps you brainstorm the content of the newsletter or annual report or the look of various pieces, make sure you use them. They may have wonderful new ideas to bring from their experience with other organizations or their workplace. If you don't have an editorial committee, consider developing one. Two or three volunteers from your program or board can provide consistent help in brainstorming and then checking content, style, looks, and continuity with other written materials.

You may also want to use someone inside or outside the organization to give you feedback on written pieces. This may be a key volunteer or board member, the executive director, or the public relations person (for larger organizations). When planning your production schedule, make sure you include time for these people to read drafts and suggest revisions.

Ready, Set, Outline

Now that you know why you're writing something, who is going to read it, and who is going to help you along the way, you can start writing. But do you dread facing the blank sheet of paper or blank computer screen? Do you expect yourself to pour forth with lucid, sparkling prose? Most writing doesn't begin that way. You can help yourself begin by making a list of the principal points you want to cover. For a newsletter article there may be only one or two points: something happened and your organization had a role in it. For an educational brochure, there may be four or five, or more: the need for your services, what the services are, how they are paid for, how to use them.

For example, to develop an educational brochure on the sexually transmitted disease chlamydia, I met with a group of health providers and asked them to tell me everything they thought their patients needed to know about the disease. As they talked, I took copious notes. When I got back to my office, I developed a list of statements that had emerged from the meeting. From there it was easy to build paragraphs around each of these statements.

When you know your key points, state each one in a short declarative sentence. This may be more difficult than it sounds, but it will save you from hopeless muddle in the end.

If outlining in this way is antithetical to your personality and the only way you can start is to just get writing, then try checking what you have written by outlining it afterward. Read each paragraph and write in the margin what the topic of that paragraph is. If you find that each sentence in the paragraph is a topic in itself (a common finding of this method), then you'll know you have too many ideas in one place and you can begin to separate them into their own paragraphs. Keep in mind that presenting ideas and information clearly usually means offering one well-developed thought at a time.

If you've started by making an outline of what to say in simple, clear, and concise statements, then you can evaluate and revise them until they are appropriate to your purpose and interesting to your readers.

The First Draft

Now you're ready to write a first draft. Take each of your topic sentences and flesh out the idea with supporting data and illustrations. Consider how one paragraph flows into the next, and add some phrases to relate them to each other. Phrases and words such as "on the other hand," "moreover," "furthermore," "in addition," "or," and "meanwhile" create bridges from one idea to the next and keep the reader moving through the story.

When your draft is done, let it sit for a few days. If you don't have a few days, give it what I call "the 24-hour rule" by not looking at it at least overnight. After you get away from it, you will come back with a fresher eye. I follow this rule even with correspondence that's of any substance; say, a letter to a researcher or to a donor or legislator. The next day, or a few days later, I guarantee you'll find ways to say things more concretely, briefly, and clearly.

While the piece is sitting in your in-box, start thinking about how you want it to look when it's printed. Keep in mind the graphic elements discussed in the first part of this article. Thinking about layout and design issues now will have an effect on how you approach the length and organi-zation of the piece when you come back to your writing.

If you are not doing the layout yourself, now is the time to meet with the person who is. For example, while writing a brochure about agencies for runaway youth and their families, I met with the designer. Together, we decided that a strong statement on the cover could introduce what the brochure was about and lead the reader inside. That meant composing the right number of words to fit on the cover, having them say just the right thing with just the right emphasis, and getting approval from the client. This step took time. Fortunately, it was time we had while the draft was going through revisions.

When you take your piece out of your in-box again, you'll be ready to start revising. As you reread it, look for common obstacles to clear writing; these include wordiness, ambiguities, jargon, lack of focus, abstract rather than concrete images, misplaced thoughts or elements, and passive rather than active wording.

After you've done at least one revision, you're ready to show the piece to others for comments. When you're ready for advice, seek it openly. Rid yourself of that time-consuming ego trip called "pride of authorship." This isn't the great American novel. Ask your editorial committee or people most familiar with the topic to read and comment on what you've written.

Despite busy schedules, it doesn't take long for someone to review even a relatively long piece, such as an annual report, and the piece will benefit from another perspective. Not only can your reader correct any facts that might be wrong, they can also point out problems with the writing and suggest additions that might strengthen the piece. With comments and suggestions from your readers, decide which suggestions to incorporate and revise the piece again.

As you work on it this time, keep in mind how it will look on the page. Does it need shorter paragraphs? Are there places where you can break up the text with subheadings? For longer pieces, such as educational brochures, it's critical to direct your reader's attention to the different points of information so that someone who only wants to know, for example, about treatment of a condition or service hours of your agency or your legislative strategy can find it easily. To get them there, use subheadings as a guide to the text.

Style

Style involves those elements that make the writing clear, help it to move along smoothly, maintain your reader's interest, and show the reader your respect for their intelligence and their time. Anyone who has written a term paper has probably used Strunk and White's classic reference, *Elements of Style*. There are, in fact, a number of books relating to style that you might want to dip into from time to time to sharpen your writing (see box). Here are ten style elements relevant to the type of writing we're talking about.

1. Keep in mind exactly who your reader will be. For example, when I was hired to write a text on how to write a grant proposal, my instructions included the following paragraph:

> Write it as if it were written to volunteers, most of whom have two years of college at a community school, have not traveled widely, think foundations will save them, and want to start or get more money for their humane society, church school, health clinic, food bank, homeless shelter, Big Sisters program, etc. Imagine them also to be primarily in small towns or rural areas, with limited or no access to other reference materials.

This tells me just how to approach a piece in terms of tone, style, word choice, and breadth and depth information.

2. Keep your message brief. Even an ardent supporter has only a few minutes to focus on your message. This is where knowing just what you want to get across comes in. In addition, keep all the elements short: short words, short sentences, short paragraphs.

- Membership and appeal letters need not be more than two sides of one page.

- Keeping an informational brochure short will allow for white space and make room for art — either photos or graphics.

- Annual reports should spend one or two sentences on background, one or two sentences on program description, and use two to four sentences for accomplishments (for each program).

- Newsletter articles should also follow these rules.

3. Use active verbs and active construction; eliminate the passive voice. Passive voice is a favorite of deadly dull bureaucratic language. (See box).

4. Use examples and illustrations — verbal and visual — to make your material come to life.

5. Don't tell people what they must do — assume they can think for themselves when they know the facts about the situation, then give them an understanding of what action can help. Wouldn't you rather feel you're making your own choice than being preached to, threatened, or "guilt tripped"?

For example, don't tell people that unless they vote for Proposition A libraries all over the state will close. Tell them the importance of the library to their community, the impact of funding cuts, the remedies that Proposition A promises. Then let them know they have a chance to keep the libraries open by voting for the proposition.

6. Weed out jargon, alphabet soup, clichés, and flowery adjectives. Keep it simple.

Useful Books and References on Writing Style

Theodore Bernstein, *Do's, Don'ts and Maybes of English Usage,* Random House, 1995 ($6.99).

Casey Miller and Kate Swift, *The Handbook of Nonsexist Writing,* 1980 (Print on demand, about $15; order through your bookstore).

William Strunk, Jr., and E. B. White. *The Elements of Style,* 4th Edition, Allyn & Bacon, Inc., 1999 ($6.95).

Francis-Noel Thomas and Mark Turner, *Clear and Simple as the Truth: Writing Classic Prose,* Princeton University Press, 1994 ($16.95).

University of Chicago Press, *The Chicago Manual of Style,* 14th Edition, 1993 ($45).

Jan Venolia, *Write Right! A Desktop Digest of Punctuation, Grammar, and Style,* Ten Speed Press, 1995 ($6.95) .

Passive versus Active Voice

Passive: Five bills are selected each year by the Advisory Board as priority issues.
Active: Each year the Advisory Board concentrates on five top issues.

Passive: Representatives are sent by each committee.
Active: Each committee sends a representative.

Passive: Grazing standards on ranches was the subject of a workshop led by the Advisory Commission.
Active: The Advisory Commission held a workshop on ranch grazing standards.

Passive: Miriam is going back to school. She will be missed.
Active: We will miss her.

Passive: Contributions from clients to further expand the program are invited.
Active: Client contributions will help us provide service to even more people.

7. *Instead of fancy words, use easy, familiar words.* A plain tone is more forceful. I once saw a corporate memo forbidding "portable personal consumption confectionery units" at workers' desks. Honest. They were talking about candy bars. An employment program for seniors described itself by writing, "The purpose of the program is to provide, foster, and promote useful work experience activities for seniors." Why not say, "The program finds work for seniors"?

8. *Remember that each paragraph should begin with one clear point, with the next sentences providing examples or supporting facts.*

9. *Revise, and, if you have time, revise again, cutting out all unnecessary words.* Look at your second paragraph. Chances are it says what you meant in your first paragraph once you were warmed up. Many pieces do much better to start with their second paragraph. A corollary to this principle is to avoid introductory remarks. Get the reader right into your story or your appeal or report. Here are some ways to do that:

- Use a startling statement, such as a little-known fact, to catch the reader's attention.

- Give a piece of news, such as a legislative breakthrough or something that has happened that affects the reader's life.

- Use a quotation from a known person (Daniel Webster, Ben Franklin, Simone de Beauvoire, etc.).

- Use a story, such as about a client you have helped (a real story).

10. *Let others brag for you.* If you're trying to impress potential donors or supporters with the value of your services, use real testimonials from real people. Don't write an endorsement and then ask someone to put their name to it. It will undoubtedly sound "canned." Ask a few clients or a few volunteers to say in their own words what your service or organization has meant to them.

Clear writing is a matter of knowing what you want to say and working with the words to get it right. Clear writing will get your message across and enhance your organization's cause.

1998

Ten Ways to Get More from Your Printing Budget

By LINCOLN CUSHING

Every organization needs printing, and it can be a large portion of its budget. Having seen thousands of jobs come across our counter over the years, we find that there are recurring issues that would save both clients and printers a lot of expense and aggravation. In our ongoing effort to save trees, tempers, and timelines, we offer the following tips.

1. Be organized. One person in an office should be responsible for handling all printing orders. It is not uncommon for two different people to place orders for the same job because of vacation overlaps, or for one person in an office to order a single set of business cards without knowing that their entire business printing design is to be revised the next week.

2. Plan out the big picture. Know your audience and delivery method. What is it that you are trying to achieve? Efforts to reach upscale donors or informing membership usually call for different levels of flashiness and expense. Perhaps the best way to publicize your open house is a simple flyer rather than a three-color poster. Knowing the end recipient of the printed piece and how it will reach them is the first step in making smart printing decisions. Often getting advice from direct-mail professionals and mailhouses will save you a lot of time and money.

3. Use standard sizes and formats. A 7" × 9" program booklet may be cute, but it could also cost you almost double what a 6" × 9" one will. Don't make assumptions about standards — one common mistake is to base booklets on a legal-size sheet (8.5" × 14"), which is not efficiently available in papers other than 20 pound bond. Let your designer/printer know that you are flexible and interested in cost-saving suggestions.

4. Accurately assess your numbers. Nothing is more frustrating for a print buyer than to order a mailing of 5,000 and then be told when the job reaches the mailhouse that the actual mailing list is 6,500. Rerunning a job is slightly cheaper than it was to print the first time, but it is still dramatically more expensive than a longer run to begin with. If you need exact count, be sure to let your printer know — trade customs allow that quantities of 10% over or under your order are acceptable.

5. Try to use the most appropriate reproduction method. Roughly speaking, the best way to reproduce small quantities (1–500) of a document is by photocopying or docuteching; the next step up (500–2,000) is "quick printing" (disposable plates), then offset printing with metal plates (500–10,000), and finally web printing (for very large numbers), running from rolls of paper. Other technical factors that will affect your options include use of photos, desired print quality, choices of paper, and ability to gang parts of a job together. It is important to note that as organizations get bigger (or smaller), their printing needs change. The corner copy shop that printed their small-run four-page newsletter may not be the best place to handle their larger-run eight-page newsletter. Also, just because something is physically small doesn't mean it should be printed on a small sheet — it is often most efficient to run large numbers of flyers several up on a large sheet.

6. Not all donated paper and services can be used. Sometimes nonprofits can get expensive portions of a job donated, such as paper or color separations. In all cases, be sure that you work with your designer/printer to make sure that the materials supplied meet their technical specifications. For example, paper should be of a type suitable for the job, it must be an appropriate sheet size, it must show up in time to print and be in good condition. Be prepared to use a house sheet as backup in case the supplied donated paper doesn't work.

7. **Get appropriate graphic design.** Good design can make or break a printed piece, but be sure that whoever you use is familiar with your budget and audience. A classic printer's nightmare involves equal parts designer fresh out of school looking to create an award-winning product, an overworked client giving said designer free rein in putting together an annual report, and an unspecified budget. Using volunteer design and type can be a great idea, but be careful. Not all designers are attuned to the slim budgets of nonprofits, and the recurring costs of producing overdesigned printing may be far more than a single fee to a professional who has the long-term interests of the organization at heart.

8. **Avoid late changes.** It may seem obvious, but make sure that copy is proofread before it goes off to the designer. Catching a misspelled donor's name at a blueline proof could easily cost you $50 or more.

9. **Avoid rush work.** Again, planning helps. Aside from additional charges, rushed work lead to shortcuts and hasty proofing, which lead to errors, and then everybody is unhappy. This problem has actually gotten worse with the advent of "desktop publishing" (digital page composition), because clients now expect instant results. In some ways this has created new and greater opportunities for errors, such as a minor font substitution reflowing text and knocking out a final sentence. You must allow time and attention for all proofing stages. It is especially important to see a blueline, which is made from the final film and reveals the actual pagination and folding. Tight schedules work best when you call ahead to schedule time and have the technical people talk to each other to make sure there are no nasty surprises.

10. **Price is not everything.** Saving a few dollars on a job is usually no reason to drag your printing all over town. Other factors to consider in a long-term relationship with your printer include volume discounts, the convenience of having film or type on file, their familiarity with your work and staff, and the support of union shops and affirmative-action vendors. If you are a regular account, letting your printer know that a particular project needs some financial support may well result in a discount.

SOME USEFUL TERMS

Most printers will work with you to understand technical issues affecting a job; knowing some of the basics will help get you off to a good start. These are some common terms in the trade:

Bleed — when the ink "runs off" the edge of the sheet (like the cover of this magazine); in reality it is printed on a larger sheet and then trimmed.

Folds — some folds are easier (and cheaper) than others. Simple folds are half-fold, letterfold, Z-fold, accordion (like a Z-fold but more panels), and barrel or roll fold. The trickiest parallel fold is a double gate fold, in which the two outside edges fold towards the center twice; this adds time and expense.

Cracking — this is the result of the paper surface and/or ink film breaking on a fold, and is most undesirable where there is heavy ink. Heavy stocks and coated paper aggravate this situation; special scoring minimizes it.

Register — the fit between the edges of a multicolor job. Images with very tight register over large areas are more difficult, especially for small press work.

Trapping — similar to register, it is where one color of ink slightly overlaps another to give the illusion of fitting together exactly.

Halftone — the technical trick used in printing to reproduce a range of shades with a single color of ink by breaking up the image into tiny dots. All printed photographs use some version of halftoning. It is increasingly common for documents created in electronic format to have the photos scanned in, which halftones them. However, beware of poorly done scans; when in doubt, ask for a proof before printing and allow time for fixes. A related item is a screen tint, which is filling in an area with a percentage of solid ink. Very dark tints (over 70%) tend to "fill in" to solid when printed.

Pinched type — the filling in of small lettering that reverses out of a solid background.

Ghosted image — "screening back" (halftoning to a lighter shade) of an image or solid to allow for type to be legible in front of it. This type can sometimes be hard to read if the background image is busy.

1996

Fundraising Strategies

I. RAISING MONEY BY MAIL

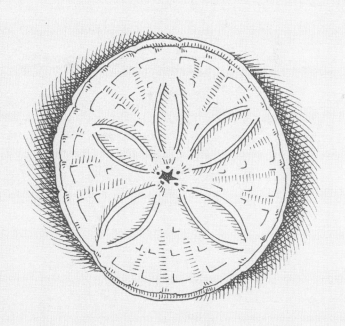

The Direct Mail Fundraising Letter

By KIM KLEIN

Most people who are good at fundraising are also good writers. Since most of our work is done through writing, a grasp of decent writing skills is essential. However, being a good writer will not automatically make you a good writer of direct mail letters, or indeed of many kinds of letters. The basic tenets of direct mail writing are often not the basic tenets of good expository writing. A brief look at what a fundraising letter is and is not will show why this is so.

A fundraising letter is not literature. It is not designed to be lasting, or to be filed away or to be read several times with new insights emerging from each reading. It is disposable, and it is part of a culture increasingly acclimated to disposable goods of all kinds — from diapers and cameras to contact lenses. The function of the fundraising letter, then, is to catch attention and hold it just long enough for a person to decide to give.

Keeping this in mind, whenever you decide to sit down to write a fundraising letter (or, indeed, a grant proposal, which is basically a really long fundraising letter), first think for a minute about who you are writing to. Ask yourself these questions: Do the recipients of the letter read well? Do they like to read? Where will they receive the letter (i.e., home, office) and what are those environments like?

For example, imagine a person coming home from work, picking up the mail, figuring out what to make for dinner, making sure the kids are doing their homework, and perhaps vacuuming or dusting while dinner cooks. How receptive will such a person be to your request? When will he or she even read your letter?

Think of the mood of the whole country. Working people are concerned about losing their jobs, paying their bills, crime, health care, the declining quality of schools, pollution — to say nothing of the international scene, with its daily pictures and articles about war, starvation, murder, refugees, etc. How crucial or relevant is your message given all the other things going on in people's lives and in the world?

On top of all this, be aware that your letter arrives with anywhere from one to six other fundraising letters. What will make yours the one that is read?

And finally, keep in mind that the recipient of a fundraising letter reads this letter on their own time, for free, as a volunteer. It is not their job to read the letter, and if the letter has its intended result, they will wind up paying money for having read the letter.

THE PSYCHOLOGY OF LETTER READING

A fundraising letter has a very difficult job with no power whatsoever. Using letters to ask for money, whether on a mass scale or in one-to-one personal appeals, requires reflecting on the psychology of letter reading. Before you even begin to write, keep in mind the following three premises:

1. When reading, watching TV or a movie, listening to a lecture, or even to a lesser extent listening to someone they care about, adults subconsciously go back and forth between two questions. The first question is, "So what?" If this question is answered satisfactorily, they move on to the next question, which is, "Now what?" This "So what? / Now what?" seesaw is a strong screening device for filtering out trivia, boring details, and rhetoric.

To be sure, what is trivial or boring to one person may be profound or lifesaving to another, so the answers to these questions will vary somewhat from person to person.

However, details about when your organization was founded or the permutations of your organizational structure may not pass the "So what?" test, and the myriad problems that led to your current budget deficit will only bring on a fit of "Now what?" questioning. As you write your letter, imagine your reader asking at the end of each sentence, "So what? What does this have to do with me, my problems, or the people I care about?" If the sentence stands up under that scrutiny, then read the next sentence while asking, "Now what?" Does this sentence offer a solution, provide more information, create confidence in the group?

2. People have very short attention spans, particularly for the written word. A person should be able to read each sentence in your letter in 6 to 15 seconds. Each sentence must be informative or provocative enough to merit using the next 6 to 15 seconds to read the next sentence.

3. More than anything else, people love to read about themselves. This is partly because of #1, the "So what — Now what?" question. "What does this have to do with me?" is an underlying question. But it also reflects a desire to be treated personally. The reader of a fundraising letter wonders, "Do you know or care anything about me?" "Why do you think I would be interested in this?" "Will giving your group money make me happier or give me status or relieve my guilt?" "Did you notice that I helped before?"

Therefore, the letter should refer to the reader at least twice as often and up to four times as often as it refers to the organization sending it. To do this requires drawing the reader into the cause by saying, "You may have read," "I'm sure you join me in feeling," "If you are like me, you care deeply about..." When writing to someone who is already a donor to solicit another gift or a renewal, use even more references to what they have done. "You helped us in the past." "Your gift of $50 meant a great deal to us last year." "I want you to know that we rely on people like you — you are the backbone of our organization."

Of course, in the case of a form letter, the person receiving it knows it is not directed to him or her; but at a less conscious level, there is a belief that he or she is being addressed personally. The subconscious cannot tell fact from fantasy and believes everything to be real. (That's why dreams seem very real, why affirmations work, and how you can make a child smarter or more graceful by telling her that she has those qualities.)

Work with those three premises as you write your letter. Notice letters that you read, and try to figure out why you take the time to read them. Notice also what parts of the letter you read, and why. As a consumer of fundraising letters, you are not so different from the people you will be writing to.

THE FORMAT OF THE LETTER

People generally read fundraising letters in a specific order: the opening paragraph (or only the opening sentence if the paragraph is long), the closing paragraph, and the postscript. As many as 60% of readers will decide whether or not to give based on these three sentences and will not read the rest of the letter. The remaining 40% of people will skim the rest of the letter. Only a tiny handful of people will read the letter all the way through.

Given this pattern of letter reading, you should spend most of your writing time on the sentences that are most read. Write the rest of the letter to make sense if skimmed.

The Opening Paragraph

Use the opening paragraph to tell a story, either about someone your group has helped, some situation your group has helped rectify, or about the reader of the letter. There is a saying in fundraising, "People buy with their heart first, and then their head." Programs and outcomes need to be described in "people" terms (or animal, if that is your constituency). This can be done without being condescending or melodramatic. The stories should be short and should end with something about your organization. Here are some examples:

Someone the group worked with:

Tony and her children, five and eight, have been homeless for two years, moving in and out of shelters. Tony occasionally gets work, but is never able to save enough to pay the security deposit on an apartment or to afford child care while she is at work. This week, because of Homes Now, Tony and her children will move into a two-bedroom home, and Monday morning she will start a full-time job. Her children will be cared for at our day care program.

The paragraph ends here. The body of the letter goes on to explain the philosophy of this group and provide a description of their work, which includes helping people find and move into appropriate housing, and use job placement, job training, and day care services.

A situation the group helped rectify:

To some people it looked like a vacant lot, full of weeds, old tires, and paper trash. Kids play baseball there and sometimes families have picnics there, but when Dreck Development proposed a parking lot, few objected. After all, it is a poor neighborhood and a parking lot would be useful to the commuters who work in the industrial park a few blocks away. To Joe Camereno, the lot looked like a park. He called Inner City Greenspace and asked us how to go about protecting this vacant lot. How did this come about?

The opening ends here. The rest of the letter lets people know how Inner City Greenspace can help them transform vacant lots, treeless streets, and abandoned buildings into more livable community spaces.

Where the reader of the letter is part of the story:

As a resident of Rio Del Vista, you were probably as shocked as I was to learn of the toxic waste dump proposed for Del Vista Lake last year. Working together, we were able to save this lake, but now the dump is proposed for Del Vista Canyon. We've got another fight on our hands.

The letter goes on to explain how and why this town must gear up and fight this dump battle again.

The Closing Paragraph

The last paragraph of the letter tells people what to do. It is specific and straightforward:

Send your gift of $25, $50, $75, or whatever you can afford. Use the enclosed envelope and do it today.

Or,

Don't delay in responding. Your gift will be put right to work. We need it as soon as you can get it to us. Thanks.

The P.S.

The postscript ties people back into the letter by telling a story or offering additional incentive for acting immediately.

A story:

An independent study showed that the quality of our schools has improved because of Community Concern. It also showed we have a long way to go. For the sake of the children, please make the donation today.

Incentives:

We have a donor who will give $1 for every dollar we are able to raise between now and Oct. 1.

Or,

If we hear from you by April 15, we will send you two free tickets to our dance May 1.

The Rest of the Letter

The rest of the letter is used to tell more stories, provide backup statistics, describe philosophy, and stress the need for money. The letter needs to be two to three pages long so that readers get the sense that you have enough to say, and that all of the information they might want is in the letter. This length also gives you room to make the letter easy to read, with wide margins, decent-sized type, and space between paragraphs.

The tiny percent of response that we can expect from a direct mail appeal shows how little power the appeal has. However, appeals do educate the public, raise consciousness, and plant the idea that your organization deserves to be supported. By using mail carefully, you will not only gain new donors, you will also build a network of people who have heard of your organization and might support its work.

1993

Mail Appeals:
Will They Open the Envelope?

By KIM KLEIN

Many mail appeals fail because, although much attention has been spent writing an effective letter, it is enclosed in an envelope that no one opens.

Mail appeals are called "packages" because they are more than letters in an envelope. The entire unit consists of the letter, the return form and return envelope, and the outside envelope in which the contents are sent. Each is an important part of the package.

Personal and business mail that is sent first class can arrive in a plain envelope with little doubt that the person receiving the letter will open it. In the case of first-class mail, the envelope is simply a convenient way to carry the message.

In a fundraising appeal sent by bulk mail, however, the outside envelope has an entirely different purpose. It must grab the prospect's attention and then intrigue them enough that they want to open it and see what's inside. The envelope in this case is like gift wrapping. Everyone wants to know what's inside a present. In fact, gift wrapping works so well that even when you know what a gift is, the wrapping still provides the thrill of discovery in opening it.

That thrill and that curiosity is what you should strive for with mail appeals. Your job is to make the prospect want to know what is inside the envelope.

There are many ways to entice someone to open an envelope; different ways will be effective with different audiences. For the purposes of this article, we will concentrate on the effective use of an outside envelope for small mail appeals (200–5,000 pieces) sent by bulk mail to new prospects.

GETTING PERSONAL

The main idea is to make the envelope look as if it contains a personal letter. There are two ways to make that happen: Make the envelope look as if it was sent by first-class mail, or make it different from other mail appeals the prospect will be receiving.

The methods you choose to accomplish this purpose will depend on how many volunteers you have to help with the mailing, your judgment about whether this is the best use of volunteer time, how many pieces you are actually sending, and your goal for the mailing.

BULK MAIL INDICIA PRE-CANCELLED
BULK MAIL STAMPS

Look First Class

The best way make a mail appeal look as if it came first class is to write the address by hand. If you have an appeal going to fewer than 1,000 names, this is not too arduous a task.

In addition to or instead of handwriting the address, you can use a precanceled bulk-mail stamp in place of the common postal indicia. These stamps may be purchased at the post office where you send your bulk mail. The rules for sorting and handling the mail are the same as for any other bulk mailing. Sometimes the presence of an actual stamp will make the piece look more important.

Consider the rest of the envelope. If you are in a major metropolitan area where a lot of mail appeals originate, don't put your name and return address in the upper-left hand corner of the front of the envelope. Either use only your address without your organization's name in that space, or put the name and address on the back flap of the envelope. In either case, the prospect asks, "Who is this from?" and opens the envelope to find out.

On the other hand, if you are in a rural area, it is likely that the people receiving your mail will open all letters that originate in their county or small town. In that case, you want your return address to be fairly prominent on the front of the envelope.

ADDRESS ON BACK FLAP

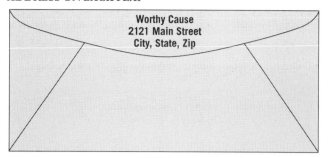

Worthy Cause
2121 Main Street
City, State, Zip

ADDRESS ONLY ON FRONT OF ENVELOPE

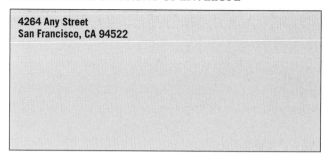

4264 Any Street
San Francisco, CA 94522

NUMBER 10 OFFICIAL

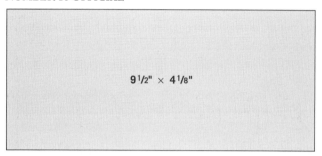

$9^{1/2}" \times 4^{1/8}"$

NUMBER 7 OFFICIAL

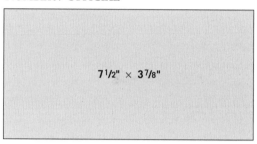

$7^{1/2}" \times 3^{7/8}"$

NUMBER 6 ANNOUNCEMENT

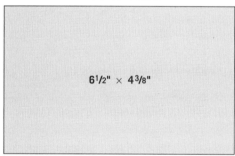

$6^{1/2}" \times 4^{3/8}"$

NUMBER 6 COMMERCIAL

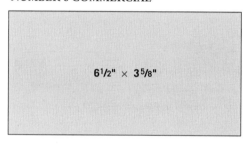

$6^{1/2}" \times 3^{5/8}"$

Look Different

Most mail envelopes are sent in standard business-size envelopes (called No. 10). Your appeal will stand out if it arrives in a smaller or an odd-sized envelope. Personal letters are not generally sent in business-size envelopes, so to make your appeal look more personal, send it in a No. 6 or No. 7 envelope, or in an invitation-style envelope. One word of caution: If you use smaller envelopes, make sure your return envelope is smaller yet, so that it will fit into the carrier envelope without needing to be folded. Also, letters that must fit into smaller envelopes may be more expensive to print.

The least effective method of gaining attention is "teaser copy." However, this strategy should not be totally disregarded. "Teaser copy" involves including a phrase, a drawing, or using a photograph on the envelope itself, which intrigues the reader or causes some emotional response that will make them open the envelope. So many direct mail appeals use this strategy now that it will not make your envelope stand out unless the teaser is very unusual. The examples below show the most common uses of teaser copy.

You may wish to experiment with various styles of outside envelopes to find which methods work best for your organization. Save mail appeals from other groups that you open, and figure out what it is about the envelope that caused you to open it. The more creative you can be in getting the recipient to open the outside envelope, the greater chance you will have of the prospect reading your appeal.

WORDS & PHRASES, AS WELL AS THE STYLE OF THE GRAPHIC, GIVE AN IMPRESSION OF URGENCY

John Goodgiver
1234 Anywhere Street
San Francisco, CA 96678

PRIORITY MESSAGE • PRIORITY MESSAGE • PRIORITY MESSAGE • PRIORITY MESSAGE

John Goodgiver
1234 Anywhere Street
San Francisco, CA 96678

PICTURES OR DRAWINGS USED EXTENSIVELY FOR CHILDREN, ANIMAL OR WILDERNESS APPEALS

John Goodgiver
1234 Anywhere Street
San Francisco, CA 96678

John Goodgiver
1234 Anywhere Street
San Francisco, CA 96678

PHRASES THAT ARE "COME-ONS" PROMISING SOMETHING FOR NOTHING

Survey Enclosed

John Goodgiver
1234 Anywhere Street
San Francisco, CA 96678

John Goodgiver
1234 Anywhere Street
San Francisco, CA 96678

1993

Trading Mailing Lists

By KIM KLEIN

For organizations that use direct mail to acquire donors or raise money, one of the biggest challenges is getting names to use for these appeals. Small organizations that are generally doing small mailings (fewer than 5,000 names at a time, and sometimes barely more than the 200 needed for bulk mailing) quickly run out of names when they simply seek to generate them internally. There are only so many names on raffle tickets, door prize drawings, or the sign-up sheet at a community meeting (although every group should make sure to use the names gathered in these ways), and board, staff, and volunteers eventually exhaust their lists of friends' names. This shortage is compounded in rural communities, where board members' lists of ten friends may all include five of the same people!

One of the best ways for a small group to expand their universe of names is to trade lists with similar organizations. This suggestion almost always generates a number of objections from the organization whose list you would like to use. Here are many of them, with answers you can give when groups balk at trading mailing lists with you.

COMMON OBJECTIONS

All the objections begin with assumptions about the donors of the group whose list is sought and all expose fears of losing their donors.

Our donors will feel inundated with appeals, and since they belong to our group, they probably won't join yours anyway. It is important to remember that most people who give away money donate to between five and eleven groups. These groups will all have something in common; in fact, you can learn a great deal about a person just by knowing what organizations she or he supports. Of these five to eleven groups, two or three will change every year. So in fact, some people will choose to belong to both our groups. Further, we are only seeking to use your list once, so it is unlikely that your donors will feel inundated by the presence of one extra letter.

All my donors will like your group better and will leave my group and join yours. On the contrary, studies show that the loyalty of a person to the first group of a type of organization (such as feminist, environmentalist, peace,

community organizing, antiracist) increases with every subsequent appeal from a similar group. People want to feel that they made a good decision the first time in joining your group, and they also enjoy feeling part of a whole movement when it is clear that there are similar groups working on these issues.

All our donors prefer giving locally/regionally/nationally and your group is _____ (whatever is the opposite). Many of your donors belong to your organization because you work at the local/regional/national level, and it is true that they will not join us. As you know, we only expect 1–3% of your donors to respond to our mail appeal, so 97–99% of your donors won't give to us for various reasons, including that one. However, your donors are not all alike, and some will understand that this issue must be addressed at both the _____ and the _____ level.

Our donors will wonder why there need to be so many of the same kind of groups and might stop giving for that reason. Again, this is a common misperception and can be cleared up by looking at businesses. If you have an intersection in a busy part of town with gas stations on each corner, what happens? People buy more gas! For example, they are stopped at a red light, and look to their left and see a Chevron station. They glance at their gas gauge and see they need gas. Now the light changes so they drive across the street and pull into the Exxon station that is on their side of the road. Another example is the plethora of stores selling cell phones. This has not led to a glut of stores, but to the perception that everyone should have a cell phone. The more organizations there are working on a cause, the more clear it is that this is a pressing social issue. Also, we would be clear in our letter about our work, which is not the same as yours. We are not duplicate organizations; we are complementary and each of us is stronger because of the presence of the other.

Those are the more common objections. The only other common objection is that the mailing list is confidential. That is a policy decision and there is little you can do about it, except see if the policy can be changed. In some cases, there are good reasons for confidentiality and those should be respected.

TERMS OF THE TRADE

Once you get past the objections to the idea of trading mailing lists, you now must work out the terms of the trade. There are several possibilities. The most straightforward is simply to trade name for name. "We'll give you 300, and you'll give us 300." Make sure that all the names you get are of *donors*. Many groups keep on their lists names of people who are not donors. Only trade for donor names. You will probably also want to specify that the donors must be individuals and not foundations or corporations, since these grantors will not respond to mail appeals.

If the group you are trading with has a larger list than yours, you can "trade in advance." This means you will get their names now, and when your list is the same size, they can use yours, or they can use the names you have now and get new names as you acquire them. This requires careful record keeping and for that reason is not ideal.

A third possibility in working with groups who have bigger lists than yours is to trade your names for others without counting. Because you have a smaller list, your donor names won't have been traded very often, if at all, and so your list is fresher and your names are worth more. You could also trade for the number of names you have and pay a fee for the rest of the names. If you have a list of 1,000 donors and you are working to get a list of 2,000, trade for the first 1,000 and then pay $75–$110 (what you would pay a list broker) for renting the second 1,000.

Other terms you will want to consider are whether to include all donors or specify only donors giving under $100, thus leaving out major donors of both organizations. The advantage of this agreement is that donors who give less than $100 are more likely to respond to mail appeals; major donors tend to give because of personal contact.

You must also specify and agree that each group will only use the names once. You are borrowing (or trading) lists for one-time use. You will get some new donors from their list. The rest of the list is worthless to you. Don't photocopy the other group's list or cheat on this part of the agreement in any way.

HOW TO PREVENT OTHERS FROM REUSING YOUR LIST

To ensure that groups you trade with don't reuse your list or use it for purposes other than those you agreed upon, add three or four names to your list that are coded in some way. For example, if I trade my list with Good People's Good Group, I will code three names (mine, a friend's, and the office address) with the middle initial "G," or have one of the last names be Good or spell my name wrong. That initial or that name will only appear on the list I traded with Good Group. If I get more than one appeal from them, or from some other group, I will know that they violated our agreement.

While you won't be pressing charges against this group, you will know not to trade with them again, and confronting them with your evidence may make them stop. Since most groups know that every group has a few of these "dummy" names in their list, cheating on these agreements is fairly rare. As a precaution, you can tell them it is your policy to have three dummy names in every list traded.

GET AND GIVE DELIVERABLE NAMES

You also need to ensure that you give and get "clean" lists; that is, lists where the addresses up to date; don't use a list that hasn't been updated in more than four months. You can also look on their newsletter or other regular mailing to see if they pay for "address correction requested" from the post office. This is the only way to ensure that mail sent bulk rate is returned to the sender for correction. Bulk mail that is not deliverable won't be returned without this request, which costs the organization a small amount for each piece returned.

Make sure you are ready to use any list you borrow within ten days of getting it, so that it doesn't get old sitting in your office. If you wait any longer than two months to use it, 3–5% of the addresses will have become undeliverable. About 15% of the population moves every year, so time is of the essence with mailing lists.

Finally, specify the format you want to receive the list in: Do you want it on labels, computer disk, or e-mailed in a specified format?

FINAL CONCERNS

Ultimately, some groups will still refuse to share lists for fear of losing donors. These groups don't give donors credit for loyalty or thoughtfulness. Groups like these also seem to assume that their donors are reclusive nonreaders who don't get any information besides what their group sends them. Of course, they will claim they are trying to protect the donors, or that they "hear" complaints from their donors about how much mail the donors get already, or any number of other seemingly thoughtful motives.

It is imperative to remember that you cannot manipulate people with direct mail or invade their privacy or force them to take an action. Mail is passive. Most direct mail is thrown away before it is even opened. The worst that will happen is that the other group's donors will feel momentarily annoyed. In the meantime, some of them will be happy that your group has found them and will become willing and involved donors.

1989

Spring Cleaning:
When to Take Names Off Your Mailing List

By KIM KLEIN

I am on the mailing list of upwards of 40 groups to which I don't contribute in any way, nor have I ever contributed to them. I am on the mailing list of another 20 groups that I have made one or possibly two contributions to more than three years ago. How did I get on all these lists? I could flatter myself that I am just very popular and everyone wants my name on their list, but a more realistic guess is that staff or board members of these groups have been in fundraising workshops or meetings with me, or my name has been traded from a group I do give to.

I have been on some of these lists for ten years, and a few of them for even longer. This is amazing because I have moved seven times in three states since 1989. These groups have changed my address and found me in my new digs. They have no idea if I am interested in their work or if I care about their existence at all. They never ask me if I want to stay on their mailing list, although they do ask me for money two or three times a year. I guess they don't want to find out that I don't have time to read their stuff, and even though I wish them well, I will never give them money no matter how many years they keep me on their list.

Over the past 20 years of working with thousands of organizations, I have witnessed this persistent problem: Organizations keep names on their mailing list when they have no evidence that the person is even alive, let alone interested in their work. The mailings that continue to go out to these names — unread and unresponded to — are costing these organizations hundreds and sometimes thousands of dollars that could be used for real fundraising.

To really evaluate your mailing list, you first need to figure out what is called your "fulfillment cost" — that is, what it costs the organization to keep someone on the mailing list. Take the cost of the newsletters you send out and divide it by all the people you mail to. Be sure to include postage. Assign a small amount per name for entering them into the computer and changes of address. Most organizations' fulfillment cost is $2 per person per year, even if all they send is a four-page newsletter twice a year, printed inexpensively and sorted by volunteers to be sent bulk mail.

Recently, I was with a group that had 3,000 people on its mailing list, of which only 400 were donors. The other 2,600 were there, they explained, for "outreach purposes." They calculate their fulfillment cost to be $3 per person per year. The group, with a budget of just over $110,000, is thus paying $7,800 a year for this "outreach." After realizing this, a committee of the board, in a very brief discussion, decided $7,800 could be used for more effective outreach than mailing to people who have shown no interest in the group in several years.

Every year, your group should examine each name on its mailing list and decide whether or not that name should stay. The way to decide is to identify those who have given to the group, then examine the rest of the names carefully. Here's how to do it:

- Identify everyone who has made a donation of any size in the last 18 months. They stay on the list.
- Identify everyone who has given time or in-kind donations or advice as a volunteer in the last 18 months. They stay on the list.

- Identify everyone who has given money in the last three years, but not the last 18 months and prepare a mailing for them that says, "We miss you. We don't want to take you off our mailing list. Please let us know if you want to stay on our list by sending a contribution in the enclosed envelope. If you want to stay on the list, but cannot give at this time, simply indicate that on the card and return it to us. If you don't want to stay on our mailing list, please take a moment and tell us why." Include a paragraph or two about all the exciting things your group is doing. Basically this letter resells your group to these lapsed donors. Give these people another six months to send their contributions or response card in. Remove everyone who doesn't respond.

- Now look at every name that doesn't fall into one of these categories and decide, name by name, whether or not they should be on the list. Names you may want to leave on your list include funders, politicians, past volunteers and staff, organizations doing similar work, and people important to your group for one reason or another.

- For everyone who isn't in any of the above categories, send a letter saying, "In the interest of good stewardship of resources, we are cleaning up our mailing list and removing anyone who doesn't want to hear from us. Please use the enclosed card to let us know that you want to stay on the list. If possible, please send a donation to help with costs. If you don't want to be on the list, please check the category, Take me off your list.

After two months, remove everyone from the list who hasn't responded. Six to eight months later, after they have missed at least two issues of your newsletter, write them one final letter, saying, "Have you missed us? We have missed you. A lot of exciting things have happened in the past six months (enumerate a few). Please join us and be part of our wonderful work." Structure this like a mail appeal. You will probably get a 1–2% response from this list.

After the responses from the final letter that come in, delete everyone who hasn't responded to any of your mailings.

Paying systematic attention to your mailing list ensures that you are doing proper outreach and not wasting donor money mailing information to people who don't seem to care about it. This frees up money to recruit new donors and do real outreach.

1990

Testing and Tracking Your Results:
Fine-Tuning Your Direct Mail Package To Yield the Best Returns

By PAT MUNOZ and AMY O'CONNOR

This article discusses direct mail testing and how to track and analyze the results of your mailings. To do well at direct mail, it is essential that you experiment, both with lists and with various elements of your "package," to find out which lists, and which "spins" on your package, produce the best results.

TESTING, TESTING

Testing various elements of your direct mail program will result in much better returns. It is important to test not only the lists you are thinking of mailing to but also the elements of the direct mail package. Testing these aspects on smaller numbers will help you create a more successful mailing when it goes out in large quantities.

List testing

When you are using any large list (5,000 names or more) for the first time, no matter how well you think the list is going to perform, you should first test a random sample of 2,000 names to see what results it produces. Because most lists available for rental on the market have minimum orders of 5,000, you will want to work with a list broker who is able to provide quantities of fewer than 5,000 names per list to you.

If your test of 2,000 names does well, you can then mail to the entire list with a fair assurance that the results will mirror your test results. Many small groups have been badly burned by conducting mailings with large lists they thought would do well and getting a dismal return. Don't let this happen to you.

Testing Elements of the Package

If you are serious about your direct mail program, you should be testing elements of your new member package to see if you can reduce your costs, increase your response, or both. The only rules you need follow are

1. Test only one variable at a time.

2. Be sure that the test groups are truly comparable.

3. Mail all pieces that are part of a test at the same time.

The reasons for these rules are obvious. If you test two or more variables at once (such as the color of the envelope and the type of postage), you won't know which variable has influenced the results. If you use two different lists (instead of two random segments of the same list) you won't know if the difference in response is attributable to the list or to the variable. And if your test packages are not mailed at the same time, your results will be meaningless, since the date you drop your mail is a variable in itself and can significantly affect your response rate.

While there are many variables you could test, the most important are

- Outer envelope copy, design, and type
- Letter
- Cost of membership (what you charge to be a member)

Other variables you might want to test are the use of a first-class stamp vs. bulk-rate postage, premium vs. no premium, enclosures such as press clippings vs. no extra enclosures, and handwritten addressing vs. labels. (The super-personalized handwritten envelope will almost invariably produce better results, but is logistically difficult to implement, especially if large quantities are involved.)

Let us consider what is involved in testing just one of these potential variables: the letter. If you have been mailing out the same basic letter for some time and response rates are beginning to drop, you might consider testing a new letter against the old "control" letter to see if you can improve results. As with list testing, you will need a list of at least 4,000 names that you can split into two comparable test groups. To one segment of the list you will send the "control" letter; to the other, you will send the new letter you have just developed.

To track the results of this test, you will need to code the reply cards or reply envelopes in order to distinguish between responses from each group. For example, you might have access to 4,000 Sierra Club names. For your test mailing you could have the merge/purge service use a computer program to randomly select 2,000 names for test package one and 2,000 names for test package two. Each sub-list would then be coded on the mailings labels, say as "1" and "2," to ensure that you can distinguish the returns by a source code once new members are entered into your database.

It is ideal and most efficient for you to use numeric codes printed on the label that can simply be recorded in a "source" code field in your database. You should do everything in your power to get your database to accommodate a source code field so that you can track the lists in each of your direct mail campaigns.

If all else fails, you can resort to coding your lists by running a magic marker down the edge of a stack of return envelopes or labels that are to be attached to return cards. Both the position and color of the markings can be used to indicate which test group the piece belongs to, provided you keep a record of what the markings mean and tally the responses as they come in.

Once all the responses are in, you will be able to see whether the new letter has generated more responses, or a higher average gift, or both, than the old "control" letter. If the new letter outperforms the old, then it is time to use it as the "control" letter, at least with that particular list.

THE TRACKING GAME

As with testing, there are several things you should track when studying your direct mail campaigns: the responses to each package or version of a package, the costs of each mailing, and how each list performed.

Tracking Responses

As you go through the process of designing your package and arranging for your mail to be sent, it is vital that you put in place a system by which you can easily track returns from your mailing. This is usually done by coding the reply cards so that when checks come in, you can look at the accompanying card and tell which list the new member came from. This is then recorded in a "source" code field in your database. If you are buying or exchanging your lists through a list broker, it is easy to ask the broker to put a code on the labels you are acquiring. Make the codes mnemonic if possible so that they remind you of the name of the organization the list came from (for example, a Sierra Club list could be coded SC100 or something similar).

With small lists, you may have to get more creative and keep a sample of the labels (if the typeface is distinctive), run a magic marker down the labels, or use some other device to let you know which labels came from which lists.

Whatever system you use to identify each list, be sure that you record it carefully. And if you repeatedly mail to the same list, be sure you use a different code each time so that you can analyze the results of each individual mailing to that particular group. That way you'll know if and when the list stops working for you.

It is important to try to track the results of your mailing on a daily basis. Just as depositing all checks should become a part of the daily routine, so should logging in

Weekly Membership Acquisition Report for the Week of: _____

List name: _____ **Code:** _____ **Quantity Mailed:** _____ **Mail Date:** _____

MONDAY		TUESDAY		WEDNESDAY		THURSDAY		FRIDAY		PREVIOUS TOTAL		CUMULATIVE TOTAL		AVERAGE GIFT	RESPONSE RATE	NUMBER OF LARGE GIFTS		
number responses	amount received	number responses	amount received	number responses	amount received	number responses	amount received	number responses	amount received	number responses	amount received	number responses	amount received			$500	$250	$100

List name: _____ **Code:** _____ **Quantity Mailed:** _____ **Mail Date:** _____

MONDAY		TUESDAY		WEDNESDAY		THURSDAY		FRIDAY		PREVIOUS TOTAL		CUMULATIVE TOTAL		AVERAGE GIFT	RESPONSE RATE	NUMBER OF LARGE GIFTS		
number responses	amount received	number responses	amount received	number responses	amount received	number responses	amount received	number responses	amount received	number responses	amount received	number responses	amount received			$500	$250	$100

List name: _____ **Code:** _____ **Quantity Mailed:** _____ **Mail Date:** _____

MONDAY		TUESDAY		WEDNESDAY		THURSDAY		FRIDAY		PREVIOUS TOTAL		CUMULATIVE TOTAL		AVERAGE GIFT	RESPONSE RATE	NUMBER OF LARGE GIFTS		
number responses	amount received	number responses	amount received	number responses	amount received	number responses	amount received	number responses	amount received	number responses	amount received	number responses	amount received			$500	$250	$100

responses to direct mail. If you do this faithfully, you will soon get familiar with the pattern that the results follow and, after a few mailings, be able to predict with a good deal of accuracy what the final outcome of a mailing will be by looking at the first few weeks of results.

Usually, the returns follow a bell-shaped curve over a four to six week period, with dribs and drabs coming in for many weeks after that. You can make your daily tallying easiest if you enter your new members directly into your member database, recording the source code for the particular list that member came from in a specific field dedicated to that information in your database. Your system should then be able to take this daily information and produce daily reports. If your system does not allow this, or if you do not have the time to enter all of the names into the database daily, try using a simple form like the one shown here ("Weekly Membership Acquisition Report") to record your information daily.

Tracking Costs

As you pursue testing, you will find that some tests are more expensive to implement than others. Therefore, it is especially important to record all costs incurred so that, in your analysis, you can determine which approaches being tested are the most cost effective. As you handle the various aspects of the mailing, keep copies of all your receipts together in a file so that, when the mailing is over, you can put together a full picture and do an accurate cost/benefit analysis. If you are renting some of your lists, record these costs separately for each list.

A sample cost sheet for a direct mail might look as follows:

Sample Cost Sheet for a 20,000 piece Direct Mail

ITEM	COST
Design	$ 500
Printing:	
Letter	340
Outer Envelope	360
Inner Envelope	240
Reply Card	240
List Rental:	
5,000 American Rivers @ .05/each	250
5,000 Sierra Club @ .08/each	400
3,000 WV Magazine @ .05 each	150
List Processing/Merge/Purge	400
Postage	2,200
Premiums	0
Stuffing and Mailing	2,000
Fulfillment Costs (Thank yous)	200
TOTAL COSTS	**$7,300**

Tracking Lists

When doing direct mail, you must keep track of how your lists perform so that you know which ones to go back to and which ones to abandon because they are too expensive or ineffective for your group. We recommend starting a list history like the one shown below in which you track the performance of your lists over time. (See example on following page.)

Keeping track of your lists will allow you to quickly weed out the unproductive lists from the productive ones and make your mailings more and more cost effective as you learn which lists work best for you. It will also be invaluable to new staff taking over the membership function who may not be familiar with past list performance. (It would be good if your database will produce such a history using the source code data that you enter for each new member; if not, just set up a table on your computer following the format shown below.)

If you keep track of how lists perform over time, you can learn a lot about both the lists and the time of year when they perform best. You can also determine which segments work best for you (for example, which geographic areas) and how often you can mail to individual lists and still obtain good results. (You can often mail to good lists two to three times a year and get the same high response rates.)

RECORDING AND ANALYZING YOUR MAILINGS

When the mailing has run its course, it is important that you immediately record and analyze the results. You should keep at least one complete copy of each package (letter, outer envelope, reply card, reply envelope, any enclosures) in a binder or folder with all records and analysis pertaining to the mailing. This will prove invaluable for creating an institutional memory of the work you're doing.

The information that you should consider keeping in your binder includes the source codes of lists mailed to, organization names corresponding to the source codes, number of pieces mailed, number of pieces returned, date mailed, cost, income, response rate (for each list and overall), average gift (for each list and overall), net loss or gain (overall and by list), and cost/benefit ratio.

Look at the hypothetical report below on a 20,000-piece mailing. By analyzing this mailing, we can see that the cost benefit ratio is about 1/1. This means that every dollar spent on direct cost brought in another dollar. Another way of saying this is that the mailing broke even, which is extremely good and increasingly rare in today's direct mail market. This happened because most of the lists mailed to were sure bets, with only one test list, the *WV Magazine,* which we will not use again because of its poor performance.

Sample List History

NAME OF LIST (source code)	TOTAL OF NAMES	NUMBER OF NAMES USED	LIST SEGMENT	DATE USED	RESPONSE RATE	AVERAGE GIFT	TOTAL COST	TOTAL INCOME	GAIN/ LOSS
American Whitewater Affiliation (AWA 101)	30,000	3,000	(MD/DC, WV)	2/20/98	1.5%	$35	$975	$1,575	+ $600
American Whitewater Affiliation (AWA 100)	25,000	2,500	(MD/DC, VA, WV)	5/3/97	1.5%	$32	$750	$1,440	+ $690
American Rivers (AR 100)	25,500	5,000	(MD/DC, WV)	2/20/98	2.0%	$28	$1,875	$2,800	+ $925
Sierra Club (SC 101)	500,000	5,000	(WV)	2/20/98	1.0%	$25	$2,025	$1,250	− $775
Sierra Club (SC 100)	475,000	2,500	(WV)	5/3/97	1.0%	$24	$950	$600	− $350
WV Trout Unlimited (TU 100)	40,000	2,500	(WV)	2/20/98	.8%	$30	$600	$813	− $213

Even though the Sierra Club and the Trout Unlimited lists did not break even, their response rates were good by today's standards, and we will definitely use them again in the future, particularly since both these lists are large. We might want to test a different letter with the Sierra Club list, to see if we can improve the response rate, the average gift, or both by using a more environmentally oriented message. The Sierra Club list was more expensive than some of the others because we had to buy it for $80 per 1,000 names, so we might see if we can exchange for the list next time to cut costs.

When you begin soliciting members via direct mail, your goal will be to make your mailings break even, or even to make a small profit. Later, as you begin to do larger mailings, your response rate will probably go down, and you will begin to lose money on these initial mailings. Just remember that you are investing in members who, if properly treated (with newsletters, member involvement, appeals, major donor programs, and renewals), will pay back the investment and provide core funding for your group in the long run.

Nevertheless, it is vital to keep track of how much you lose on any given mailing, how individual lists perform, and what the cost/benefit ratio for the mailing is. Over time, you may even want to track when the mailing breaks even and you begin earning "dividends" on your initial investment, if your computer system can handle this level of analysis.

ACQUISITION IS ONLY THE BEGINNING

Because members tend to become more loyal and more generous over time, investing in members is much like counting on compound interest. The more the initial investment, the greater the returns in the long run. But much like a stockbroker who watches over and fine-tunes his accounts, we in the nonprofit sector must always take care of and properly cultivate our hard-earned new members. This is especially important in light of the fact that acquisition costs are high and a member sometimes begins to pay for himself or herself only after two or three years.

After you break even on members, any contributions they make, except for basic maintenance costs, can go toward general operating costs, such as salaries and rent. That's why membership retention is so critical to a successful membership program. In addition, all along the way your members provide a powerful source of political clout, community involvement, volunteer labor, board prospects, and other less tangible resources for your group.

As you pursue your direct mail membership acquisition program, remember that you can pursue the program at whatever level your organization's leadership is comfortable with and your cash flow allows. Whether on a large or a small scale, your efforts will help build a more stable funding base as well as solid public support for your cause.

REPRINTED WITH PERMISSION FROM, "RIVER FUNDRAISING ALERT," A PUBLICATION OF RIVER NETWORK. 1998

Direct Mail Report

NAME OF LIST (source code)	QUANTITY MAILED	NUMBER RETURNS	AMOUNT RETURNED	RESPONSE RATE	AVERAGE GIFT	TOTAL COST	GAIN/ LOSS
American Whitewater Affiliation (AWA 101)	3,000	45	$1,575	1.5%	$35	$975	+ $600
American Rivers (AR 100)	5,000	100	$2,800	2.0%	$28	$1,875	+ $925
Sierra Club (SC 101)	5,000	50	$1,250	1.0%	$25	$2,025	− $775
WV Trout Unlimited (TU 100)	2,500	20	$600	.8%	$30	$813	− $213
WV Magazine (WV 100)	3,000	6	$120	.2%	$20	$1,125	− $1,005
CCA (CCA 100)	1,500	30	$900	2.0%	$30	$488	+ $412
TOTAL	**20,000**	**251**	**$7,245**	**1.3%**	**$29**	**$7300**	**− $55**

Point/Counterpoint:
The Direct Mail Debate

By AMY O'CONNOR and ANDY ROBINSON

The following articles present two viewpoints on the efficiency of direct mail as a membership acquisition strategy. This dialogue was stimulated by the article, "Testing and Tracking Your Results," by Pat Munoz and Amy O'Connor. Andy Robinson first presents the case against small nonprofits using direct mail to acquire new donors and Amy O'Connor, one of the authors of the original article, responds. These viewpoints are followed by Andy's suggestions for ways to acquire new members without using large direct mail campaigns. The *Journal* is grateful to these two writers, both excellent fundraisers, for being willing to air their differences in this public forum.

THE CASE AGAINST DIRECT MAIL FOR SMALL GRASSROOTS GROUPS

BY ANDY ROBINSON

Over the years, the *Grassroots Fundraising Journal* has published a number of articles about mass mailing strategies for nonprofits. Topics have included composing the letter, designing the mail package, how to rent or borrow outside mailing lists, and so on. A recent story, "Testing and Tracking Your Results," by Pat Munoz and Amy O'Connor, offered thoughtful and comprehensive guidelines for tracking direct mail responses and refining your mailing strategy based on these results.

I have raised money for social change since 1980 and, along the way, I filled a lot of mailboxes. The more I mailed, the more uncomfortable I felt. After years of trial and error, success and failure, I've come to the conclusion that sending mass mailings to strangers is a less and less effective way for grassroots organizations to find new donors.

I'm not alone in this opinion. Even Mal Warwick, one of the most respected direct mail consultants in the country, has his doubts. In the July 1998 issue of his newsletter, *Successful Direct Mail and Telephone Fundraising,* he wrote, "To put it plainly, larger organizations can better afford to use the techniques explored in these pages. A smaller or local nonprofit may lack the means, staff resources, or opportunity to do so."

For the purpose of this article, "grassroots" refers to groups with fewer than 2,000 active donors, and especially those with fewer than 1,000 members. For larger organizations, the mechanics and economics of mass mailings are more manageable, although the environmental impact increases with the size of the mailing.

My primary concern involves using direct mail to acquire new donors; renewing current or lapsed donors through the mail remains quite effective, especially if you make the effort to personalize the package.

The Case against Direct Mail for Small Grassroots Groups

1. Lousy odds. These days, a "successful" acquisition mailing — which we use to reach prospects and request their first gift — generates a 1–2% return. In other words, for every 100 pieces you send out, you get one or two new members. The other 98 or 99 pieces fail.

Consider this carefully. When was the last time you succeeded one time out of a hundred and felt good about it? To put this in fundraising perspective, asking qualified prospects face-to-face has a success rate of 25–50%, while sending them personalized letters from people they know will generate at least a 10–15% return. (Follow-up phone calls increase this percentage dramatically.) Even grant proposals — a dubious way to raise money — have a better rate of success: Between 6% and 15% of all proposals receive funding.

Are we so hard up for cash, or so desperate for new ideas, that we fail 98% of the time and call it success?

2. High cost. If you break even acquiring a new member through direct mail, you're doing well. When you factor in the cost of design, printing, list rental, mailing preparation, and postage, the first gift typically costs more than it's worth. (Don't forget staff time to write the letter, organize the mailing, and track the results. Staff expenses are generally not included in direct mail cost calculations.)

Using this strategy, you don't begin to net money until the third or fourth gift. Unfortunately, many grassroots groups are squeamish about resoliciting their membership three or four times annually, so it can take years to make back the initial investment.

3. Competition. In addition to charitable solicitations, your mailbox is filled with catalogs, magazines, newsletters, insurance pitches, credit card offers, flyers, free samples, sweepstakes forms, and even an occasional letter from a friend. The average college graduate is on 300 mailing lists. Declining direct mail results are directly related to the sheer volume of competition. You can rent a better list or write a better letter, but you have no control over all the other materials moving through the post office.

4. Cash flow. Because of the high costs associated with direct mail, you need money in the bank. In fact, to run a successful mass mailing program, you have to plow much of the income into additional mailings to eventually make money. For many cash-starved grassroots groups, this is unrealistic.

5. Lack of self-discipline. As pointed out in the *Journal's* June story, any effective mass mailing strategy requires scrupulous record keeping: how many pieces were mailed to each list, when the mailings were sent, which items were included in each package, how many donors responded, how the response rate changed when one variable was changed, etc. Without this level of detail, it's difficult to know what's working and what needs to be fixed.

Alas, I know very few grassroots organizations with sufficient discipline (not to mention staff or stamina) to track mass mailing returns adequately. When other crises — real or imagined — pop up, donor tracking is one of the first things to go. What remains is instinct and guesswork, which are poor tools to manage a direct mail program.

6. Environmental impact. First there's the paper, most of which still comes from trees; then, the energy used to design, print, and distribute the mailing; finally, the pollution associated with dumping all those unwanted letters (and plastic decals and mailing labels and heaven knows what) into the landfill or burning them in incinerators. Even folks who recycle their junk mail still create environmental impacts through recycling collection and reprocessing.

We live in world of paper, at least for the time being, and I'm realistic enough to accept that we need paper (and electricity and gasoline) to raise money. Nonetheless, we should minimize our use of paper and energy whenever and wherever we can. It's hard to justify a 98–99% failure rate when our failures diminish the natural world and affect human health.

THERE'S STILL LIFE IN DIRECT MAIL

BY AMY O'CONNOR

Direct mail membership acquisition is just one important tool in any fundraiser's toolkit. I believe that every nonprofit group should use alternatives to direct mail to the degree possible and appropriate. Such alternatives, as Andy Robinson describes them in the article above, include personalized mailings, hand-addressed envelopes, face-to-face solicitation by existing members, events, tabling, and soliciting friends, relatives, and acquaintances by the board and staff. However, I would recommend that such alternative tools be used in addition to, rather than as a replacement for, direct mail as a membership acquisition strategy.

A Wider Net

While direct mail may not be appropriate for every nonprofit, most can benefit from the significant infusion of new members that it can bring. It is vital that those who use the alternatives to the exclusion of direct mail understand the consequences. When we look at membership acquisition, the alternative approaches will only allow you to reach a relatively limited prospect pool and may severely limit the size of the organization — something that may not be in the group's best interest. By contrast, direct mail reaches far beyond this "inner circle" of prospects. While one eventually runs into limits here as well, direct mail helps groups reach far more prospects, gain far more donors/activists/volunteers, and spread their message to a much larger population than any of the alternatives alone or taken together.

Setting Goals First

It is critical that any organization determine its membership goals before it spends a lot of energy or money on any kind of recruitment. A group should begin by determining what kinds of members it needs (taking into account such factors as ethnicity, gender, geography, political clout, etc.) and the number of members in each category necessary to achieve its program goals.

Some organizations, such as those that primarily serve other nonprofits and are able to sustain themselves on existing funding, don't need a lot of members. They may be content with a few hundred. Others may need thousands to achieve their political goals.

A good example of an organization that benefited from significant growth is the Southern Utah Wilderness Alliance. In 1988 the group had about 1,000 core members. Through a strong direct mail campaign, which involved sending as many as 300,000 pieces of mail each year for five years, the membership grew to 10,000. The average renewal rate remained high at 70–75%. A second, three-year recruitment effort involving door-to-door canvassing brought the membership to 20,000.

The membership success of the alliance would not have been possible without the help of direct mail. And the significant progress that has been made toward protecting Utah's magnificent canyon country may well have been far more limited had there not been a sizeable membership to back up the organization's goals with letters, phone calls, attendance at public hearings, funding, letters to the editor, and general political clout.

Typical Concerns about Direct Mail

Below are some questions that correspond to the six specific issues Robinson raises in "The Case against Direct Mail," along with some responses. These questions are typical of those that cross many board and staff members' minds when they consider using direct mail to acquire new donors.

1. IS A 1–2% RETURN A FAILURE OR A SUCCESS?

While it is true that the return rate for nonprofits is usually around 1% or 2%, once you've captured the people who are interested in what you do you have the potential of realizing a great deal of income from this group of people over their "membership lifetime."

2. IS THE COST OF DIRECT MAIL REALLY PROHIBITIVE?

It generally does cost more to acquire new members through direct mail than they pay in dues and contributions in the first year. However, it is far less expensive to get subsequent gifts, upgrades, and renewals from these members than it was to acquire them in the first place, making each successive gift more and more profitable. The key is that the organization must do the work required to renew and upgrade members. That's where personalization, hand-addressed envelopes, personal contact, volunteer programs, major donor programs, house parties, and the like play a critical role. (Keep in mind that these strategies, too, cost money.)

If an organization makes no effort to upgrade members and average gifts remain at $25, then the organization should definitely not pursue direct mail, since its cost will be prohibitive. If the organization is willing to treat its members as part of the team and to upgrade their giving, direct mail is a viable option even for small groups.

3. IS THE FACT THAT MANY NONPROFITS TODAY FIND MEMBERS THROUGH DIRECT MAIL DETRIMENTAL TO EACH GROUP'S SUCCESS?

Given the proliferation of nonprofits (there are well over a million in the United States), competition is often brought up as a reason not to do direct mail membership acquisition. There are a lot of nonprofits and an awful lot of other mailers fill our mailboxes. No doubt this has resulted in overall decreased returns for everyone. Direct mail is not as profitable as it used to be. But as long as the returns are still bringing in new members who remain donors and, on average, increase their giving over time, then it would be unwise to leave this useful tool out of our repertoire.

Furthermore, while more nonprofits are using direct mail membership acquisition each year, giving by individuals also continues to increase. Last year, according to *Giving USA,* individual donations surpassed $144 billion. In addition, there is evidence that overall giving increases when people are given more choices of groups to give to. The best examples can be found in the arena of workplace giving. When companies increase their workplace giving options from United Way only to United Way plus other federations of nonprofits, charitable giving has been shown to increase.

4. DOES THE FACT THAT MOST NONPROFITS ARE STARVED FOR CASH MEAN THAT THEY CAN'T ENGAGE IN DIRECT MAIL MEMBERSHIP ACQUISITION?

It is true that smaller nonprofits may find it hard to come up with the cash to do direct-mail membership acquisition on a significant scale. If you only need a few hundred members, you don't have to send hundreds of thousands of pieces of mail to find them. If you do need to get thousands of members, however, then consider what it would take to do some large-scale mailings. Some foundations are willing to provide funds for raising membership. The more compelling a case you can make by linking the need for members to your program objectives, the more likely your grant proposals will succeed.

I strongly encourage nonprofit leaders to take advantage of the Revolving Loan Fund offered by the Washington, D.C.–based Environmental Support Center or similar programs in other fields. While many nonprofits are skittish about borrowing any money, this kind of loan fund provides an incredible opportunity for nonprofits. Just as small businesses need venture capital, small nonprofits need capital to invest in their future financial stability. Direct mail is the most efficient way to acquire large numbers of new donors who readily renew their membership through the mail; no other strategy allows you to do that.

5. ARE THE LOGISTICS OF RUNNING A DIRECT MAIL PROGRAM TOO COMPLICATED FOR SMALL NONPROFITS?

Direct mail does take staff time and is usually just one of numerous responsibilities. My own experience at the Southern Utah Wilderness Alliance convinced me that it is possible to juggle numerous tasks in addition to doing direct mail and tracking the results accurately. In any case,

as an organization grows, it will need additional support staff to serve and upgrade the memberships. Staffing levels should be evaluated periodically if a successful direct mail program is implemented.

Small organizations can do direct mail and deal with tracking lists and maintaining simple statistics if they are committed to the program. They will be greatly helped by acquiring a database program that allows for accurate coding and by availing themselves of a small amount of consulting help or training to get them started.

6. DO THE BENEFITS OF ENGAGING IN DIRECT-MAIL MEMBERSHIP ACQUISITION JUSTIFY THE ENVIRONMENTAL IMPACTS OF USING THIS TOOL?

While I consider myself a die-hard environmentalist, I don't agree that the environmental impact argument justifies ending direct-mail membership acquisition. It is true that we all contribute to waste and pollution. While one might argue that this does not justify knowingly wasting resources such as paper (i.e., trees), we must also look at the benefits of our nonprofit activities. In my mind, the benefits of saving southern Utah's irreplaceable canyon country, protecting the last 5% of our remaining old-growth forests, promoting responsible family planning, and advancing a million or so other causes justify using some of our precious resources to find the members who make it all happen.

ALTERNATIVES TO DIRECT MAIL FOR ACQUIRING NEW DONORS

BY ANDY ROBINSON

You have many other options for recruiting (and, over time, upgrading) new contributors, including using the mail for more targeted, major donor fundraising. Consider the following:

1. Small, targeted mailings. In the June 1997 issue of the *Journal,* my article, "Finding Major Donors by Mail," (see page 80) outlines my experience with The Wildlands Project, a grassroots conservation group. During 1996 — the first year of our major-donors-by-mail program — we raised $65,000 from a pool of only 700 donors and prospects, nearly all of whom were solicited by mail. The main components of this program included

- Personalizing letters to all previous $50+ donors (about 250 people) by mail-merging their names, addresses, and salutations, then having a board member add a real signature.

- Passing these letters around at a board meeting and asking all board and staff present to write personal

notes to any donors they knew.

- Hand-addressing all envelopes; affixing a big, colorful first-class stamp; and enclosing a response card with check-off amounts beginning at $100 and going up.

- Asking board and staff to identify additional prospects from their own personal mailing lists, Rolodexes, etc.

- Asking board and staff to review published donor lists photocopied from the annual reports and newsletters of other conservation groups, to see if they personally knew any of the donors. We reasoned these folks would make excellent prospects for The Wildlands Project because they 1) had a relationship with the solicitor, 2) had proven their concern about environmental issues, and 3) had demonstrated the ability and inclination to make a charitable gift.

- Repeating steps a, b, and c with the 400+ new names gathered during steps d and e.

This process produced a 33% renewal rate for previous donors and a 15% acquisition rate for new donors, far outperforming any kind of mass mailing. Even better, the average gift from both prospects and donors was well over $100. In 1997, using the same approach, we raised $116,500 from a pool of 800 donors and prospects.

I have shared this strategy with several small nonprofits, all of whom report acquisition rates of at least 10%. Remember, "acquisition" means new members and new money. Let's do the math: You can mass mail 5,000 "Dear friend" letters to strangers and get a 1% response rate, bringing in 50 new members. Or, you can send personalized mail to 500 people who have a relationship with someone in your circle — board, staff, volunteers, members, former board and staff — and get a 10% response rate, acquiring 50 new contributors.

Either way, you add the same number of supporters. With the first approach, you lose money, you waste resources, and you're still dealing with strangers even after you receive their gifts. With the second approach, you make money, you use less paper and energy, and you begin with some personal knowledge of your donors, which makes it much easier to identify their interests, increase their loyalty, and upgrade their gifts.

Of course, this personalized approach requires a lot more time from a lot more people, and you can only squeeze so many names out of your board and staff. Try casting a wider net: Ask volunteers, former board and staff, and your most loyal donors to also contribute leads. Some will allow you to use their names, will sign letters and/or add personal notes, and even visit the best prospects. We call this "peer-to-peer" fundraising.

All effective fundraisers look for opportunities to involve more people in "the ask." This major-donors-by-mail strategy is a great way to begin.

2. Telephone follow-up. Several years ago, when I was working for Native Seeds/SEARCH, a nonprofit seed-conservation group in Tucson, I conducted an experiment. We mailed out a batch of regular membership renewal notices to 200 donors. After waiting a week or so, we randomly split the list. Half the recipients received reminder telephone calls from me or a board volunteer; the other half did not.

Not surprisingly, these phone calls doubled our response rate. Members reached by telephone also gave larger average gifts than those who were not called. While this experiment was conducted during a renewal drive, you should get similar results when soliciting prospective new donors.

While I would never, ever encourage you to call strangers — "cold calling" is a complete waste of time — the phone works wonderfully when you have a relationship with the donor or prospect. These relationships come in three flavors:

a. You're calling a current or lapsed member, so what connects you is your shared commitment to the organization and its mission.

b. You know the prospect personally.

c. You're referred by a mutual friend: "Hi Sally, I'm Andy Robinson with That Cool Group. Juanita Sanchez asked me to call and tell you about our work. Do you have a minute?"

Personalized letters and personal phone calls are both effective. When you combine these strategies, however, they work even better.

3. Recruitment events. House parties are one of the most widely used and effective fundraising strategies. Many, many political campaigns have been funded with contributions solicited at coffees, brunches, cocktail parties, and private dinners. Independent film and video makers often use house parties to show excerpts from their works-in-progress and request gifts to complete the projects. Affiliates of the National Abortion Rights Action League (NARAL) have successfully adapted this strategy to recruit both donors and activists at the same time.

At Native Seeds/SEARCH, we organized a series of recruitment dinners in private homes. These events featured a unique menu based on traditional Southwestern foods — tepary bean paté, posole stew, mesquite meal cookies, prickly pear punch — a slide show, and lots of hands-on show-and-tell, including multicolored ears of corn, gourds, and baskets of beans. (This kind of educational component is essential for any successful house party. It provides the "hook" that draws people in.)

Fifteen or twenty people attended each event, paying $50 per person in advance. The host or hostess provided half the invitation list; we pulled the remaining names from our prospect pool.

Our fundraising dinners netted only $400 each, but were easy to organize, requiring 20 hours of staff time per dinner. However, the real financial benefits were realized later on: After spending an evening with these folks, it was easy to identify the most enthusiastic prospects. We later approached several for major gifts, receiving donations of $500 to $1,000. One dinner guest recommended us to a corporate donor, who has made annual $5,000 contributions for six years (and counting).

Any time you hold a public event — rally, news conference, educational workshop, auction, dance, field trip, etc. — capture the names and addresses of everyone present.

Pass around a sign-up sheet. Even better, give people an incentive to provide their names. Organize a drawing for a free door prize — perhaps a T-shirt or a gift membership — and ask participants to write their names, addresses, and phone numbers on the ticket. Then add these new prospects to your database and solicit them by mail, by phone, or in person.

4. Donor visits. The most effective way to recruit new donors and raise money is face-to-face. While it isn't cost effective to set up meetings for $25 gifts, at higher levels — perhaps $250 and up for local prospects — it's an efficient use of both volunteer and staff time. (Remember, a $250 annual pledge works out to about $20 per month, which is affordable for a wide range of people.)

The *Grassroots Fundraising Journal* has published many articles describing how to set up, rehearse, and conduct donor visits. The reprint collection, *Getting Major Gifts,* is a good place to start.

5. The Web and the Internet. Like direct mail, Web-based fundraising still costs more than it earns. The expense of designing and "hosting" your Web site, including handling secure credit card transactions, is likely to exceed your initial income.

Unlike direct mail, where response rates are declining, the Web shows great promise for the future. Mal Warwick believes that, by 2000, any organization without a Web presence will miss out on a huge pool of potential donors.

While the Web is unlikely to replace other, more personal strategies, it offers a whole range of new options. You can solicit gifts from a dedicated page within your Web site. Donors make payment at least three ways: by submitting credit card information electronically, by phoning in a pledge, or by printing out your membership form, filling it in, and sending a check through the mail. An increasing number of prospective contributors have accounts with online banks, such as FirstVirtual, which provide another avenue for electronic giving.

The best way to learn about Web-based fundraising — how to reach prospective donors, get their attention, and involve them in your work — is to go online and see for yourself. In the June 1998 issue of *ReSources*, the newsletter of the Nonprofit Resource Center in Sacramento, Bill Tucker of the Support Center suggests taking a look at the following sites:

- For ease of giving by filling out and submitting a membership form online: the Sierra Club (*www.sierraclub.org*), and The Wildlands Project (*www.twp.org*)
- For providing a secure way to make a gift by credit card: The American Red Cross (*www.redcross.org*)
- For linking your home page to special gift forms, such as memorial and honorary gifts: the American Cancer Society (*www.cancer.org*)
- For having donors "adopt" something important, such as a hungry child or a nature preserve: The Nature Conservancy (*www.tnc.org*)
- Using quizzes and surveys to grab interest and capture names and e-mail addresses: The Nature Conservancy
- Creating a flashy site and updating it frequently, so donors will want to visit often: Rainforest Action Network (*www.ran.org*)

For most groups, the Web is not yet cost effective for fundraising, but you should consider establishing a Web presence now to reap the rewards later.

There you have it: five alternatives to mass mailings. None of these strategies alone will equal the new supporters you can get through a comprehensive and disciplined direct mail program. Implemented as a package, however, they can bring in lots of new members at a much lower cost. Because of the personal contact used with these approaches, you should see greater donor loyalty, higher renewal rates, and larger average gifts. Your list may not grow as big or as fast, but you'll identify high-quality supporters and you'll net a lot more money for your programs.

1998

Asking Current Donors for Money:
Why, How, and How Often

By KIM KLEIN

In organizations' constant search for better ways to recruit new donors, they sometimes overlook the possibilities for raising additional money from current donors. In fact, grassroots groups often act as though their current donors are precious and fragile, like Grandmother's good china, and should only be brought out on special occasions. Consequently, many organizations appeal to their donors at most once or twice a year.

Years of fundraising experience, however, show that many donors will respond well and generously when asked for extra gifts, and that organizations that ask their donors for money three to six times a year will have a higher renewal rate overall as well as all that extra income.

WHY DO MULTIPLE APPEALS WORK?

Many groups are hesitant to send several appeals to their current donors because they have heard donors complain about being asked too often. In fact, even you may dislike being asked repeatedly for money from the same organization. So the fact that multiple appeals work is a little counter to our experience and bears exploring.

We need to remind ourselves at the outset that the purpose of fundraising is building relationships. Every year, an organization should have more donors, and every year its donors should be more loyal. This will occur if the donors are treated like whole people and not just ATM machines, if they are thanked in a timely fashion with a personalized note, and if they are invited to the organization from time to time through an open house or other event.

Obviously, most of the donors to any organization will simply send their donation and wish the group well and the organization will never meet them. But a donor should have the impression that if they were to want to meet staff or board members, or get more involved with the organization, they would be welcomed. In fact, as much as possible, donors should be integrated into the work of the organization by being invited to be volunteers or attend events.

With this principle in mind, if a donor calls to complain that their name has been spelled wrong or that they are getting two copies of the newsletter, their complaint is dealt with swiftly and they are treated respectfully. If a donor attaches a note to a donation that says, "Only ask me once a year because I will only give once a year," then the organization complies with that request. The name of that donor will be coded accordingly in the database and suppressed for multiple mailings. Similarly, donors who write, "Don't phone me," should not be phoned. These are reasonable requests and a group can accommodate them.

In the absence of such a directive, however, donors should be asked for gifts several times a year. In addition to helping you raise more money, the requests help to educate the donor about the work of your group. Studies have shown that about 10% of donors will give each time they are asked. Some donors will give every time they are asked, and some may only give one or two extra times, but each time you send a letter you will have a response from at least 10% of the list. Interestingly, even donors who give only once a year are more likely to renew their gifts if they are asked several times during the year than if they are asked only once annually.

Multiple appeals are successful for any number of reasons. First, a person's cash flow can vary a great deal from month to month. In one month a person may receive an appeal from a group she supports, but she had just replaced all the tires on her car and can't afford it. Two months later, she may have gotten a raise and be able to make a donation in response to the appeal that comes then.

Second, sending only one or two appeals a year does not allow for much variety. Some people respond better to some types of appeals than to others. Organizations that send four or five appeals will discover that donors who regularly give $25 will give $50, $100, or more to a special appeal. They like the idea of buying something for the organization — media spots, an organizing drive, new computers, and the like.

We rarely know why people don't respond to appeals, but we usually make the assumption that the donor doesn't want to give when any of the following might be just as true: The donor has been away on vacation and mail has piled up, so he throws anything away that is not a bill or a personal letter, including your appeal; the donor is having personal problems and cannot think about anything else, even though she might be very committed to your group; the appeal is lost in the mail; though he meant to give, the donor loses the appeal in a pile of papers that got thrown away. Sometimes organizations report receiving donations for an appeal that is six months or a year old, showing that the donor has saved the appeal until he or she had some extra money, or misplaced it and decided to give when he or she saw it again.

Donors have a sense that a lot is going on with a group that sends several appeals a year. Multiple appeals keep your organization on the donor's radar screen and ensure that your group will be taken into account as the donor makes his or her charitable gifts. Remember that your group is not the only one the donor gives to and may in fact be one of a dozen or more groups they support. The donor needs to know that your group continues to do good work throughout the membership year.

HOW DO MULTIPLE APPEALS WORK?

Once we have established that multiple appeals do work, we have to look at how they work. Clearly, if so many people dislike being asked many times a year, it is possible to overdo appeals or to do them badly. So how do you do them well?

When you make a donation to a large national organization that appeals to its donors a dozen or more times a year, which is not unusual, this is what will often happen: You send in your gift. You may or may not get a thank-you note; if you do, it will not be personal. But six weeks or so after your first gift, you will get a request for another gift. This request will not acknowledge your previous gift at all. In fact, it won't be clear from this appeal that the group even knows that you gave before. Whether or not you send in another gift, you will get another appeal. This is what makes people dislike multiple appeals — the sense that whatever they send is not enough.

To counter this problem, always begin an extra appeal by thanking the person for their previous gift. This can be done even in a form letter by saying, "Dear Friend, Thank you so much for what you have given so far this year. We have used your donations to further our work. Now we have a chance to expand our work and need your help with an exciting project." The letter explains what work you are going to do and asks the donor for an extra gift: "If you can help us with an extra gift of $35, $50, $100 or whatever you can afford, we will be able to…" The letter ends by thanking the donor again, "Thank you for your previous support, and thank you in advance for helping in whatever way you can now."

HOW OFTEN SHOULD WE SEND APPEALS?

Grassroots organizations generally find that sending four appeals a year works well. The appeals can be sent quarterly, with a description of the exciting work coming up in the fall, winter, spring, or summer. Some groups plan to send three appeals and hold one appeal as a "floater." The floater appeal will be sent whenever something really exciting is happening and may not be sent at all during a year when nothing lends itself to description in a mail appeal. Some groups send three appeal letters and one invitation to a special event, and some groups send two appeals, and an invitation to a special event, and call donors once a year.

What you do will depend on how widely scattered your donors are (national groups will hesitate to run up their long distance bills by calling and generally will not be inviting donors who live far away to a special event), how many volunteers you have to help you with the appeal, and how many donors you have. Incidentally, return envelopes put in newsletters, although a good idea, do not take the place of multiple appeals.

To find out what works best, you may want to segment your donors and try different methods on different donor segments over the course of the year.

WHAT SHOULD WE SAY IN OUR APPEALS?

Once an organization has accepted the idea of doing multiple appeals, they often wonder what they are going to say in each different appeal. The following list of 26 ideas with sample text should help you choose some approaches that will work for your organization. Some of these ideas will be better suited to one organization than another, but almost any organization should be able to find one or two ideas that they could modify and use for their group.

Seasonal Appeals

1. Beginning of Year (written as a testimonial): "One of my New Year's resolutions is to give more money to

Verygood Group. I realized that, like many of my resolutions, this one could fade if I didn't act now. So I sent an extra $35 on Jan. 5. Will you join me and act now? Verygood will put the money right to work, right in our community."

2. End of Summer: "This fall our organizing efforts in Southend are going to result in the cleanup of the now closed Foul Factory. Getting the factory closed was one of our most important victories, but we must keep the pressure on to make sure the site is properly and thoroughly cleaned. Will you help us get a head start on our fall fundraising with an extra gift right now? Knowing that we have the money for our organizing campaign to monitor the cleanup process will make planning for it much easier."

3. End of Year: "If you are like many of us at Very Effective Group (VEG), you are gearing up for Hanukkah, Christmas, Kwanzaa, or the Winter Solstice. As you think about gifts for your loved ones, please think about VEG as well. This is your last chance to make a tax-deductible gift and count it against this year's taxes. We appreciate all you have done and wish you all the best in this holiday season."

4. Spring Appeal for New Members: "In the spring, everything seems to put on a new look — new leaves, new flowers. Everything starts growing again. Our organization is growing, too. You have been a big part of our growth and we thank you for that. This year we hope to recruit 500 new members — people like you. So, instead of asking you for a contribution, we would like you to send us the names of five people you think would be interested in joining our group."

Holiday Appeals

5. Martin Luther King's Birthday: "It is no secret that Dr. King would be both pleased and appalled at the progress America has made toward ending racism. Pleased, because much that is positive has happened. Appalled, because in some ways racism has gotten worse. We at Do Right Organization live and work by the principles of Dr. King and other civil rights leaders who gave their lives for their beliefs. Help us continue the legacy of Dr. King with a tribute gift to our organization in his memory."

6. Lincoln's Birthday: "President Lincoln was only one of the more famous people to be killed with a handgun. I know you want to end this senseless and continuing outrage of handgun violence. An extra donation from you, sent today, will give us the extra funds we need to work on a special program to stop the sale of handguns in our city."

7. Valentine's Day: "Do you often think of important people on Valentine's Day? Do you remember them with flowers, candy, or cards? I know I do. This year, I thought of other important people in my life — the people at

Working for Good Organization. They really depend on us, the members, for the financial support they need. Will you join me in sending an extra donation? You can send flowers or candy as well."

8. April: "Taxes. That's what's on everyone's mind right now. How much you owe. How you're going to pay it. Whether you are getting a refund. And where the tax money is going. At People Against Military Waste, we try to stop wasteful spending on weapons no one will ever use and we question the size and scope of our military. This year, we are asking people who have supported our work in the past to consider sending us a donation equal to 10% of what you owe the government or what you will get back in a refund."

9. Memorial Day: "We invite you to remember someone important to you with a gift to OurHospice Group. We will send a special card to the family of the person you are honoring and put the money right to work helping people cope with terminal illness."

10. Flag Day: "Flag Day. Most of us don't even own a flag anymore, but when I was a kid everyone put out a flag on June 14. At Center City Organizing Project, we were reminded by one of our senior members of the principles the flag stands for: freedom of speech, liberty, democracy, equality, pursuit of happiness. With your help, we will continue to work for these ideals. We aren't putting out a flag, but we are putting out a request — will you help us with an extra gift? You cherish these ideals as much as we do, and with your help they can become reality for all people."

11. July 4: "We are inviting all our members to a special July 4 barbecue at Phyllis Wheatley Park — the park we fought to save and worked to restore. Suggested donation: $15 a person, $25 for two; children under 12 are free. All you can eat, games, and fun! If you can't come, be with us in spirit by sending a donation in the enclosed envelope."

12. Mother's Day/Father's Day: "On this day, we remember our own parents and celebrate parents we know. For many people, these are fun times, surrounded by loving family. But what happens when this vision of a loving family turns sour, as it does for more than half of married women, who suffer from domestic abuse, or for the millions of children beaten, humiliated, or sexually assaulted by relatives? Mother's Day/Father's Day becomes a cruel irony. Mark this holiday in a different way this year — with an extra donation to the Abuse Prevention Project."

13. Labor Day: "Labor Day is a wonderful day to rest from work. But what about all the people who want to work and can't find jobs? For them, Labor Day is another reminder of their joblessness. We provide training to thousands of people so that they can get good jobs in areas needing workers. Help us make sure that we are able to provide training to everyone who wants it with your extra gift this Labor Day."

14. Columbus Day: "'Columbus discovered America.' This is one part of American history that nearly everyone knows. The problem is that this is a half-truth — Columbus discovered America for white people. There were already people here — our people. We are Native Americans. Yet our history since Columbus has been one of genocide, displacement, and oppression. Our latest project at Native American Advocacy Fund is free lesson plans, games, and plays for people who work with young children to teach them who Columbus really is and who we really are. Your donations in the past helped us develop this curriculum and your donation now will ensure that it is widely used."

15. Thanksgiving Day: "Your donation of $14.50 will provide a family with turkey and all the trimmings. Give whatever you can."

16. Any Holiday: As this holiday approaches, we are just $1,000 short of our goal to provide an important service to all the seniors in our community. Help us celebrate this holiday with your extra gift."

Old Stand-Bys

17. Anniversary: Our organization is now entering its ___ year of service to the community. Celebrate with us by sending $10 (or more or less) for every year we have existed. For your gift, we will be pleased to send you our special anniversary calendar. For those donating $1,000 or more, there will be a special reception with Famous Person at the home of Important Person."

18. Pledge: "Did you ever wish you could give more? Would you like to be a major donor, but can't afford it? Now you can. By joining our Monthly Donor Club, you can give $10, $20, $50, or whatever you wish on a monthly basis. You can do this by automatic charges to your credit card or direct debit from your checking account, or we can send you convenient reminder envelopes."

19. Famous Person: "I'm _____ . You may have seen me on television. In my personal life, I am very concerned about _____ . From your support of Good Work Organization, I know you are too. Will you join me in making an extra gift and ensuring that this important work continues?" (Famous Person can be truly famous, like Jimmy Smits or Oprah Winfrey, or it can be someone well known and well respected in your community.)

20. Another Member: "My name is Joe Murphy and I have been a member of Right On Group for five years. In that time, I have witnessed the malicious efforts of our elected leaders to deny us our rights. All that stands between us and them is Right On Group. In the past five years, Right On has succeeded in _____ , _____ , and _____ . That's why I am giving a little extra this year. My additional gift of $15 is not a lot for me, but if all our members gave at least that much, it would really add up."

21. The Story That Might Have Been Sad, but Ended Well Because of Your Group: "Ruthie is ten. Two years ago, she ran away from her violent stepfather. She was brought to our program from the streets of New York City, where she was found wandering alone, penniless and dazed. Today she is a good student and has found friendships with her classmates. She needs the support of our structured program, but with continued counseling, Ruthie can achieve her dream of becoming a judge. You have helped Ruthie and 500 children like her. Help us help more. Please send your extra donation today."

22. Urgent Need: "We have an urgent need to raise $2,000 to alert the public to the efforts of our city council to sell Vacant Lot to developers. We have been working for four years to have that lot turned into a community center. The developers want to make it into condos that no one in our neighborhood could afford. Help us stop this gentrification. Send your extra gift today."

23. Specific Project: "Our day care center is in desperate need of new playground equipment. The quality of day care is threatened by the dilapidated swing sets and slides that are all the children have to play on. To replace the whole playground will cost $5,000. Will you make an extra gift today toward that goal?"

Combination Appeals

24. Monthly Donor to a Specific Project: "Please join our Food for Thought Donor Club. For $10 a month minimum donation, you will help us keep serving 100 meals daily at our parish hall. In return, we will be pleased to send you our special newsletter, *Food For Thought.* "

25. Request for Funds and New Members in Honor of an Anniversary: "In honor of our second anniversary, we are forming a 2 X 4 club. Send us any combination of money, as long as it has twos in it — $2, $2.22, $222, $22.22 — and send us the names of four people who you think will be interested in joining. To thank you, we have had a special anniversary pin designed by one of our members. It is a 2 X 4, in a shape that will surprise and delight you. Join today."

26. Any of the Above Appeals with a Premium: "If you send your special gift before ___ date, we will send you, with our thanks, an autographed copy of *A Great Book* by A. Famous Person."

2000

Finding Major Donors by Mail

By ANDY ROBINSON

Most grassroots groups tend to focus their fundraising on two inefficient and risky strategies: grant proposals and benefit events.

Grants are problematic for at least two reasons. Foundations and corporations, which distribute grants, provide only 12% of the private-sector money available to U.S. charities, so groups that rely on grant funding are chasing a small piece of a very large pie. Furthermore, fewer than 15% of all proposals submitted are actually funded, which makes for lousy odds.

Benefit events, on the other hand, are great for identifying new donors and increasing the visibility of your group, but as a pure fundraising strategy they're terribly inefficient. Consider the "work-to-profit" ratio: If you applied the same number of staff and volunteer hours and the same expense budget to other strategies, could you raise more money hour-for-hour and dollar-for-dollar? In most cases, the answer is a resounding yes.

So where should you put most of your fundraising effort? Find and cultivate individual donors, especially potential major donors. In a typical annual campaign — seeking unrestricted individual gifts that all groups need to survive and prosper — just 10% of the donors provide a whopping 60% of the money. If you identify the right people and approach them in the right ways, you can build an effective major donor program to cover a big piece of your budget.

PUTTING THEORY INTO PRACTICE

To understand how this works, consider The Wildlands Project of Tucson, Arizona, a nonprofit conservation group working to establish a network of linked wilderness reserves across North America.

When I began working with Wildlands in January 1996, the organization had an annual budget of $300,000, most of which came from three foundations. Board and staff were understandably nervous about relying on such a narrow funding base, and sought help both to diversify foundation support and to build a major donor program that would increase their small donor pool.

In designing a fundraising strategy to reach individual donors, we were restricted by two factors:

• *The Wildlands Project is not a membership group and, for two reasons, did not want to become one.* First, it is not equipped to manage and service a large membership base of $25 donors. And, perhaps more important, because one of the organization's primary goals is to improve cooperation among national conservation groups, the board chose to avoid mass mailings and the perception of competing with other groups for their members.

• *The project could not solicit many major gifts in personal meetings.* The Wildlands Project works throughout North America and has an international board that meets just twice each year. Given the vast geographic distance between staff, board, and prospective donors, and the relatively low buy-in they had decided on for the major donor program ($100 and up), it would have been too costly and logistically difficult to solicit many prospects in person.

As a result of these considerations, we decided to build the campaign around small, personalized mailings. Our goal: 200 individuals donating between $100 and $5,000 each, for a total of at least $50,000 in 1996.

WORKING THE "HOUSE LIST"

For starters, we reviewed the group's donor list and found 265 people who had given $50 or more during the previous two years. This was the first, and best, pool of prospects for major gifts.

To solicit them, we mail-merged their names into an appeal letter using the office laser printer. The mail merge allowed us to personalize each letter with name, address, and salutation: "Dear Fran" instead of "Dear Friend." The letter also requested substantial gifts: "Whether you can contribute $100, $1,000, or more, we need your help."

The letter was a page and a half long — front and back on board letterhead — and included signature spaces for both the chairman and the board president. (One is a prominent biologist, the other a nationally known conservation activist.) Both men signed all letters by hand in colored ink.

So far, so good — personal letters signed by real human beings. We took this stack to the next board meeting and read off the names with the request, "If you know any of these people, raise your hand and add a note." The blank half-page on the back would accommodate their personal greetings.

At least 100 of these letters ended up with personal notes. A few contained five or six notes, which makes for a compelling request (talk about peer pressure!). Board and staff enjoyed this exercise and were eager to learn which of their contacts contributed.

As a final touch, we hand-addressed the envelopes and applied a first-class stamp. Hand-addressing is the most effective way to ensure that the envelope is opened; a "live" stamp also helps. We included a response envelope and a remittance card, with check-offs beginning at $100 and going up to $2,500, to indicate that we were serious about receiving a substantial gift.

This appeal generated an impressive 33% return and nearly $30,000, including one gift of $10,000 and another of $5,000. After subtracting these two big contributions, the average donation (including 34 gifts of less than $100) was $164. This one mailing produced more money from individuals than everything Wildlands had tried during the previous two years. This group of donors was solicited again in December, seven months after the first letter, and the checks continued to come through March, generating more than $20,000 in additional gifts.

BRING US YOUR NAMES

Once the first mailing was completed, we asked board members to go through their personal address books, Rolodexes, and databases to identify prospective donors. Their instructions: Put aside any concerns about whether these prospects can afford to give $100, and focus on their relationship to you and their concern about the environment.

We also contacted several national conservation groups (The Nature Conservancy, National Audubon Society, The Wilderness Society, etc.) to request copies of their annual reports. These booklets contain pages and pages of major donors, sorted by the size of their gifts. After photocopying these donor lists — 62 pages of names — we distributed packets to all board and staff and asked them to check off anyone they knew.

We reasoned that these people would make excellent prospects because they had a relationship to the solicitor, they had proven their concern about conservation issues, and they had proven their ability to make a big gift. The process of reviewing these lists "triggered" other names, which increased our pool of prospects.

Needless to say, list screening is miserable work: boring, time-consuming, and seemingly pointless. One board member was embarrassed to review more than 5,000 names and find only five people he knew — but one of those five came through with $1,000. Now he doesn't need to be convinced.

In the many cases where board and staff knew prospects but did not have an address or phone number, we used a CD-ROM product available at the public library. PhoneDisc, an electronic compilation of most phone books in the country, provided good addresses for at least two-thirds of our "missing persons." As an alternative, try one of the many online databases. Our local library's Web site — www.lib.ci.tucson.az.us — links to several directories, including AnyWho, Switchboard, The Ultimates, WhoWhere?, and Yahoo. Click on "Web links," then "directories."

After gathering names and addresses, we again mail-merged them into an appeal letter signed by the person who knew them best. After the signer added a personal note, other board and staff were asked to add notes where appropriate. As before, we hand-addressed the envelopes, affixed a first-class stamp (from the Endangered Species commemorative series!), and included a response card and remittance envelope. For these new prospects, we also enclosed a brochure about The Wildlands Project.

Through this process, board and staff identified and solicited more than 400 additional prospects; most received two letters six months apart. The result: Forty donors provided $11,650 in large gifts, with two dozen sending smaller donations.

All told, we contacted 700 major donor prospects; 177 responded with nearly $65,000 in contributions of $100 or more. About one-third of these gifts were received from board members and at benefit events, and a few others were unsolicited, but the rest were raised through the mail.

WHAT WE LEARNED

1. Personal attention makes a big difference. The old cliché is true: People give money to people, not organizations. The more personal the contact, the more effective our fundraising. Next year, we plan to approach selected donors and prospects by phone and, when feasible, in person.

2. You don't need rich people. Most of our contributors are college faculty, nonprofit staff, doctors, activists, teachers, homemakers, retired people, etc. We have very few "name" donors.

3. Small is beautiful. Big national groups will not give this much attention to $100 or $500 donors, but grassroots groups can and should. This is the strategic advantage of being small.

4. Don't try for more major donors than you can service. Our goal was to enlist 200 major donors in 1996. Given our limited staffing, we figured this was the largest number we could maintain strong relationships with. We continue to send them personal notes and treat them as part of the family.

5. You can't save time. Every stage of this process—screening lists, mail-merging and hand-signing the letter, writing notes, hand-addressing envelopes, etc. — is time consuming. If you want to build a successful major donor program, you can't take shortcuts.

6. It works. This successful major donor strategy tripled income from major donors of The Wildlands Project within one year. Try these techniques with your own organization and watch what happens.

The Wildlands Project

PROPOSED GIFT-RANGE CHART FOR $50,000 MAJOR DONOR CAMPAIGN

RANGE OF GIFTS	NUMBER OF GIFTS DESIRED	NUMBER OF PROSPECTS (RATIO) NEEDED	TOTAL DOLLAR AMOUNT PER RANGE EXPECTED
$5,000 +	1	10 (10:1)	$5,000
$2,500–$4,999	3	15 (5:1)	$7,500
$1,000–$2,499	10	40 (4:1)	$10,000
$ 500–$999	15	45 (3:1)	$7,500
$ 250–$499	30	90 (3:1)	$7,500
$ 100–$249	125	250 (2:1)	$12,500
TOTALS:	184 donors	450 prospects	$50,000

RESULTS FROM MAJOR GIFT CAMPAIGN

GIFT AMOUNTS	NUMBER OF GIFTS	TOTAL DOLLAR AMOUNT RECEIVED
$10,000	1	$10,000
$5,000	2	$10,000
$1,500	2	$3,000
$1,243	1	$1,243
$1,000	10	$10,000
$600	1	$600
$500	17	$8,500
$400	4	$1,600
$350	1	$350
$300	5	$1,500
$250	18	$4,500
$225	1	$225
$200	18	$3,600
$150	4	$600
$125	2	$250
$100	90	$9,000
TOTALS:	177 donors	$64,968

1997

Fundraising Strategies

II. PERSONAL SOLICITATION

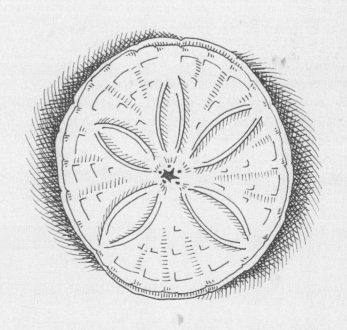

The Fine Art of Asking for the Gift

By KIM KLEIN

People who are active in an organization, particularly board members and key volunteers, are natural candidates to solicit major gifts in person from contributors or prospects. An organization may even conduct or provide training sessions to increase volunteers' skill and comfort in making such personal solicitations. Many people have discovered that doing face-to-face fundraising reminds them of the true depth of their commitment to an organization. They remember why they became involved with the work in the first place and why they think the work is important. Occasionally, people discover in the process of asking for gifts that their commitment is not that strong and that they would be happier in another organization.

People soliciting major gifts for an organization must, first and foremost, believe thoroughly in the cause of the organization. Second, they must have demonstrated that commitment with a financial contribution. The size of that contribution is not important, but it must be an amount that is significant for that individual. Having made their own gift, they convey the message to their prospects (whether simply in attitude or in words as well), "Join me. Do what I have done. Give a large contribution to this organization because it is really important." Once a solicitor has demonstrated their own commitment, they can approach their prospects with confidence.

TYPES OF PROSPECTS

There are three types of prospects for face-to-face solicitations:

- People who have given before and are prospects for a repeat or upgraded gift
- People who have not given before, but are close to someone in the organization
- People who are interested in the cause but don't know anyone in the organization. For these people, some kind of cultivation is necessary before actually soliciting the gift. Inviting the person to a special event, house meeting, or educational evening, or asking to see the person in order to describe the program, should precede the meeting at which a gift is requested.

In this article, we will assume that the prospect is ready to be asked for the gift.

APPROACHING THE PROSPECT

There are three steps in approaching the prospect:

1. A letter describing the program and requesting a meeting to discuss it further

2. A phone call to set up a meeting

3. The meeting itself, in which the gift is usually solicited

Obviously, if you are approaching your spouse or your best friend, you can skip the letter, and perhaps even the phone call. In some cases the letter will be enough and there will be no need for a phone call and meeting; in others a phone call alone will suffice. Requests for gifts of more than $1,000, for capital gifts, or for multiyear pledges will almost always be more successful in a face-to-face meeting. Further, even when prospects decline to meet, they are pleased that you were willing to take the time to meet with them had they so desired.

Letters to Current Givers

The simplest letter is the one to prospects who have given before. You thank them for their support in the past and ask them to give the same amount or more again. In the letter, describe some of your achievements during the past year and some of your future plans. Tell them you will phone them in a few days and, if they are in your area, offer to meet with them. Enclose a stamped return envelope.

After a few days, phone them. Often you will discover that the check is in the mail. Over time, you will learn who prefers not to be phoned, but just wishes to be reminded when it is time to renew their gift.

If you do meet with the prospect, ask for a larger gift than they gave last year, or use the meeting as an opportunity to ask for the names of other people who might be interested in giving major gifts.

As you get to know the donors, you can see if they would make good board members, or if they would be willing to solicit some large gifts on behalf of your organization. Meeting with current donors tells people that they are valued and helps build their loyalty to the organization.

Letters to People Close to the Organization

Letters to prospects in this category should be signed by the person who knows them best. Letters to prospects you know rest heavily on the amount of respect and affection the prospect has for you. When writing to someone you know, use the same tone and format you would use in writing to him or her about anything else. If you normally call the person by their first name, do that in your letter. Mention to your friend that you are a donor yourself. You don't have to say how much you give — just the fact that you give will tell your friend that you are asking them to do only what you are already doing.

If the person who knows the prospect is unable or unwilling to write the letter, then the person actually soliciting the gift may be a stranger to the prospect. In that case, begin the letter by making the connection clear: "Jane Friendswithyou gave me your name. She said you might be interested in our work because…." Go on to describe the work of the organization and ask to meet with the person.

Indicate in the letter that you will be asking for money. The letter can describe how much the organization needs and what kind of gift you hope the prospect will make.

In writing the letter, remember that people have short attention spans. Make your sentences interesting, evocative, and short. Avoid using jargon or complicated explanations. Statistics are fine, if used sparingly. The idea of the letter is to spark the prospect's interest so that he or she will want to meet with you. The letter does not have to

convince fully, and in fact, should just raise the person's interest. The face-to-face meeting is the time to convince the prospect to give.

Sample Letter

Dear Theodor,

You and I have talked about my work with the East Side Senior Advocates, and I have appreciated your support over the years for our various projects. We are now entering one of our most exciting ventures yet — a project to put a Senior Advocate in every neighborhood where more than 10% of the population is over 65. This project will involve hiring three more staff and renting one more office. The benefits far outweigh the costs, however.

I am hoping you will consider a major gift to this project. We are looking for gifts in the range of $2,000, although gifts of all sizes are needed. I don't expect you to decide based on this letter — what I want is for us to meet and talk about the project. I will call you in a few days to see when we can get together. Sincerely, Anastasia

The Phone Call

If you say you are going to call, call. Rehearse the phone call beforehand to anticipate possible questions or objections the prospect might have. The following examples show three different problems that arise during phone calls and ways they could be handled.

SCENARIO ONE: THE EASY PROSPECT

You: Hello, this is Worthy Cause. Is this Mary Prospect?

Ms. Prospect: Yes, it is.

You: I recently wrote to you about…. Did you get my letter?

Ms. Prospect: Yes, I think I did.

You: Do you have a minute now? (Or, Is this a good time to talk?)

Ms. Prospect: I have just about one minute. Now remind me of what your organization does. I get so many letters.

You: Our organization…(two sentences at most). What I would really like to do is get together with you for about half an hour to explain our project in more depth. I know you are busy, so is there any time next week that I could come see you?

Ms. Prospect: I think I could fit you in next Wednesday at 10.

You: Great. I'll be there. Thanks so much.

SCENARIO TWO: TIME AND LOGISTICS PROBLEMS

Ms. Prospect: This is really a bad time of year for me. I'm doing an inventory and then I have to fly to Washington, D.C., and I just can't fit in another thing.

You: I can certainly understand that. Why don't I call you next month and see if things have settled down, and you might have some time then?

Ms. Prospect: That would be fine.

Or,

Ms. Prospect: This is just too busy a time for me. I'll call you when I can work you into my schedule.

You: I know you have a lot on your mind. I'll call you in a month or so to see if things have settled down.

Or,

Ms. Prospect: I never make decisions to give away such large gifts without talking it over with my husband. We do all our giving jointly.

You: That seems reasonable. May I come and talk to you both?

SCENARIO THREE: DISAGREEMENTS WITH THE ORGANIZATION

Ms. Prospect: I got your letter, but I have to tell you honestly that I think the government should be taking care of this, and you all should be lobbying for restored government funding in this area.

You: We agree that the government should be taking care of this problem, and we're working with a coalition of groups to pressure for restored funding. But in the meantime, these people are without services, and we have to turn to people like you who understand the need so clearly. I'd like to talk with you about our government strategy, since I know that it is an area of interest to you, in addition to discussing our program. Could we meet next week?

Or,

Ms Prospect: Aren't you the group that had to fire your Executive Director for incompetence a little while ago?

You: Yes, our executive director was released when the board discovered....I know you'll be pleased to learn that Much Better Person has taken her place and things are now completely back to normal. I really want to talk about our programs in more detail. Is it possible to set up a meeting in the next few weeks?

Or,

Ms. Prospect: I have other priorities at this time and I'm not sure your organization falls within my present commitments.

You: I know that you have other priorities. I would really appreciate it if we could discuss our organization's program because I think it falls within your concerns. Jane Friendswithyou indicated that you are strongly committed to...and we do work in that area now.

Ms. Prospect: I'm afraid you'll be wasting your time.

You: I'm not worried about that. I don't want to waste your time, but I do think a brief meeting would help us both to see if we have any goals in common.

THE IMPORTANCE OF BEING ASSERTIVE

Most of the time when people put us off we assume that they are trying to say no but are just too polite to come right out with it. This is a false assumption. Prospects are looking for signs that you are really serious about your organization. They appreciate persistence, assertiveness, and an attitude that what you have to offer is critically important and worth taking some time to discuss.

If you are easily put off and take the first no as the final answer, it tells the prospect that you are not terribly concerned about the organization, or that you don't really care whether or not the prospect gives. Clearly, you don't want to be rude, but you need to be willing to push the prospect a little; don't take the first resistance as the final word.

The Face-to-Face Meeting

Once you have an appointment, you are ready to prepare for the face-to-face solicitation. This is not as frightening as it seems. First of all, the prospect knows from your letter or your phone call that you will be talking with them about making a contribution. Since they have agreed to see you, the answer to your request is not an outright no. The prospect is considering saying yes. Your job is to move them from "I'm considering giving" to "I'd be delighted to give."

The purpose of the meeting is to get a commitment to give. Everything else revolves around this purpose. It is fine for the conversation to go off on a tangent, but you must keep bringing it back to the financial needs of the organization and the possible role of the prospect in meeting those needs.

As the solicitor, you must appear poised, enthusiastic, and confident. If you are well prepared for the interview, this will not be too difficult. Many times, board members and volunteers are afraid they will not appear knowledgeable about the organization. It is perfectly fine for them to bring along a staff member or someone who has been with the organization for a long time and who can answer difficult questions. Sometimes going with a partner also helps you feel more relaxed. It is also fine to answer a question with, "I don't know, but I'll be glad to get you that information."

In the meeting, your role is to help the prospect to see that giving to your organization is a logical and natural extension of his or her interests and concerns. Ask the prospect questions, and carry on a conversation with him or her. "Do you agree with our approach?" "Did you see the article about us in last week's paper?" "Has Jane Friendswithyou talked much about our organization?"

When you finally ask for the gift, look the prospect right in the eye and in a clear, bold voice say, "Can you help us with a $300 contribution?" or, "We are hoping you can give $500–$1,000." Keep looking at the prospect, and don't say anything after you have asked for the gift. It is the prospect's turn to speak. Although it may seem like a long time between your request and his or her response, it is only a matter of a few seconds.

Sometimes the prospect will say, "I'd like to help, but that figure is way out of my range." Your response can be, "What would you feel comfortable giving?"

After you ask for the gift and get an affirmative answer, discuss how the prospect wants to make the gift. Perhaps they will give you a check right there, or mail it in the return envelope you brought. For larger gifts, prospects (now donors) may want to transfer stock, or make other arrangements that will cause the gift to arrive in a week or two. Once these arrangements are made, thank the donor and leave.

Immediately after the interview, send the donor a thank-you note. Another thank you from the organization should be sent when the money arrives.

BUILDING A STRONGER ORGANIZATION

Although it can be anxiety producing to ask for money the first few times you do it, it is thrilling to get an affirmative commitment from a major donor. It is also a good feeling to know that you were able to set aside your own discomfort for the greater purpose of meeting the needs of your organization. Knowing that you can talk comfortably about the financial goals of your organization is empowering. Boards of directors find that they are immeasurably strengthened when each of their members feels able to ask for money.

1983

Getting Over the Fear of Asking

By KIM KLEIN

Early last spring a number of people met at the head-quarters of Californians for Justice on a Saturday morning. We had volunteered to walk some precincts and talk to people about two of the initiatives on the California ballot that we opposed: One would prohibit gay or lesbian marriages from ever becoming legal; the other targeted young people of color for increased penalties in the criminal justice system.

The day dawned raining and windy. At the office of Californians for Justice, we were told that, because it was so stormy, we could phone people instead of going door to door, although the organizer felt that visiting people personally was more effective. Several people said they didn't mind the rain and wanted to walk. They were clearly the diehards, in my opinion. I had opted for the less effective but definitely more comfortable option of phoning.

Then the organizer said that they had found it effective to ask people for money at the door as part of the rap. She said, "Just ask for a dollar. We have found that people who give even a small amount of money are more likely to vote on election day." At that announcement, half of the group that had been willing to walk decided to phone. "I'll do anything but I can't ask for a dollar," said one volunteer. Another chimed in, "I don't mind rain, falling branches, even loose electrical lines, but I draw the line at asking for money."

I have seen this behavior over and over for many years. When it comes to asking for money, the amount doesn't matter, the cause doesn't matter, the gender, race, or class of the person reacting doesn't matter. Asking people for money continues to be the most difficult, but also the most important part of fundraising.

Every community-supported organization uses a variety of methods to raise money from individuals, such as direct mail appeals, special events, pledge programs, products for sale, and so on. But the fastest and most efficient way for an organization to raise money is for board members, staff, and volunteers to ask people directly — in person — for donations. Unfortunately, this is also the hardest way, since it requires that we directly confront our learned discomfort with asking for money.

For an organization to have an effective donor program, the people in the group must get over their fear of asking for money. The purpose of this article is to discuss some of the reasons that asking for money is difficult and to provide some exercises that will help you let those difficulties go.

SOURCES OF OUR FEARS

Asking a person for money face-to-face is an acquired taste. Few people love to do it initially; in fact most people are afraid to do it. If you are afraid to ask for money, that's normal. If you are not afraid, that's great. Stop reading this article and go ask somebody for a donation!

People are afraid to ask for money for a wide variety of reasons. However, it is important to understand that everything we think and feel about money is learned. Children have no trouble asking for anything. They ask over and over, and don't even seem to hear the word *no* until it has been said several times. But by the time most of us have reached the age of ten, our ability to ask for what we want has been trained out of us.

In discussing some of the reasons people fear asking for money, I will focus on the United States because that is where I am from and where most *Journal* readers live. It is also because our feelings about money are particular to our culture. There are many countries in the world where people have a very different relationship to money than we do.

Most of us are taught that four topics are taboo in polite conversation: politics, money, religion, and sex. The subjects of age, illness, and death are often taboo as well, and in some parts of the country or within different cultural groups, other topics may also be off-limits. Of all these topics, the taboo against talking about money is the most firmly in place. We have ecumenical councils to break down barriers between religions, we have support, education, and advocacy groups on issues of sex and sexuality, hospice programs to deal with death and dying, and a disability rights movement, but there are few serious efforts to break down our taboo about talking about money.

For example, many of us were raised to believe that it is rude to ask someone what their salary is or how much they paid for their house or their car. In many families, one person (traditionally the man) takes care of all financial decisions and transactions. It is not unusual, even today, for spouses not to know how much each other earns, for children not to know how much their parents earn, and for close friends not to know one another's income.

The net effect of these taboos about discussing money is that money takes on the air of being both mysterious and bad. The hidden message is that "good" people don't deal with money except insofar as they must in order to live. Many people, misquoting the Bible, say, "Money is the root of all evil." In fact, Paul's statement to the Philippians in the New Testament is, "The love of money is the root of all evil." In the *Letter of James,* we see the much more Biblical admonition, "You have not because you ask not."

Money, in itself, has no good or evil qualities. It is not a moral substance. Money facilitates people getting what they want or need. As such, how money is used, where it is obtained, and the inequities of who has it and who does not have moral implications. This is a very different situation from money itself being evil.

As long as money remains private and mysterious, only people who are willing to learn about it can really control it. In that case, systems can remain discriminatory and people without knowledge about how money works will have far fewer choices and much less power than those willing to break the taboo. For example, when it is common practice not to ask about salaries, institutions can conceal the fact that women are paid less than men or that people of color receive less than white people for the same work. Banks can deny loans on the basis of race or

gender with little fear of repercussions because most people have little idea of what they are entitled to.

In America, an elite upper class controls the majority of the nation's wealth, either by earning it or inheriting it, or both. It serves the interest of this ruling class for the mass of people to continue not to know about money.

As political activists and participants in social change, however, we must learn about money, not only for fundraising, but for all organizing purposes — how to raise it effectively and ethically, how to manage it efficiently, and how to spend it wisely.

EXAMINING YOUR ATTITUDES

I recommend you take some time in your organization to explore feelings and anxieties about money in general and asking for money in particular that may be getting in the way of successfully carrying out your fundraising plans. The following are three exercises that will help you do that. To do the exercises, you will need a blackboard or flipchart and markers.

Taking the Charge Out

The first step in getting over your anxiety about asking for money is to remember that you weren't born with this anxiety and that what you have been taught about money perpetuates a system that, in the rest of your work, you are trying to change. Take some time in your group to discuss your personal experiences with money — what each person learned as a child and what they think now. This does not have to be a heavy, deeply personal discussion. The purpose of the following exercise is to take some of the "charge" out of the word *money* and help get some distance from it.

Each person in the group takes a minute or two by themselves to write down the answers to two questions:

1. What is your earliest memory of money?

2. What messages, ideas, and attitudes about money were conveyed to you by parents, peers, and others in your community?

Next, people pair up and each person takes a couple of minutes to tell their partner what they have written. After a few minutes, the group comes back together and people share key points, with someone writing them on a flipchart or blackboard.

You'll probably hear such things as

- Money talks.

- Money doesn't grow on trees.

- Money doesn't buy happiness.

- We were taught to give it to "the needy."
- Don't ask for it.
- We never had enough of it.
- Money is power.
- Never ask someone what their salary is.

Looking at the list, notice how many of the messages are negative or about privacy and power.

Next, the group discusses what a healthy attitude toward money might look like by considering together the following questions:

1. In an ideal world, what would people be taught as children to think about money?

2. How would this change how we feel about money as adults?

Again, record answers on a flipchart. At the end of this discussion, compare this list to the previous one. You'll probably see that what a healthy attitude might include and what people learned as children are very different.

DISPELLING FEARS ABOUT ASKING FOR MONEY

Fears about asking for money are related to our anxiety about talking about it. For the following two easy exercises, one member of the group can act as facilitator or you can ask someone outside the group to facilitate. These exercises can be done privately, but they are more effective when group members share with each other in recognizing and letting go of fears about money.

The Worst That Can Happen

In this exercise, the group looks objectively at everyone's fears about asking for money. Confronting fear in this way is like confronting any fear. When you hear a loud, unfamiliar noise in your house at night, an immediate, normal reaction is fear. You have two choices about how to respond to this fear: 1) You can give in to the fear, huddling under the covers and imagining all the worst things the noise could mean, or 2) you can take the more sensible, but much more difficult, action of getting up and turning on all the lights until you discover that the noise was as simple as the cat knocking something over while leaping from one surface to another, your child playing a noisy computer game when she is supposed to be sleeping, or a car backfiring on the street.

In the same way, looking at everyone's fears about asking for money in the "light" of discussion with others will show that many of these fears are irrational and that for most, the feared outcome is far less likely to happen than they think.

To begin the exercise, each person imagines asking someone for a relatively large amount of money (anything over $100). Then each person says out loud what they are most afraid might be the outcome of their solicitation. This includes not only what the prospect might say or do, but also what the prospect might think of them and what they will think of themselves. The facilitator writes down all the feared outcomes. After four or five minutes, there will probably be a list that includes the following:

- The prospect will say no.
- The prospect will yell at me (or hit me).
- The prospect will give me the money, but won't really want to, and will resent me.
- I will feel too nauseated to continue.
- I know the prospect doesn't have the money.
- It is imposing on our friendship for me to ask, and we won't be friends anymore.
- The prospect will think that the only reason I was nice to her was to get money.
- The prospect will say yes, then ask me for money for his cause.
- I don't know if my group really deserves the money as much as some other groups might.
- The prospect will ask me questions about the organization that I can't answer.

After this brainstorming session, the group looks at the fears they have listed. They will probably notice that they fall into three categories:

- Fear of things that will definitely happen some of the time (the person will say no).
- Fear of things that might happen but could be dealt with if they do (the person will ask me for money; the person will ask questions I can't answer).
- Fear of things that are extremely unlikely to happen (I'll be punched, I'll be sued, I'll throw up).

Now, examine the fears starting from the top. For most people, the worst thing that can happen when they ask for money is that the person will say no. This is a possible outcome: Everyone who does fundraising will be told no almost as often as they will be told yes. Remember, just as it is your privilege to ask for money, it is the other person's privilege to turn you down. The person being asked may have just spent $1,000 on their car, or been asked to give to five other organizations, or have other priorities. Sometimes people will say no because they have other worries just then and can't take the time to think about your request. Perhaps they trust your friendship enough that they feel they can say no to you with no hard feelings. While no one likes to be turned down, it is important not to take being turned down as a personal rejection, because it almost never has anything to do with you.

The fear that someone will give to your organization and then ask you for money for his or her special cause requires remembering that if someone gives to your cause, you don't personally owe them a favor. The organization the check was made out to must now write them a thank-you note and do the work you said the group would do. The obligation to the donor (to the extent that it exists) is paid by these actions.

Fundraising is about an exchange: Donors provide money in exchange for work being done that the donor believes in and wants to see happen. If the person you ask then asks you for their cause, you should think about whether it is a cause you believe in. If it is and you have the money, make the gift. If not, then don't. If you believe that a person's main motive for giving money is to be able to ask for money, exclude that person from your prospect list. You want to create a base of donors who are loyal to the organization, not to you, and not to an idea that they can now raise money from you.

Questions you can't answer can be responded to with "I don't know" or "I'll find out and let you know."

Fears such as "I know the person doesn't have the money" are very common. However, unless you have a financial statement from the person you are asking, or unless you know he or she has recently experienced a devastating financial setback, you don't know that the person doesn't have the money. Although most of us have had times when our financial situation has been bleak, the fact is that how much money we feel we can give depends mostly on what mood we are in at the time we are asked and little on objective reality. Some days a person feels generous or feels flush and some days they don't.

The group should discuss each of the fears listed. Are they real? If they are real, do they matter? What is the worst thing that can happen?

Looking at our fears makes them less scary and allows us to prepare ourselves properly for what might actually happen during a solicitation.

Sometimes it is not appropriate to ask someone for money, but this is true far less often than we think. When you consider asking someone for money and decide not to, ask yourself, "Do I have a reason not to ask, or just an excuse based on assumptions I am making about the other person?"

The Yes and No Lists

When thinking about why a person would give money to an organization, think about why you give money to any organization. Your reasons for giving and not giving will be much the same as everyone else's and will help you understand what motivates people to give.

In this exercise, participants imagine that an acquaintance — someone they like and respect, but don't know well — has come to them, explained a cause he or she is involved in, and asked for a gift. Imagine that the gift is an affordable amount, but not an amount you could give without some thought. For most people, this amount is somewhere between $50 and $250.

Each participant takes 30 seconds to write down privately on a sheet of paper all the reasons they would say yes to this request. Then, for the next 30 seconds, they list all the reasons they would say no. Asking participants to share their results, the facilitator then writes the "yes" and "no" reasons on two separate sheets of paper, or two columns on a blackboard. Generally, there are more "yes" reasons than "no" reasons. The following are the most common reasons:

WHY I WOULD SAY YES

- Like the person asking
- Believe in the cause
- Get something for my money
- Tax deduction
- I feel generous
- Just got paid
- Know my money will be well used
- Want to support my friend
- Feel guilty saying no
- Know other people in the group
- Don't have time to volunteer, so give money
- Liked the approach

WHY I WOULD SAY NO

- Don't believe in the cause
- Don't have the money
- Bad mood that day
- Organization has a bad reputation
- Give to other things
- Already been asked several times that week
- Don't know what my money will be used for
- Think person asking is naive or pushy

The group discusses the two lists. Looking at the "no" list, these answers fall into two categories:

A) Reasons that are not the asker's fault and that could not be known ahead of time.

B) Responses that appear to be "no" but are really "maybe."

In the first case, the asker usually cannot know that the prospect does not have the money right now, or that they are in a bad mood, or have been asked several times that week. When this is the reason for the rejection, the asker can only thank the prospect for their time and go on to the next prospect.

In the second case, if the prospect knew more about the organization, knew how the money was used, knew that the reasons for the organization's bad reputation have been cleared up, he or she might give. These "no" answers are really "maybe." "Maybe I would give if I thought the organization did good work." "Maybe I would give if I knew what the money is being used for."

Possibly the asker can discuss the prospect's reasons for saying no and change the answer to an affirmative. If this is not possible, the solicitor can still see that the rejec-tion has little to do with them or their group.

A few of the "no" reasons reflect badly on the asker. For example, if the prospect thinks the asker is naive or pushy or dislikes the asker altogether, then this was an unfortunate choice of a person to solicit the gift.

The point of this exercise is twofold: to illustrate why people give and don't give and to illustrate that people have more reasons to say yes than to say no to a request for a contribution.

These exercises and the subsequent discussion they involve will help people in your group understand that asking for money is not as frightening as they may have thought. The worst thing that can happen is that the person asked will say no, and usually they say no for reasons outside your control or knowledge.

Taking the time to have this discussion to help people let go of their personal barriers around asking, as well as understanding how asking for money is an important political act, will free your group to ask for the money it needs to do the work that needs to be done.

2001

Asking in the Age of the Machine:
How to Deal with the Electronic Moat

By KIM KLEIN

It's hard enough just to make the call. Whether you are new to personal solicitation or a veteran with dozens of "asks" under your belt, you probably spend a fair amount of time preparing to work your way through your list of calls.

First, you have to decide whom to call and what to ask for. Depending on the size of your donor base and the number of people available to make these calls, I recommend calling people who have given at least $100 and whom you want to ask for more money. You may also call people who have given $100 or more simply to ask them to renew at the same amount, if you believe the person has reached their capacity or if they have recently increased the size of their gift. However, it takes so much energy to call that, unless your information indicates otherwise, it is best to use the call to ask for more money. Of course, you can also use phone calls to ask donors to host a house party or to recommend other people who might become donors.

Your database needs to be able to list people who have given frequently over a long period of time (three or more years), people who have given significantly at least once (the exact size of "significant" varies from group to group), and people whose giving is increasing without being asked. These are the people to concentrate on. Another group not to be overlooked is people who have given a major gift, then decreased their giving. You need to find out if their decrease has anything to do with you.

Now, to the phone. You take out your 3 × 5 card or computer-generated form with the information about the person that you are calling. You review his or her giving history and the gift you are to seek. You recall what you know about this person — is she garrulous or brusque? Is he likely to be receptive to your call or will he resist? You review what you are trying to do with the phone call — get a meeting, get the money on the phone, set up another phone date, etc. If you are like me, you make some notes about what you want to say and you review how to answer objections that may be raised. You take a deep breath, wish yourself luck, and call.

WHO ANSWERS?

Ring, ring. Until the last ten years or so, if you were calling someone at home, you either reached a person or the phone kept ringing. If you called the person at work, you might have encountered a secretary or receptionist of varying degrees of friendliness. In that case, you had to decide what kind of message to leave, particularly in response to the slightly hostile question, "Will she know what this is regarding?" or the even more haughty, "Will she know who you are?" As you left your name and tried to summarize in ten words what you wanted, you kicked yourself for not preparing more thoroughly for such an encounter.

For the last decade or more, you would have prepared yourself not only to speak to the prospect, but also to leave a message on an answering machine if the prospect wasn't home. In leaving the message, you would have had to decide how reliable the machine sounded. Did it have that underwater quality that indicated your voice would be too distorted to be understood? Did the tape run out without warning mid-message, leaving you feeling really foolish? Did it make weird clicking and blipping noises that caused you to keep stumbling over your words, unsure which were being recorded? Veterans of calling got used to all that.

But in the last two years, message machines have gotten more complicated. Now you may be confronted by a menu of choices that requires pen and paper just to keep track of, let alone select from. "Hello, you have reached the Smith family. We are either on the phone or not available to take your call right now. If you know who you want to talk to, you may press the number at any time. For Kevin, press one, for Moira, two, for Shelley, three, for Alfred, four." Beep. Now, your dilemma, which must be resolved in one nanosecond: You want a meeting with Kevin and Moira, which box do you leave that message in?

Or, you call the prospect at work. First you are routed electronically to a staff directory. You can enter the first three letters of their last name. Someone else has the first three letters of your prospect's last name, and you are put into the wrong box. You call back and press zero for an operator. There is no operator, but you can get to another directory that gives everyone's name at the office, along with the code you must use to reach them. "For Mary Jones, press 157 followed by the pound sign." Everyone, we hope, knows which is the pound sign by now.

If a live person at an office answers the phone, his or her job is mostly to put you through to voice mail. Forget getting anyone who can tell you whether the person you want to reach is out to lunch or on sabbatical! At the voice mailbox, some people are very nice about leaving an outgoing message that describes their whereabouts; "I'll be out of my office today, and back tomorrow," which would help except you don't know which day is "today" and which "tomorrow."

To be sure, what I have just said applies to a particular demographic profile of donor: people who have jobs. Organizations whose donors are mostly retired people will not have most of the experiences I am describing. Similarly, what I am describing is more true in urban areas than in rural ones and more likely in big cities than small towns. But for many groups, the majority of their donors match this demographic profile. So, for the phone call you make today, your chances of actually getting your prospect on the phone the first time you call are down to almost zero, and your chances of ever speaking to them in person at all (unless they are also a good friend) are down to about 20%!

Now another complication has arisen: An increasing number of people prefer to be reached by e-mail or fax. Although they are not unwilling to engage in a conversation, you may never have one with them. A friend of mine successfully concluded a $5,000 request recently all by e-mail. It took three days and six messages, but she says it actually took very little time.

EVERYONE IS ON THE PHONE

A second and related problem is the degree to which raising money by phone has become seemingly universal. Whether it is commercial telemarketers making "cold" calls to sell everything from long distance phone service to credit cards and mortgages, or nonprofits promoting a cause that will save, prevent, promote, stop something bad or start something good, the phone is suddenly the chosen first method of contact. The fax machine is not far behind, and unsolicited advertising over e-mail is already beginning.

Even though people find phone solicitation annoying, it does work, as attested to by the income generated. A study commissioned by the Direct Marketing Association in 1998 showed that some $65 billion was raised the previous year by nonprofits through telemarketing. Compare that to giving by foundations of $11.8 billion and you have an idea of the impact of the strategy. Telemarketing is not likely to go away any time soon.

It's no wonder that many people are choosing to surround themselves with gatekeepers: Machines that screen messages or display the caller's phone number allow many calls to go unanswered. I call this the "electronic moat."

From now on, and as far into the future as we can see, it is clear that as fundraisers we need to spend less time psyching ourselves up to talk to the prospect and more time preparing to talk to the various electronic voices that inform the prospect what is wanted of them.

THE PERSONAL TOUCH

Along with total strangers calling people to invite them to join groups they do not currently belong to, many nonprofit groups are trying harder to approach current donors more personally. I endorse this activity, and many articles in the *Journal* have talked about how to do this. However, this strategy is losing effectiveness because it is being overused.

In my own experience, in 1997 I got dozens of personal notes attached to letters asking me for money. While many of these notes were from people I had met briefly, they were often from people I did not know *at all* . Many of these personal notes were followed up with phone calls — very nice messages asking me to give again or give more. In talking with friends, I learned this personalizing was extremely common. The problem with it is that as it becomes more common, it becomes less effective.

So, what are some solutions? First, I reaffirm that any personal note or phone call is more effective than none. That it is less effective than it used to be does not for a minute mean it is not much more effective than an impersonal letter with no follow-up message.

However, many people engaged in personal solicitation have lost sight of the meaning of the word *personal*. As Funk and Wagnalls reminds us, personal means "pertaining to or concerning a particular person, not general or public." The key word here is "particular" person. We need to be increasingly conscious of trying to match solicitors with prospects whom they know personally.

For many years, the connection between prospect and solicitor could be simply that they were both donors to the same group. Many of us have made successful calls to people by introducing ourselves as board members or volunteers and saying, "We don't know each other, but we both give to Verygood Group, and I'm hoping I could talk with you about renewing your gift." While this can still work, it doesn't fly as well as "Hi, George, this is Mary. Will you call me when you have a chance? I want to talk with you about giving to Verygood Group. It was great to see you and Terry at New Year's. 444-8765. Thanks."

When deciding who will ask whom, every effort should be made to put people together who know each other socially or professionally. For many organizations, this means a larger pool of volunteers will be involved in asking for money. The development director's job more and more involves getting as many people as possible out there asking and maximizing the opportunity for people to ask particular people whom they know.

WILL THEY OPEN THE ENVELOPE?

That being said, there will still be many instances in which the relationship between prospect and solicitor is not close and true personal contact is not possible. In those cases, solicitors must think through how to leave short, interesting messages that are to the point.

Start by recalling that a person's attention span for unsolicited messages is 15 seconds at most. As someone sits at their desk or stands by their answering machine at home taking down messages, they listen to very little of what is said. "Who is it and what do they want?" is all they want to know. A person taking down messages wants to know your name, your number, and briefly what the call is about. Thus, the message you leave on voice mail or a machine is comparable to the carrier envelope in direct mail. If the prospect doesn't open the envelope, he or she will not be responding to your mail appeal. If the prospect cannot be bothered to listen all the way through a rambling message, you probably won't get any further with this solicitation.

Here's a good message: "Hi, this is Con Cise. I'm calling from the Food Bank to follow up a letter I sent last week. I'd like to talk with you about whether you might increase your already generous gift. We have a lot more people needing us, as you can imagine. If you have time to meet in person, that would be great. My number is 543-1234 and I will be available all day Tuesday and Friday. I'll also try you later this week. Thanks."

Contrast: "Hi, this is Beata Roundthebush. Hope you are doing well and that you got my letter about the Food Bank. You probably don't remember meeting me, but I think I met you at our open house. You know, there are a lot more hungry people this year than last. And we have to raise a lot more money this year. I would like to talk with you about that. Maybe we could meet for lunch and I could bring you up to date on all that has been happening. I'll keep trying you, or you feel like it, you can call me. My numbers are 876-9887 at work and 989-4432 at home. Okay, well that's it. I look forward to speaking with you soon. Take care, and I hope you are not snowed in."

Beata's message is definitely friendlier, but on an answering machine, friendly quickly becomes annoying. Con's message is terse, but if delivered in a friendly, warm voice, would seem no less friendly than Beata's and would also seem more respectful of the prospect's time.

TO MEET OR NOT TO MEET?

Having figured out how to get the prospect's attention in your message, you have to decide what you're asking for. In the old days, a few years ago, the phone call was the way to set up a meeting to ask for the gift. Now, many people are asking the prospect to make a phone date rather than to meet in person. For many busy people, a personal meeting seems like too big a time commitment, and in fact it is bound to take more time than a phone call. So the purpose of the initial phone call may become to set up another phone call, one in which you'll actually talk with the prospect and make the ask. This is particularly useful for donors in the $100–$500 range, who are as likely to agree to increase their gift over the phone as in person.

In that case the message you leave goes like this: "Hi, this is Con Cise. I'd like to talk with you about your gift to the Food Bank this year. Could we set a phone date to do that? Tuesdays and Thursdays are good for me, as well as any evening or weekend. My number is 543-1234. I'll also try you later this week. Thanks."

MAKE IT WORK FOR YOU

Another somewhat effective solution to the electronic moat is to use it to your advantage. Invite the prospect to leave a message on your answering machine anytime. Sometimes prospects will call when they are certain you are not there, and leave their response to your message. "Hi, Con. Thanks for calling. I'm not sure what else I can do for the Food Bank this year, but I will give what I gave last year." Then Con can leave a message saying, "Thanks so much for your message. That's very generous. I'll put you down for a renewal and send you a return envelope. Hope we will be able to talk in person one of these days." It is not unusual for gifts to be solicited and confirmed via machine. This same tactic can be used with donors who give you their e-mail address.

The biggest drawback to this reciprocal use of machinery is that it gives the solicitor little chance to persuade the prospect about the necessity and value of increasing their gift. On the other hand, I have heard of people negotiating an upgrade with prospects through a series of phone or e-mail messages. Again, if there is some familiarity between the solicitor and prospect, the chances of upgrading the gift, even without in-person communication, increase. For the most part, however, this strategy will result in a renewal rather than an increase in the gift.

Solicitors often make the mistake of thinking that because a prospect doesn't want to talk with them, the prospect no longer likes them or their group. This is rarely the case; far more often, the prospect simply feels jammed for time. Perhaps they don't have any questions about your work. If the Food Bank is still feeding people, that's great. That there are many more people to be fed can be discerned by walking down the street or reading the paper. If your group actually has a complicated or controversial issue, then the prospect may wish to talk with you because he or she can learn something. Even then, the prospect may request something (by message, of course) in writing.

THE PERSONAL THANK YOU

The one type of personal contact there is still not enough of is thank yous. While many organizations use thoughtful, personal appeals to solicit money, whether in letters or phone calls, their thank you often comes in a form letter, without even an extra note attached. This does not make for prospects who want to meet and talk in the future. They feel they are appreciated up until the time they give their money, and then not until they are asked again. Do not neglect that thank you — by phone and by mail — and make it personal!

Time is our most precious nonrenewable resource. With few exceptions, people feel as if they have too little of it and they must be very careful about giving it away. Working with that understanding allows you to work with the electronic voices, instead of resenting them.

1998

Donor Cultivation:
What It Is and What It Is Not

By KIM KLEIN

In a number of my recent fundraising workshops, I have asked participants to give me a definition of donor cultivation. Here are the five worst and five best descriptions people have offered.

Worst

1. Cultivation is where you act like you like the donor, whether you do or not, so they will give you more money.

2. Cultivation is like gardening — you feed the donor a lot of manure, water with flattery, and pick the fruit as soon as you can.

3. Cultivation is like going on a date. You want to have sex, and your job is to get the other person to want it too.

4. Cultivation is where you go and visit a rich person three or four times without talking about money, and then you finally bring it up. I don't know how you get to the money part, though, or what you talk about on those other visits.

5. Cultivation is a nice word for the games you play with donors, where you try to win a lot of money and they try to give you less than you want.

Best

1. Cultivation means you treat the donor like a whole person, instead of just a checkbook.

2. Cultivation is where you get to know your donors to find out things you have in common, especially what you each most like about the organization, so you can talk about something besides money when you see them.

3. Cultivation is what I tell myself I am doing when I am actually procrastinating about asking for the gift.

4. Cultivation is what you have to do to get the donor to trust your organization, so he or she will give you a really big gift.

5. Cultivation refers to the things you send your donors, especially more personal things, like birthday cards.

I had been in fundraising for more than ten years before I started to understand what donor cultivation was. I would hear the word at conferences and read it in articles, especially in relation to big gifts. "She gave $10 million, but of course, that gift was cultivated over many years." Or, "They left their entire estate to our institution because we had been cultivating them for a decade or more."

The tone of these comments seemed predatory rather than simply descriptive, and I was put off by them. In the meantime, I was asking for — and sometimes getting — gifts of $100, $500, and $1,000 and teaching other people how to do what I was doing. Since I was able to raise money, I didn't spend a lot of time thinking about cultivation one way or the other.

UNDERSTANDING CULTIVATION

Although my understanding of what cultivation meant didn't come to me in a big revelation, two incidents stand out in my mind as helping me to clarify what cultivation is.

The first incident occurred when a longtime donor to a group I was working for told me she appreciated how I and the other members of the development committee cultivated her. I didn't tell her this, but I was not aware that we were cultivating her and had never thought of her or any of our donors in those terms. When I asked her what she meant, she said, "You often send me articles on topics you know I am interested in, you always add a personal note at the bottom of any form letter or invitation, and I was particularly touched that you remembered that my cat was having surgery and called to see how she was doing."

By her response, I could see that she was referring to my policy of personalizing as many pieces of correspondence with all our donors as I could and of keeping track of donor interests, so that I could send them information related to our group that spoke to their particular interest.

The second incident occurred at a workshop I was teaching with the late Hank Rosso, founder of the Fund Raising School. In an exercise during his session on "The Big Gift," he asked participants to tell him which of the following four activities fundraising was most like: seduction, hand-to-hand combat, sales, or stalking. To my surprise, most people in the class identified fundraising with seduction, and a few even chose stalking. Only a handful related fundraising to sales. Fortunately, no one chose hand-to-hand combat.

Hank explained that seduction is not a bad thing in its place, but that its place is not in fundraising. "We don't want the donor to be swept away with passion, particularly if there is to be any regret later. We want a donor to make an informed choice to give — a choice he or she will continue to feel good about, and which will lead to another gift."

Stalking, of course, was ruled out not only because of the image of the donor as a victim, but because stalking implies that the donor would not willingly come near the organization, but must be hunted down and trapped into giving.

Sales was the correct analogy because there was a quality product — the work of the organization — to be sold to a customer seeking that product. The product merely had to be described in words that the customer could understand, with a price attached that the customer could pay. While the sales analogy has it shortcomings, it does place appropriate emphasis on the organization and its work, whereas all the other analogies focus solely on the donor.

CULTIVATION AND FUNDRAISING

Now, what does cultivation mean in the context of fundraising? In the five best definitions above, the one that is the most accurate is the one that admits that, much of the time, cultivation is a code word for procrastination, as in, "I can't ask for the money yet, because I haven't cultivated the donor enough." The definition that best summarizes cultivation is, "Cultivation is where you treat the donor like a whole person."

The analogy to sales is also critical here. You and the donor are in a partnership because of your organization. The staff, the people who give time — board members and other volunteers — and the people who give money (who ought to include but not be limited to the staff and volunteers) are all committed, to greater and lesser degrees, to the goals of the organization. People who donate money help to build the organization and also the movement the organization may be a part of. Donors need to be seen as integral to the framework of the organization rather than as a separate group to be dealt with differently than other constituencies.

So, cultivation is what you do to build the loyalty and commitment of the donors to the organization. Obviously, the more highly a person thinks of your group, the more they will be willing to do for your group. A person thinks highly of a group for one or both of two reasons: First, as the person understands the work of your group and sees it as successful, important, and well planned, and perceives that you spend money (their money) wisely, they increase their respect and admiration for what you do. Second, as a person feels appreciated by your group, believes that their gift makes a difference, that they are noticed individually and cared about individually, they will also increase their respect and admiration for what you do. Both of these perceptions of your group build loyalty, but the two combined build the most loyalty.

Let's look at what this actually means. Cultivation usually begins after a gift has been made. While you may read and hear many stories of donors who were "cultivated" for years before they finally gave millions of dollars, I think these are the fundraising equivalent of fishing tales. Grassroots organizations in particular do not have people like this whom we can "cultivate." We don't have buildings to name after people, academic positions to endow, or esoteric pieces of medical equipment or research projects to underwrite. Just as in sales, you want to attract new customers, but most of your energy should go into keeping customers you already have. Your greatest energy should go toward those customers who buy the most frequently and who buy the most.

So, to begin thinking about cultivation, sort your donor list into three categories: frequency of giving, recency of giving, and size of gift. Your highest priority for cultivation will be people who are in all three categories: those who give large gifts often and who have given recently. The next-highest priority will be people who give large gifts frequently, even if their last gift is not very recent. Third priority will be people who give large gifts anytime, and last will be people who give frequently.

CULTIVATION TECHNIQUES

The minimum cultivation effort required is that every donor receive a thank-you note for every gift. All donors may also receive a newsletter. Those donors who do more — either by size of gift or by frequency of giving — should be given a little more attention. How much more will depend on how much you know about them and how many of them you have.

Here are some possible cultivation techniques:

Receptions for donors: An example

A group in New Mexico successfully completed a three-year campaign to have child care offered at the workplace of a local corporation. They planned a celebratory reception where one of the main organizers would give a short talk, to which they invited the following categories of donors: anyone who was a donor at the time the campaign started, all the donors who gave specifically to this campaign, and all current donors who give annual unrestricted gifts of $250 or more. To the first group, they sent a letter saying, "You may recall that we have been working on this issue for the last three years. You were helping us then and have continued to support us. Now help us celebrate."

To the donors who gave specifically to the child care campaign, the letter read, "Your financial help has paid off, and thanks to you and all the people like you, we have won. Come celebrate with us." The major donors got a similar invitation. Furthermore, anyone who was a major donor, gave specifically to this campaign, and had been a donor at any level for three years or more also received a follow-up phone call.

The organization decorated the reception venue with a timeline showing the progress of the campaign, highlighted by newspaper articles and pictures about the campaign, so people could relive the success. More than 60 people came to the celebration, giving the staff and board members a chance to meet other donors. There was no additional request for money — this was simply a time to say thank you and celebrate.

Sending articles and information

When donors send money in response to a specific appeal, or they tell you they are most interested in one particular issue, or you think that because of their job, other groups they are involved with, or other information you have about them that they have particular interests in some aspects of your organization's work over others,

make a note of these interests in their donor information file. As newspaper articles come out or reports are published, send copies of these to those donors who will be interested with a brief note saying, "Thought you might enjoy this." Or, "As per our conversation, here is the report I told you about," or whatever happens to be appropriate.

Offering to visit

The most effective cultivation technique is meeting a donor in person. Mostly, these will be times when you want to ask for a larger gift, but every so often, you should meet with a donor in order to get advice, tell them about what is happening in your organization, or simply to drop off an annual report or a premium such as a mug or a T-shirt. These visits can last five minutes or an hour — just taking the time to show that you are interested in knowing more about the person will be effective.

Other techniques

Things like birthday cards, congratulatory notes, and get well cards are not necessary. If you are the type of person who remembers special occasions or would be likely to send a special note, then do so. If this is not something you do for your own friends, then don't do it for your donors. Cultivation only works when there is a genuine desire to know the donor better. Many of us find that we become friends with some of our donors, so we treat them like friends. Those who are not friends we should consider to be colleagues — they share our values and they wish for the success of our organization's work.

If I were in charge of reinventing all the words that would ever be used in the context of fundraising, I would never choose the word cultivation. I think it is a difficult word to truly humanize, and I don't use it very often. To me the word adds a sense of something that I, as a development director or board member, do to the donor in order to get the donor to do something for the organization. I prefer concepts like graciousness, hospitality, and sharing — the idea that we are all donors, and that we are all pulling together toward the same end, which is fulfilling the mission of the organization.

Some of us give a lot of money and some a little. Some of us give what is a lot to us, and some of us give what is a pittance to us. Some of us give time, advice, or products as well as money. The way that we will keep getting whatever gifts our donors give us is to keep doing good work and to keep appreciating those who make the work possible.

1999

How to Develop a High-Dollar Giving Club

By CAROL BLANTON

Launching a giving club may be the best way for your membership organization to make a major leap forward in its annual giving fundraising efforts.

I serve as Membership Director for a national conservation group that is organized in state chapters ranging in size from fewer than 2,000 to more than 100,000 members. Most of these chapters have high-dollar giving clubs that represent between 5% and 10% of their total membership. Despite their relatively small numbers, these club members are responsible for an average of 60% of annual operating funds raised. Most of this club income comes from annual dues, not gifts raised through special appeal mailings. That makes club income dependable, predictable, bankable income. Clubs also encourage upgrading that builds an organization's major donor pool. These clubs make the job of raising operations funding — usually the hardest and most critical money for most nonprofits to raise — far more productive.

WHAT ARE GIVING CLUBS AND WHY ARE THEY SUCH MONEY MACHINES?

In our organization, high-dollar giving clubs are a subset of regular membership. Each club is identified by its own name, logo, and member benefits. Annual dues are higher than for regular membership. Though we have clubs in the $100–$999 range, we place the most emphasis, offer the greatest benefits, and dedicate the bulk of staff time to the $1,000–$10,000 level donors. Since regular membership dues begin at $25, there is an exclusivity and unique status implied in club membership. Our marketing strategy is aimed at reinforcing the notion that these are members who do more for the organization and so can expect special privileges.

Members are encouraged to think of themselves foremost as club members and to take pride in that membership. The result is that club members develop a bond with the organization and the club that encourages club renewal. Finally, the club structure encourages members to upgrade through an ascending ladder of club levels — moving to the $1,000 level and beyond — and to making major capital, planned, or annual gifts.

DESIGNING YOUR GIVING CLUB

The success of a giving club begins by defining the club as a unique, identifiable entity. The higher dues for the club underscores the value of the donor and his or her contribution to the organization. Annual dues should begin no lower than $100.

The club must have its own name, preferably one that reflects the mission of the organization. More generic names, such as "Patrons Circle" or "Benefactors Society" are less inspiring. It is also wise to have a club name that lends itself to names for the giving levels within the club. Our club is called the "Conservators," which reflects the land conservation work the organization does. Within that range we have four giving levels. Each is identified by a plant or animal associated with our state: the "Poppy Conservators," the "Golden Trout Conservators," the "Kit Fox Conservators." These names are roughly in increasing order of rarity among the species, adding to the perception of increased status at each higher level.

With a name — or set of names — you may want to develop a logo for the club. Again, this image should reflect the organization's mission yet be distinctive enough to identify the club. You may want to go further and design logos for each of the levels, but this can often lead to additional printing and other related costs that may be unnecessary for a relatively small group. An overall club logo, however, is critical for building visual recognition and member identification. One caution: Make sure you continue to reinforce your organization's logo so there is no confusion in the donor's mind and so that when they move up they continue to understand and appreciate that their ongoing connection is to the organization at large.

Determining benefits is the next step. Each club level should have benefits that reflect the hierarchical nature of each level, with more, and more valuable, benefits at each level. They should also, if possible, be appropriate to the organization's mission and relate to the work it does and sufficiently insignificant in value not to trigger tax consequences associated with the donation.

Benefits that offer unique or exclusive opportunities not available to all members reinforce the exclusivity of club membership. These might include opportunities to meet senior staff, board members, or other important individuals associated with the organization or its mission. These opportunities can often occur at special events varying from an open house to black-tie receptions. You might offer a chance to go behind-the-scenes, to see works-in-process, or go on special tours of your facilities.

Unique privileges are another possible benefit: special parking places for club members visiting your facility, first chance for reservations for events, discounts at your organization's store, catalogue, café, or an affiliated enterprise. In our organization, invitations to participate in special field trips with uniquely knowledgeable naturalist guides give club members both a privileged opportunity and reinforce the importance of the organization's work by showing members tangible evidence of our efforts and their support. We also offer a special club newsletter. This is both a marketing device for club benefits and a way of publicizing club activities. Most benefits should be reserved for $1,000+ giving levels.

Premiums, which, as opposed to benefits, are tangible items offered to members, may also be appropriate, but are often not as effective at bonding the member to the organization. (Again triggering tax consequences must be considered.) Furthermore, expensive premiums (valued at more than 5% of the donation) tend to encourage members to join only for the premium rather than to support the organization. The result is often a lower renewal rate for premium-solicited members. If you do decide to try to a high-end premium — a costly coffee-table book or framed print, for instance — track these members separately to determine how well they give and renew. A better strategy might be to offer lesser-value premiums that reinforce the mission and work of the organization, partic-

ularly items that have the club logo on them. We use a bumper sticker, a set of wildlife note cards, and a lapel pin in the design of the logo. None cost more than $3 to produce and fulfill. Consider very carefully how difficult it will be to fulfill a premium. Avoid items that offer a choice of colors or sizes, or that are difficult or expensive to mail.

PROSPECTING FOR CLUB MEMBERS

Who are your prospects? Any member who has given $50 or more should be asked to join at the $100 level. Those who have given more than $100 should be asked to join at a higher level. You may want to test members in the $25 to $49 range, but our experience is that this is not a productive group unless you apply demographic or psychographic overlays that select out members with a higher giving potential. Members whose cumulative giving is $100 or more over a single year may be good prospects, but again this is not as good an indicator. Look also to your board members, life members, those members who have indicated that your organization is in their will, special project donors — in short, any member who has made a special commitment to your organization.

At the $100 to $999 and even the $1,000 to $9,999 levels, the most efficient way to manage a membership club is through the mail. Initial solicitations, renewals, ongoing communications, and extra gift requests will come to members through the mail. Therefore, I recommend establishing mail as the primary vehicle for initial solicitation. While personal solicitations by board members and staff can be effective, mail should always be part of the solicitation process. First, it gives you a chance to underline the fact that the donor is joining a club and committing to an annual gift, not making a one-time donation. You have the opportunity to build visual identification with the club by using the logo. And it gives you the chance to describe the benefits and the various giving levels.

Donors who come through one-on-one relationships with board and staff often require continued personal contact and do not respond well to renewals. This strategy should be reserved for donors who are making (or have the potential to make) $1,000+ gifts. A personal relationship that augments mail solicitation with a personal note on the solicitation letters or follow-up telephone calls often works well at this level. The member has the benefit of receiving a personal endorsement while fully understanding that he or she is joining a club whose membership will need to be renewed.

The initial solicitation can be a letter or invitation format. It should begin building visual recognition through use of the logo. It underscores the importance of the club in support of the organization's mission, and it describes the club benefits. It should talk about the work that will be accomplished as a result of this support, but emphasize particularly the ongoing role of club members in providing a foundation of support for the organization institutionally. The package must, of course, have all the standard direct mail components: letter, reply device reemphasizing the club benefits and levels, and reply and carrier envelopes. Consider using a live stamp on the reply envelope to boost response.

Do not shy away from putting any regular member who makes a qualifying gift into the club, whether or not the gift was made in response to a club solicitation. These donors may not be aiming to join the club, but continuing cultivation and marketing to them will encourage many to maintain their membership. After all, they did self-select as donors able to give at the necessary level. By being treated as club members, they will be assured of continuing cultivation, which will only increase the possibility of their ongoing and increased giving. If they do not want to be club members, they will certainly notify you.

RENEWING AND UPGRADING CLUB MEMBERS

The keys to a successful renewal program are ensuring that members realize that they are part of a club and reinforcing the critical importance to the organization of their participation in the club. If members have been recruited appropriately, their club membership reinforced, and opportunities to take advantage of benefits offered, the renewal process will be successful.

We have tested two renewal formats. The first is a one-page invoice-style form that briefly describes the work of the organization and the club's role in that work. It has a tear-off return section at the bottom asking for the gift. Gift amounts listed vary according to giving history. The second, and currently more successful, format more closely mirrors the recruitment package: a two-page letter with a reply device nearly identical to that used for initial solicitations. This allows you to talk about your organization's accomplishments and needs and to reinforce the mission.

Four renewal notices are sent, beginning two months before the renewal month. Responses to each notice are on average as follows: first notice 34.3%, second notice 17%, third notice 14.4% and fourth notice 5.4%.

We improve the renewal effort by mailing a final time to those whose membership has lapsed for four to six months. We are also able to conduct a professional telemarketing effort to lapsed donors in the $100 to $999 club

because our club membership is large — more than 7,000 total club members, with 200 to 300 lapsed members each month. Smaller organizations should consider doing lapsed calling in-house. Conversations with lapsed members can begin by asking why the member decided not to renew and if there are ways that the member would like to see the organization change. Often the member does not realize that their membership has lapsed and will renew immediately. Donors who are as dedicated to the organization as these club members often require very little persuasion to renew their commitment.

As a follow-up to the call or instead of the call, a lapsed renewal letter should be sent. This letter follows the same format as for the other club mailings. Renewal efforts to lapsed donors can be done once or twice a year, but making it part of the regular monthly renewal process is a surer system. It is all too easy to lose track of these lapsed donors once you postpone doing a mailing to them. Our combined mail and telemarketing efforts to lapsed members raise our renewal rate by an additional 10% to a 71% total and bring an average gift of $168.

When employing the gift club strategy, upgrading is one of your greatest fundraising opportunities. In my organization, half of all our major donors come up through the ranks — most via our giving clubs. Upgrading is accomplished primarily at renewal time by asking the members in the renewal letter and on the reply device to move up to the next club level. By regularly reinforcing the club levels throughout the year — on the membership card, on the reply coupon, in publications and communications — the members become aware of the levels and the benefits for each. The levels give the members a logical way to increase their support for the organization and of progressing within the club. We have tested the club-level upgrading strategy against a more conventional strategy of upgrades based on asking for a gift of one and one-half or two times the most recent or largest previous gift, and found that the average gift increased with the club-level upgrading strategy with no negative effect on the response rate.

It is also possible to encourage upgrading by offering special benefits. As with other benefits strategies, offer opportunities that are unique to the club and the organization and that reinforce the notion of exclusivity and privilege. Oftentimes the benefit can be time specific, such as an opportunity to participate in a particular event available only to members at that higher level. I do not recommend high-end premiums for upgrading, as they too often result in one-time increases. If this technique is tried, members who upgrade should be tracked so that you know whether that strategy is cost effective over the long term.

It is important to identify those donors that have the potential for making major gifts — gifts of greater than $100 and potentially $100+ level gifts. This is most successfully done through personal cultivation. At the $100 to $1,000 levels, begin making personal contacts with the donors to determine if they have the capacity and interest in making a major gift. This can be done at events and field trips, personal visits, or in thank-you phone calls (we personally phone to thank donors for all $1,000+ gifts). You will find some donors prefer to continue a "mail" relationship, but some respond to the personal attention and relationship that leads to major gifts. Do not, however, discontinue sending renewal notices and other appropriate mail solicitations until a staff member (or perhaps a volunteer) is assigned to that donor and a plan for cultivation and solicitation is ongoing. All too often major donor prospects get forgotten when renewals are discontinued in favor of personal cultivation and solicitation and that process is not undertaken.

ONGOING COMMUNICATION AND EXTRA-GIFT FUNDRAISING

One of the biggest mistakes you can make in managing your club program is to communicate with the members only at renewal time. These people are your best donors and potentially your highest major donors. They deserve, and your organization will benefit from, all the attention you can efficiently give them. The best ways we have found to do this are through a quarterly club newsletter and our special appeal fundraising letters.

The quarterly newsletter serves several purposes. First, it is marketed as a club benefit and we have found from surveying club members it is the most appreciated one. It also serves to tell members about other benefits which, before the newsletter was launched, required special mailings. The most important of these announcements is a list of special field trips we offer the member; these trips are their next most appreciated benefit. The newsletter provides a marketing opportunity for the club levels and benefits, and is a way to reinforce the logo and other visual identification with the club. It gives the organization a place to talk about other special donor programs, like planned giving and our high-dollar fundraising trips, in a publication that targets our best donors. Each issue has a giving envelope enclosed to provide an opportunity for upgrading and extra gifts. The revenue from this envelope consistently exceeds the cost of the newsletter. Newsletter expenses are reduced by mailing the club newsletter inside of the regular membership newsletter, thereby avoiding separate postage costs.

Do not assume that club members have given all that they can or want to give through their club membership dues and exclude them from special appeals. You will be missing a tremendous fundraising opportunity. Our club members receive all six of the special appeal mailings that go to all regular members. The only exception is those club members who are in their renewal cycle, which is first priority. Club members are our best donors to these extra appeals, giving nearly 40% of all appeal income (while representing only 5% of the overall membership). Additionally, the appeal mailings serve to inform club members about special projects of the organization.

IN CONCLUSION

The key to the success of special giving clubs is to treat the members and their gifts as part of an organization within an organization. You must develop within these members a sense of commitment, participation, and obligation. With this you are guaranteed ongoing and increasing support by identifying and cultivating the very best institutional supporters within your membership. A high-dollar club really can be a money machine. Build it carefully and keep it well maintained. It will perform for you endlessly.

1993

Donor Rating for Small Organizations

By SUE MERRILEES

A rating system is a tool most often used by universities and other large fundraising institutions to organize their donors and prospective donors, usually for capital campaigns. This is not just because these institutions have thousands of people to track, although the need for a rating system does increase with the size of a database. Even organizations with relatively small lists of prospects and donors can benefit from using ratings.

Although rating systems differ in complexity, basically a donor or prospect is assigned both a letter representing their inclination towards an organization and a number representing their ability to make a donation. For example, an A1 rating can indicate someone who is highly involved with and enthusiastic about the organization (A) and can give $10,000 (1). A rating is a shorthand way of assessing a prospect using all the information you have, from giving history to remarks made during a visit or insights from board members.

A rating system is useful for a number of reasons. It represents a valuable analysis of the donor base, singly and as a whole. Knowing to the letter (and number) what kind of potential you have for raising money is always helpful.

Ratings preserve institutional memory. This is a concern to all organizations, especially with the sometimes quick turnover of development staff. When maintained consistently, a rating system remains even when staff does not. In this way, it helps ensure that the organization's relationship with a donor proceeds smoothly.

Ratings also enable an organization to sort, and therefore target, donors quickly. With a rating system in place, staff can easily identify who should be receiving attention and what kind. For example, someone whose inclination represents "Little or no involvement" or "displeased" needs to be involved first and cultivated before being solicited.

Since ratings directly correspond to "best guess" ask amounts, they are useful when setting goals, whether for an annual fund or a capital campaign. It will be easy to construct a feasible gift chart if your goal is $10,000 and you know how many of your prospects can be approached for gifts of $1,000.

Additionally, a rating system demonstrates how much information you have (or don't have) about your donors and prospects. If you find that you cannot rate your major donors, or even identify them, this is a signal that more information gathering is needed. If you cannot judge someone's inclination or ability, you are not ready to approach them to ask for a donation.

INCLINATION + ABILITY

Although many people focus primarily on the ability component of a rating, it is secondary to inclination when it comes to tangible results. Identifying someone with lots of money but no connection to your organization results in paralysis. Crafting an approach to a prospect is frustrating and ultimately futile if you have no realistic way of reaching them.

Inclination indicates a person's connection to your organization, not to the cause in general. Although Ted Turner has an interest in international humanitarian causes, he is an A to the United Nations, not necessarily to your organization. At best, ability indicates how much someone could conceivably give. However, it is inclination that gets that person to give in the first place.

Inclination

Inclination is a mixture of interest/enthusiasm about a cause and level of involvement with an organization. Together, these factors determine a prospect's inclination or readiness to be solicited. The timing of the solicitation is also affected by other information known about the person. A recent capital gift, a divorce, or business reversal may postpone the solicitation, although this is a judgment call in each case. Do not assume a change in circumstance automatically precludes a gift. Here is a sample of the inclination component of a rating system:

A High level of involvement and/or enthusiastic about the organization

B Some involvement and/or enthusiastic

C Little or no involvement and/or unhappy with some aspect of the organization

Z Not yet rated as to inclination

First, your solicitation efforts should focus on A's. In most cases, A's have given before or are good prospects for doing so. This is not to say that B's and C's should be ignored. Some B's are ready to be solicited, although probably not for the highest gift in their ability range. Their willingness to give will help determine if they are ready to become A's. Other B's and all C's and Z's are simply at the beginning of the donor cycle — cultivation. If handled well, B's and C's are your future A's.

Ability

Ability refers to a prospect's giving ability. Research — whether it includes subscribing to online computer search services, poring through local newspapers, reviewing alumni or client questionnaires, or getting feedback from board or staff who know the prospect — will provide information to help you determine ability. However, just because a person has the money does not mean they are willing to give it away. Finding out what they actually give to other organizations is a good indication of ability. Look at annual reports of other organizations, where donors are often listed by gift levels. These will be solid indicators of a prospect's possible gift range.

Here is a sample ability component of a rating system:

1 $10,000+

2 $5,000 – $9,999

3 $1,000 – $4,999

4 $500 – $999

9 Not yet rated as to ability

STARTING OUT

Assigning and maintaining ratings is labor intensive. You should only rate someone your organization considers a major donor, whether determined by the solicitation approach (usually a personal visit) or by the amount of their donation or potential donation.

For consistency, one person should assign the ratings after reviewing all the data on each person. The key that explains the rating criteria (beyond the descriptions contained in the chart) should be written down so that a future rater has a sense of how the ratings were determined. You wouldn't want a 1 rated in 1998 to be different from a 1 rated in 2002. Here are two samples from a rater's key for an A:

A = Former board member, current outreach committee vice-chair, close friend of executive director, has given every year since 1987

A = New member of alumni association, scheduled to host event in home for new students. No giving history, but has told trustee (a close friend) of intention to contribute.

The "rater" should develop the ability part of the system based on the current donor base, with room to grow. If your largest current donor gives $25,000, a 1 rating of $250,000 will be meaningless, unless you have good reason to suspect such a gift might be forthcoming in the future. Make the system work for your specific situation. It can always be revised later.

MAINTENANCE

Everyone in the development department should be aware of the rating system and what the different levels mean. Maintenance, which includes upgrading current ratings and adding new ones, should be done by either the original rater or whoever is directly responsible for managing the prospect or donor — tracking their involvement, initiating contact, or deciding upon an approach strategy.

Make a note to the file or computer record of the reason a change was made. For example, during a visit from a board member an estranged donor says, "Now that I've heard your reasoning, I'm satisfied with the shift in the organization's strategy." This encounter should be written up, however briefly, and dated with the notation, "Upgrade from C to B." Likewise, if a newspaper clipping reveals that a prospect has sold their business for a large profit, put that in their file with the note to reflect the change, e.g., "Move from 4 to 2."

A rating system can help you see the results of your work that are not reflected in money raised. Try to see each visit as an opportunity to build a relationship that will lead to a larger gift in the future. Even if a visit does not result in a gift, it will result in more information and possibly an upgrade. This is progress.

DONORS AS NUMBERS

Some may shrink from a using a rating system because they feel it turns their donors into numbers. Of course, both names and numbers are merely symbols for a person. The important thing to remember is not to treat your donors like symbols, that is, impersonally. A rating system actually can help you avoid this by forcing you to learn more about your donors, by analyzing them first as individuals, then approaching them in the most appropriate way.

One final word about rating systems. Do not use the formation of a rating system as an excuse for avoiding solicitations. Although gathering and organizing information is important, at some point you will have to approach the prospect directly. Ultimately, the only way to discover if, and how much, someone will donate is to ask them.

1998

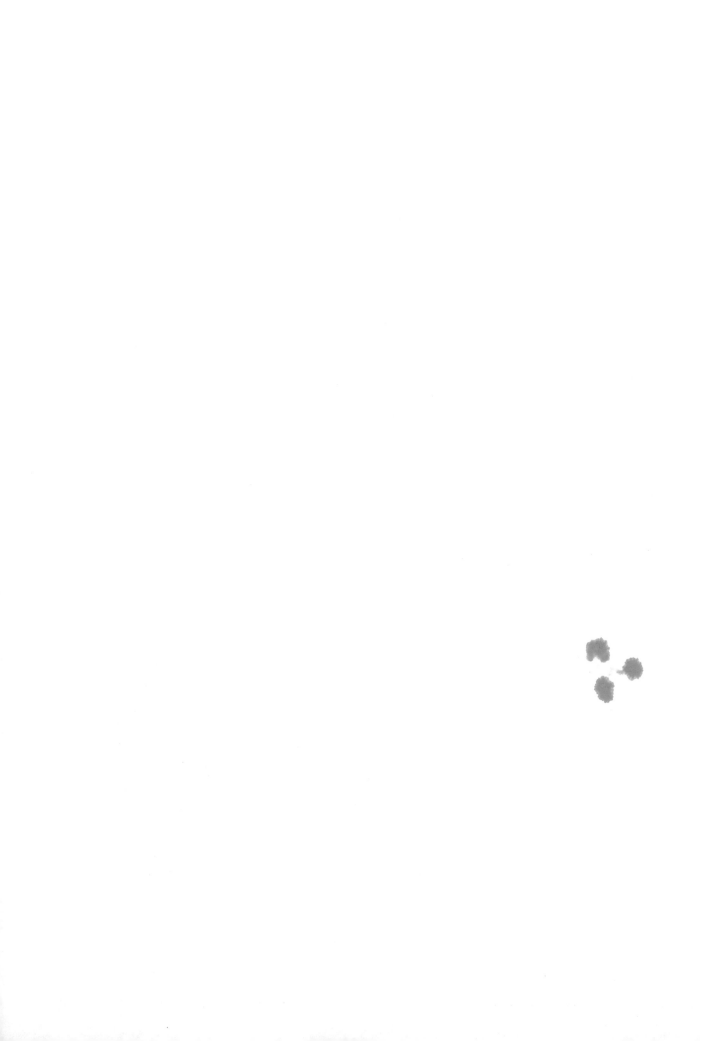

Fundraising Strategies

III. SPECIAL EVENTS

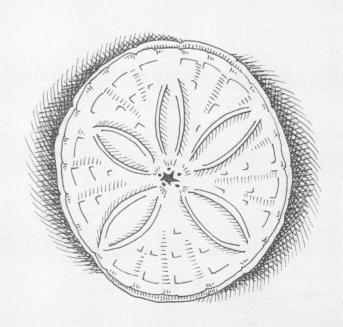

The Correct Use of Special Events

By KIM KLEIN

While you are reading this article, all over this country, and around the world, volunteers are meeting to discuss how they are going to raise money for their group. Inevitably one bright spark is going to be saying, "Let's have garage sale. I heard that the Humane Society made $15,000 on their sale." Another bright spark will say, "No, too much work, and everyone is doing them. Why don't we have a Spice Girls/Springsteen/Beastie Boys/Aretha Franklin concert?" And one person who has been through both the garage sale and the concert will think to herself, "Why don't we just have an appendectomy without anesthesia?"

Events are the most common fundraising strategy. In fact, if you ask people what grassroots fundraising is, most people will name an event as an example — bake sale, dance, walk-a-thon. In this article, we will review what events are good for and what they are not so good for.

WHY DO AN EVENT?

When choosing a fundraising strategy of any kind, whether it is direct mail, a phone-a-thon, planned giving, starting a small business, or other strategy, you need to first ask yourself a series of questions: What is it we want from this strategy besides money? Do we need money from people or places that haven't given us money before? Do we need to be better known, and if so, better known by whom? Do we need money quickly, or can we wait a while for payoff? How much money do we have to spend on this strategy? How many people are available to help with this strategy? How does this strategy fit into our overall plan? The answers to these questions will help you determine whether an event, and what kind, is right for you to do now.

The following are the reasons to do an event:

- **You need to increase your overall visibility.** Your organization is not well enough known among people who would be inclined to support you, and these people can be reached through an event. That is, they live near each other and your organization, and they tend to turn out at other organizations' events.

- **You need publicity.** To reach the people who would be inclined to support you, you need to be in the media. You choose an event that will reach the media you want to be in: your neighborhood newspaper, your alternative radio station, your local news channel.

- **You want to raise money from people or places that would not give you money otherwise,** or you want to raise money from people who are new to your organization (such as those who have been attracted by the media attention you have received).

- **You want to thank people who have done a lot for your organization by giving a party.**

- **You want to announce the beginning of or celebrate the conclusion of a campaign of some kind.**

- **You want to honor one or more people who are very important in terms of the issue you work on.** By honoring them, you will not only raise money, you will also associate your organization with them. In this way you will become known to at least some of the people they are known to.

- **You have a number of volunteers who want to help with fundraising, who like each other, and you want them to have a sense of accomplishment.** You hope that if they do well with an event, they may be willing to move into more difficult areas of fundraising, such as major gift solicitation.

- **You have a number of inexperienced volunteers and you want to train them in some aspects of fundraising.** An event provides a good training opportunity.

- **You don't immediately need the income an event will bring in, and you have some money you can spend to put on an event.**

Any one of the above may be a reason to have an event, but no reason by itself is enough. At least three of the above reasons need to be applicable for an event to be successful. For example, if you simply need more donors and need to be known among a different group of people, you could try a direct mail campaign or a door-to-door canvass instead of an event. If you need media coverage, there are other ways to get it than an event, which often won't generate more than a mention. Even needing to celebrate a victory is not reason enough to do an event. You would also need volunteers and some money to spend to make the event fun.

Answering the questions above about whether an event is the way to get what you want will also help determine, or at least narrow, the choice of what kind of event you will mount. Do you want lots of people to attend? Will there be an entrance fee? Will corporations be invited to sponsor the event? What activities are the volunteers you have most comfortable doing?

PRELIMINARY TASKS

Once you choose what kind of an event to have, you have three tasks to complete immediately. The completion of these tasks will often allow you to see ways to improve your event, or to rethink whether an event is the best way to accomplish a subset of your fundraising goals. The three tasks are to create a master task list, create a budget, and create a timeline.

1. Create a Master Task List. Make a chart with three columns: What, When, Who. Under "What," write down all the tasks — from the tiniest to the largest — that must be accomplished for this event to be successful. Under "When," write down by what date each task must be done. Later, you will assign these tasks to individuals, filling in the "Who" column. Leave it blank for now.

2. Create a budget. From your Master Task List, identify everything that will cost money and everything that will raise money. From this new list create a budget with total expenses and a projection of total income. Compare totals and see if you feel comfortable with the likely outcome.

Some events break even, or even lose money, but are still considered successful because they accomplish other goals. For example, an event to launch a capital campaign might consist of inviting prospective donors to the site of the new building, then giving them a brief and interesting look at the blueprints and the artist's rendering, and describing the kind of excellent work that will be able to happen in the new space. No money would be raised at the event, but prospects would be visited individually later.

Some events are very expensive to put on, and a budget may show income of $50,000 and expenses of $40,000. If raising $10,000 was the only goal, this would not be a good way to go about it, but if the event attracts corporate sponsors, media attention, and builds relationships with new donors, a percentage of whom can be counted on to give over and over, then spending that kind of money would be considered worthwhile.

3. Create a timeline. If after steps 1 and 2, you are satisfied that the event you are considering is the right one, proceed with this step. In this step, you plan backwards from the date and time of the event to the present to make sure you have not left out any tasks, that you have calculated all costs, and that you have allowed enough time for everything to get done smoothly.

To begin this task, imagine very specifically the place where the event is being held and the starting time. You are standing there. Look around. Is everything in place? Where will people park? Are you sure the facility is wheelchair accessible — check the bathrooms and the hallways as well as the main room. Are people going to bring children? If so, will you have child care? Does the venue look nice? Should you put some flowers on the table?

In order for everything to be in place for the start of the event, what needs to be done the day before? Two days before? The week before? The month before? And so on. Work backwards in your mind.

Do not hurry through this task because this is the check-and-balance task. Tiny details surface during this task that could have a big impact on the event.

For example, a group invited a famous person to speak. She asked for a podium and microphone. As the committee imagined her walking up to the podium, one member suddenly realized that this woman was quite short, and most podiums are built for men. In her imagination, she literally saw the speaker disappear behind the podium. Quickly, the group added "Find a riser or find a shorter podium" to their task list.

NOW THE WORK BEGINS

When these three steps are complete, you are ready to assign tasks from the task list and to actually begin the work of putting on the event. By spending time examining your fundraising needs to determine that an event is the best strategy for meeting them, and then by carefully working on the tasks outlined here, you are assured, pending some unforeseeable disaster, that your event will be successful: It will reach the people you want to reach with the message you want them to hear, the volunteers will have a good time planning and implementing the event, and the event will raise the money you need it to raise. Shortchanging these steps to save time will result in spending time kicking yourself later and regretting the ways things came out.

You will spend the time, one way or the other. You might as well do it right the first time.

1999

Putting on a House Party

By KIM KLEIN

One of the easiest special events, and sometimes one of the most lucrative, is the common house party. In some ways, it seems silly to describe how to do a house party since anyone who has ever organized a birthday party, school picnic, or anniversary celebration already knows most of what there is to know about putting on a house party. However, sometimes the events that seem easiest are fraught with pitfalls. I recently attended three house parties in a row that were dismal failures financially. For these reasons, this seems like a good time to remind readers of the obvious and not-so-obvious details about producing a successful house party.

WHAT IT IS

First, the basic description of a house party: A person invites friends and acquaintances to a party at their house to educate them about the work of a nonprofit group and ask them to make a contribution. (More than one person can host a single house party, increasing the guest list and the people available to do the work.)

The party is also a place for the guests to see old friends, meet new people, and eat good food, which provides a cordial atmosphere for the host to make the request for funds. Finally, a house party allows someone not familiar with the group to learn about it, ask questions, and get some personal attention without being obligated to give. People can either give a very small gift or not give at all without embarrassing themselves, and they can attend the house party without paying to get in.

THE USES OF HOUSE PARTIES

A house party is a good way to raise consciousness about the issues your organization is addressing. House parties are best used to explain a complicated issue to many people at once, answer questions about it, and provide the specific information people want. In the early days of the United Farm Workers movement, for example, house parties were used to explain the concept of the farmworkers union and the plight of migrant farmworkers to mainly white, nonagricultural people who were likely to be sympathetic to the issues but had little concrete information about them.

A second use of a house party is to allow a group of people to meet someone important, such as a candidate for office, a well-known activist, a member of the African National Congress, etc. This person gives a testimonial or asserts a particular viewpoint, and the host describes what people can do to respond (such as vote, give money, boycott, give money, demonstrate, give money).

No matter what else you ask people to do at a house party, you should ask them to give money. It is the only thing they can do right on the spot, and it is usually the most passive action, requiring the least amount of work on their part. The main purpose of a house party, then, is to expand an organization's donor base.

STEPS TO PUTTING ON A HOUSE PARTY

There are six steps to putting on a house party:

1. Find the person who is willing to host it at his or her house and to take on other responsibilities related to the event.

2. Prepare the guest list.

3. Design and send the invitation.

4. Make follow-up calls.

5. Choreograph the event, particularly the pitch.

6. Follow up and evaluate.

The Host

The host of a house party has several responsibilities, the least of which is providing the house and food. First, the host creates the guest list, inviting anyone he or she thinks might be interested in the organization or the topic being discussed. At the party, the host or another person gives an appropriate description of the organization and the issues. Then, the host makes a pitch for money. It is important that the host has already contributed money, as well as the party, because the host must ask people to join him or her in making a gift to the organization.

The ideal host is someone close enough to the organization to understand the importance of the group and be willing to conquer their fear of asking friends for money, but not so close as to have all their friends already be donors. A common flaw of house parties is that they draw on a small group of supporters: the same people end up attending several house parties for one organization and the organization does not succeed in expanding its donor base.

Prepare the Guest List

Once someone has volunteered to host a party, the organization's staff should help that person decide who should be invited. A house party can have any number of people, but it works best when there are at least 12 guests and not more than 50. Figure out how many people the house can comfortably accommodate. If you are planning a presentation, you will need to make sure most of the people can sit down at that time. If you are only planning a brief pitch, then having enough seats will not be so important.

Generally you need to invite three times as many people as you want to attend. In addition, there should be one person from the organization (such as a board member, volunteer, or staff person) for every five to eight guests. These people will mingle with the guests, talking about the organization and answering questions in a personal way. These people should be included in the total numbers.

Obviously, start with the host's friends and relatives. Don't forget neighbors. Think about people from church, synagogue or other religious or spiritual affiliation, social clubs, and work. Except for those people specifically invited to mingle and represent the organization, don't invite many people who are already donors. If you want to use the house party as an opportunity to upgrade some donors, only invite those who could be asked to give more money than they currently do.

Design and Send the Invitation

The invitation does not have to be fancy, and it can be printed at an instant-print copy shop, so expense shouldn't be an issue. For groups with access to desktop publishing programs, good-looking invitations can be turned out quite inexpensively.

The invitation should reflect something about the host and about the crowd being invited. This will make people want to attend. Whether serious or light, educational or assuming knowledge on the part of the invitee, the invitation should always include the following:

- *An indication that people will be asked for money.* "Bring your checkbook" is the most direct way to make this known. You might also say, "A chance to learn about _____ and contribute to this important work." Or, "As we enter our tenth year, your financial support is more important than ever."

- *A way for people to make a donation without coming to the party.* On the return card include the option, "I can't come, but I want to help. Enclosed is my donation."

- *A suggestion that people bring friends.* Ask people to RSVP so you will know how many are coming.

- *Clear directions to the house.* If finding the place is at all confusing, provide a map. Include the phone number of the host under the directions.

Make Follow-Up Calls

To assure an adequate turnout, it is important that the host follow up the written invitation with phone calls to prospective guests. Some hosts may feel that calling people applies too much pressure and that their friends will resent it. The reality is that in most people's busy lives an invitation can easily get lost in the piles of paper that accumulate at home and office. Without a phone call, people often forget about the party. Rather than resenting the call, most people appreciate the reminder.

Choreograph the Event

Where most parties fail is in not having thought through exactly what will happen at the event. To avoid this danger, imagine you are a guest at the event and play over in your mind what will happen.

You drive up to the house. Is it obvious where to park? This can be important if the host shares a driveway with people not attending the party, if there is a hidden ditch near the house, or if the neighbors are the kind that are likely to call the police about a guest parked too near the crosswalk. Is the house obvious? The house number evident? Is there a porch light? Is there a sign saying, "The _____ house party here"? This is especially important in rural communities where homes can be off the street, and in big apartment complexes where it may be confusing to find the right apartment number.

You come in to the house or apartment. Is it obvious where to put your coat? If not, someone needs to be stationed at the door to take coats or show where they belong. The greeter should also point out the bathroom if it is not obvious.

You look around for people you know and make your way to the food. Is there a traffic jam at the food table? The table should be pulled out from the wall so people can serve themselves from all sides of it. The drinks should be on a separate table from the food, to encourage people to move on from the food or from the drinks. If possible, there should be several small platters of food, rather than a few large platters, so people can help themselves from any point around the table.

Are the plates big enough? People don't want to feel that they need several helpings to get full, or to stay hungry because they are too embarrassed to keep going back for more food. People returning to the food table create a traffic jam, and people feeling hungry create a non-money-giving atmosphere. The food should be easy to eat while standing up — finger food rather than something that needs a fork and knife. And there shouldn't be anything that would be a disaster if spilled (such as red wine on light-colored carpeting, chili on the couch).

Once you get your food, you look for a place to sit. Are there enough chairs? Make sure no chair is sitting alone or obstructing people coming in and out of the entrance.

THE SPECIAL MOMENT: THE PITCH

Everything that happens at the house party should be built around the pitch. Arrange ahead of time that at least two and not more than four people will respond when the host says, "I hope you will make a donation." These people pull out checkbooks, or hand over checks to members of the organization. They don't have to be ostentatious about it, but a few people have to lead the way in giving money.

Some people object to this practice, claiming that it imposes too much pressure or is disingenuous. However, a little more thought will show that it is the considerate thing to do. Few people have the self-confidence to be the first to do anything. When the host asks for money, many people are prepared to give, but everyone has a brief attack of anxiety. "Perhaps this isn't when you give the money," they think, or, "Perhaps everyone else already turned in their money and I will look odd if I try to give my money now." Having some people go first gives permission for everyone else who wants to give to do it now.

Time the pitch so that the most people will be there when it is made. This is usually an hour into the party. The host calls for people's attention. The members of the organization discreetly get envelopes ready, and the two to four "plants" space themselves around the room. The host introduces himself or herself and welcomes everyone. If there is a presentation, the host introduces the presenter. (If there is more than one host, such as a couple, or a group, they should take turns talking so it is clear that both or all are involved.)

After the presentation, the host must be the one to give the pitch. If the presenter is a famous person or somehow special to the work of the group, that person can sometimes make a formal request for money, followed by the host saying, "I hope you will join me in helping this important cause." It doesn't matter if the host is nervous or doesn't like asking for money. The proceeds will be much lower without a pitch from the party sponsor.

Sometimes people argue that doing the party — loaning the house, fixing the food, giving the time — should indicate the host's interest. Indeed they do. But in order for the guests to give money, the host must also say that he or she gives money and wants anyone who agrees with him or her to do the same.

How the pitch is made determines how the money will be collected. This is also decided ahead of time. The best way to get the most money at the party is to pass around envelopes immediately after the host speaks. Then the host can say, "Please put your donation in the envelope we are providing and place it in the basket over there," and point to a place. Or the host can say, "You can hand me your envelope, or give it to any of the people wearing a carnation." In any case, tell people how and when to give the money.

AVOIDING FAILURE

I referred to three house parties I had attended that were failures. The first failed because the host had not made any follow-up calls after sending the invitations, and only five people showed up.

The other two failed because they had not been properly planned. In one, the host said, "I hope you will all think about making a gift to this group, which is my favorite." Then, without missing a beat, he said, "Now that the fundraising part is over, let's eat, drink, and have fun." People did exactly as they were told. For a few seconds they thought about giving a gift, then headed for the food. No envelopes were present, and no method of collection was obvious.

At the third party, the hosts showed a videotape about the group, then took the tape out of the TV monitor and went into the kitchen. People sat around chatting about the tape, then got up to get drinks and food. After a while, the hosts reemerged and went on with the party. People could be heard asking: "Are we supposed to give money?" or, "What are you supposed to do with the money?" Perhaps out of fear of being rude or out of embarrassment at not knowing what to do, they did not ask the hosts.

In all cases, the parties raised almost no money and left people feeling that house parties are a waste of time. They are if not done properly.

EVALUATION AND FOLLOW-UP

After each party, take some time to evaluate what went well and what could have been done better. Particularly if you have used a standard presentation, reflect on its length and relevance, whether it was possible to get a discussion going, and so on.

Someone from the organization should write thank-you notes to everyone who gave money, and these people should be put on the organization's mailing list. It would be a nice gesture for the host to also write thank-you notes to those who gave. If the host failed to make a pitch at the party, then the organization should immediately send an appeal letter to everyone on the guest list. If some people gave, go over the list of donors with the host. If there are people who the host thinks would have given but didn't take the opportunity or forgot, he or she should call them. If the host does not want to do that, the group should send them an appeal letter as soon as possible.

Like all fundraising strategies, house parties only work if someone actually asks for the money. Otherwise a house party is just a party — fun but no funds.

1999

Don't Just Stand There, Say Something!

By KIM KLEIN

All over America, grassroots organizations are planning open houses, receptions, cocktail parties, and the like. Meticulously they work through the details: cleaning their offices, deciding whether or not to have the event catered, how much to spend, whether to serve wine, and how dressed up everyone should get.

I recently went to such an event. It was an open house. Everything about it was politically correct: Child care was provided, no animals were sacrificed for the hors d'oeuvres, the coffee was donated by a store that buys from an organic, worker-owned coffee plantation, and all the cups and napkins were made from recycled, unbleached paper. Dozens of people came, milled around, and left.

The main flaw in this otherwise flawless party was the lack of circulation: The board members and staff members stood in clumps, talking mostly to each other or to other people they already knew. Once in a while a board member would stand with a frozen smile at the food table trying to look welcoming to strangers, but actually looking like he or she had just been struck with a tranquilizer dart and would fall over at any minute.

When, afterwards, the staff of this organization asked me what I thought, I told them they had missed a great opportunity to meet people. "But," they wailed, "how do you do that?" Since then I have talked with people in several other organizations who have raised the same question.

So, here is a step-by-step approach for meeting prospects at events that you organize, with things to think about at each stage — before the event, at the event, and after the event.

BEFORE THE EVENT

Before the event, form a committee of people who will be "greeters." This committee will draw from board members, staff, and volunteers. Ideally, there should be one greeter for every 10 to 20 new people expected to attend. The greeters go over the invitation list or the RSVP list (if there is one), identifying for each other who may be coming and who is important to meet.

Generally, there are three kinds of people who come to open houses and reception-type events: people who are friends of staff and board members; people who work for other nonprofits and want to be supportive or just want to see what your group is up to; and people who are donors or donor prospects. Certainly many people fall into all three categories, but the greeter's job is to focus on those people who are donors or prospective donors whom no one knows. Reviewing their names and whatever information is available about them will help in finding them at the event.

Next, the greeters assign themselves to "stations." Two people should be at the door or the sign-in station. They greet everyone as they come in, ask them to sign the guestbook, give them a name tag, and tell them where to put their coats. Depending on the size of the event, one or two people should stand near the food and drink tables, and one or two should be at a table with literature about the group and anything that might be for sale, such as T-shirts, buttons, books, or posters. Another greeter "patrols" any quadrant of the room that is not covered already.

Three or four other people are "rovers." One rover regularly checks in at the greeting table to note who has signed in, then goes to clue the others as to who has shown up who might be important to meet. People can take turns with this role, as it is a much easier job to be at the greeting table than to be a rover.

All the greeters should get small notebooks and pens that easily fit in a pocket. They should also have a supply of business cards with the name of the organization and a space for them to write their own name, as illustrated.

Friends of the Cactus
Dedicated to preserving the Saguaro Cactus

1012 Prickletree Road
Bakersfield, California 90027
(213) 444-9987

_____

BOARD MEMBER

The greeters should plan to wear jackets or pants with pockets big enough to carry their notebook and business cards unobtrusively.

Each greeter should have a special name tag or a flower or something that identifies them as "officials" of the organization giving the event.

DURING THE PARTY

From time to time, greeters should slip off to the bathroom or a back room and write a few notes in their notebook after meeting a person and talking with them for a while. The notes should include the name of the person and any other useful information about them. That way, the greeter is not pressured to remember everything about everyone they meet.

Here is a sample from a greeter's notebook:

Keenan Reilly — Owns Reilly Lumber. Has given off and on because his sister used to be on the board. Said if we ever needed lumber to let him know.

Mako Yashimura — Is a stockbroker down the street. Said someone at her gym wears our T-shirt all the time. Gave her a membership brochure.

Karen — Long last name beginning with T. I was embarrassed to ask her to repeat it more than once. Teaches high school civics or social studies. Talked about using our newsletter in her classes. Asked if we use volunteers for anything besides fundraising. I said we'd contact her.

Mary Oldmoney — Didn't say much, seemed glad I came up to her. Said the food looked expensive, asked if it had been donated. I told her we got a good deal on it, but had the feeling she didn't approve. Left pretty soon after

she got there. Her final words were, "I don't hear as much from you now that Sarah's not here." Who is Sarah?

Trading business cards is also useful. If a guest wants more information about your group, offer to send it to them and ask for their card. Or tell them to call you if they have more questions about whatever topic you have been discussing and give them your card.

Probably the hardest thing to figure out is what to say first. People expect the identified greeters to talk to them, so they probably won't be surprised at being approached. Allow your opening line to be pedestrian and unthreatening. "Great weather for this time of year," or, "The stuffed mushrooms are really good," or, "I'm Betty Boardmember and I'm really glad you could come." You can admire something the person is wearing: "That's a lovely pin, necklace, dress." Only do this if you really do admire it. It is important to remember that a person may be glad that you are talking to them without knowing how to respond. Shy people often don't know how to make small talk, so don't be discouraged if your conversational lines meet minimal responses at first.

After your opening, move to more direct questions or comments. "Are you a member of Friends of the Cactus?" or, "Do you live near here?" or, "I used to know everybody at these events because we were such a small group, but now we have a lot of new people, which is great." or, "Where do you work?" or, "How did you come to know about Friends of the Cactus?"

After a few sentences back and forth, use your common sense as to whether to move on or pursue more conversation. If the person is chatty, talk to them. If they have questions, answer them. Try to drive some of the conversation to your group and what it does, and what they know and like about what you do. If they answer all your platitudes with a one-sentence platitude of their own, move on. If you are talking to two people who have come together, you can move on without guilt because they have each other. If the person is alone, you may want to introduce them to someone or talk a little longer.

The point of all this is fourfold:

- *To make people who came alone or who don't know anyone in your group feel welcome.* You want them to feel that they would come to another of your events.

- *To make donors feel good about giving and thus plant the idea of giving more.*

- *To make prospects interested in giving.* This is done indirectly by answering questions, being friendly, and steering people to the information table.

- *To meet some of your donors so that they are not*

strangers. Later, if you decide to call them to ask for a bigger gift, you will have more of a sense of who they are.

There are two kinds of people who are difficult at these events: those who don't talk and those who talk so much that you can't get away from them. For the latter, the rovers are important. Rovers keep an eye on all the greeters and if they see a greeter spending an inordinate amount of time with someone, they go over and join the conversation. By a prearranged signal, if the greeter wants to be rescued, the rover says to the greeter, "Excuse me, I need to show you something," and pulls the greeter away with much apology.

AFTER THE PARTY

A day or two after the party the greeters should meet and compare notes. They look at the sign-up sheet and note who they were able to meet. If they promised anyone anything, they send it. If they had a particularly good con-versation with someone, they send that person a nice note. "Dear Mary, It was good to meet you at our Open House. I hope you will be able to come to the spring event. Vickie Volunteer."

Remember — the purpose of fundraising is not raising money, which is the end result of doing fundraising properly. The purpose of fundraising is building relation-ships. Every time you have a chance to meet people who are interested in your organization, take it. Maybe their interest was just in the free food, or maybe they just came to meet a friend and go out to dinner afterwards, but maybe they came to see if you look as good up close as you do in the newsletter, or to see if they might want to volunteer.

Friendliness will get you everywhere, and organized, planned friendliness will ensure that you don't blow this opportunity because you didn't think clearly enough about what to wear, where to stand, and what to say.

1995

The Bowl-A-Thon

By LUCY GRUGETT

My organization, a small not-for-profit self-defense and martial arts school, has had success over the past ten years with the Bowl-a-thon, which is the bowling spin on that venerable fundraising standby, the walk-a-thon.

For an organization like ours, with a small paid staff but a large pool of volunteers, the Bowl-a-thon works well for several reasons. First, it requires very little organizing from the "top." Second, the greater number of people who participate, the more money can be raised. With about 40 people bowling, our most successful Bowl-a-thon brought in more than $3,800. Third, the event can cost almost nothing to put on, which is a real plus, since expenses for many fundraising events too often take a huge bite out of the money raised.

Here is how the Bowl-a-thon works. Before the scheduled day of bowling, people solicit contributions, either on a "per-pin" basis or as a lump sum. Lump sums can be collected before or after the bowling event. A per-pin pledge is collected after the bowling event, when the pledge is multiplied by the bowler's score. (We usually choose the high score from two games, but other methods of calculating scores — like combining two games — can be tried.) For example, a 10-cent-per-pin pledge multiplied by a score of 95 comes out to a contribution of $9.50.

We find that the novelty of a Bowl-a-thon makes soliciting contributions more fun and less intimidating to volunteers than more traditional campaigns to ask for money. Once volunteers have learned to ask for small contributions from co-workers, relatives, neighbors, merchants, etc., for a Bowl-a-thon, pitching for larger amounts — perhaps through a major donor campaign — can be less daunting.

Because bowling is an activity that many people have at least some passing experience with, it's easy to get a lot of people in your group participating in this event. For those who have never bowled, the rudiments are usually picked up easily, and bowling is fun even for the most unskilled player. Kids enjoy it, too.

The day of the Bowl-a-thon offers a nice way for members of an organization to get to know one another better, hanging out in the informal atmosphere of a bowling alley and pulling together for a cause they all support.

For those of us in seasonal climates, the Bowl-a-thon is not dependent on good weather, as are outdoor fundraising events. Therefore, we like to do it in the winter and so raise some income during what would otherwise be a slow time of year.

HOW TO DO IT

If you think the Bowl-a-thon is something your group would like to try, these are the steps involved.

1. Secure a bowling alley. Many alleys here in New York City are tied up with leagues, so we make reservations a couple of months in advance; you may not need so much lead time. If you ask, the alley might donate the cost of games as a contribution. Usually, they will at least throw in the shoe rental. Here in New York, games cost about $1.50, and we ask our members to pay if the alley will not donate the fees.

When making reservations, we figure on five people to a lane because our group is usually large — 40 to 50 — so we need to be that crowded. But the game moves more quickly and so is more fun with only four to a lane. (Two games with five people per lane take about two hours.)

2. Circulate pledge sheets and "how-to" instructions. We like to allow about six weeks for people to collect pledges before the event. With more time, it feels like momentum is lost; less time has the obvious drawback of not allowing people to reach as many potential donors as possible. When to hand out pledge sheets and instructions will vary from group to group and depends on factors such as how often you meet and how experienced your group is with soliciting.

Pledge sheets should keep track of the contributors' names, the amounts pledged per pin (or lump-sum amount), and the total collected. We also ask members to collect contributors' addresses and phone numbers so that we can send them a thank-you note and add them to our mailing list for future solicitations. In the constant struggle to find new supporters, we have found this an effective way to expand our donor base.

Instructions should explain the rudiments of the Bowl-a-thon and outline the per-pin and lump-sum pledge options. We also include a couple of sample pitches, including why we are a terrific organization that they should support and what their contributions will pay for.

Include in the instructions handout the date of the event, the bowling alley's address and phone number, the cost of participating (if bowlers must pay for games and/or shoes), and the names and phone numbers of the event's organizers.

3. *Inspire members to collect pledges.* This is the key, of course, to a successful event, and the organizers' main task. Again, depending on how often volunteers connect to the group (weekly or monthly meetings, daily classes, etc.) this will vary, but momentum must build to the day of the event. We have a sign-up poster at the office where bowlers add their names and the number of sponsors they have. Sometimes we use phone trees to urge people on. But of course, the biggest motivator is that members/volunteers believe in the organization and want to help raise money to support it.

4. *On the day of....* One or two organizers are needed for the day's event, depending on the size of the group. Confirm your reservation with the alley the week before. As members arrive, assign them to lanes; when a lane has the required number of bowlers, they can begin to play.

The organizer can collect bowling fees from everyone, or she can assign a lane leader to take charge of each group. We like to give out inexpensive, funny prizes to add to the group's pleasure and also as an excuse to bring folks together, thank them for coming out and exhort them to go out and collect their pledges. Entertaining categories have been most original form, most enthusiastic bowler, best dressed, and, more mundane, highest score.

5. *Keep momentum going after the bowling day.* Bowlers now need to go back to their sponsors and collect money. As a quick visual inspiration and reminder, we keep a poster in the office that shows the amount of money collected, with the goal at top. We have started recently to put a closing date for collection of contributions (about six weeks after the event) because in some years money has trickled in for months.

6. *After pledges have been collected,* ask bowlers to turn in their pledge sheets, so that contributors can receive a thank-you note. We tell members that we will be adding their sponsors to our mailing list so they will receive a solicitation letter. If a bowler does not want a contributor to be solicited by mail in the future, she tells us. However, many who first gave through the Bowl-a-thon are now ongoing supporters of our organization.

To thank those who have raised the most money or accrued the greatest number of sponsors, we award a couple of grand prizes after all contributions are collected. But all members should, of course, be thanked for making the Bowl-a-thon a success.

The Bowl-a-thon is the most solid of our fundraising events. It consistently raises substantial amounts of money and continues to attract large numbers of participants. Because it does not drain staff or financial resources for the organization, it has not burned us out as have other events that are more onerous and expensive to mount.

So if you are looking for a novel and relatively easy event, try a Bowl-a-thon. Maybe it will become a steady and well-loved fundraiser for your group, too.

1993

Fundraising Strategies

IV. OTHER STRATEGIES

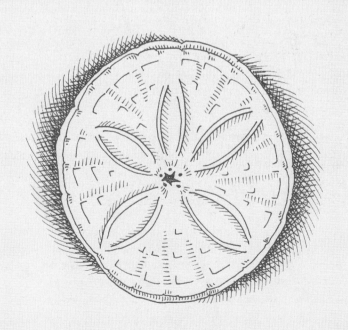

How to Create an Effective Acquisition Strategy

By KIM KLEIN

"**O**ur direct mail campaign has been unbelievably successful," the development director beamed at a board meeting. "We have acquired 2,000 members in just the last nine months, bringing our overall membership to 7,000!" Board members shook their heads in equal parts enthusiasm and puzzlement. Despite the surge in membership, the organization was facing a $20,000 deficit in an overall budget of just under $500,000; the deficit had been caused by the immediate cost of the direct mail campaign. The financial report had parentheses around numbers at the bottom of each summary of income.

"Let's move on," said the chair, either not wishing to hurt the development director's feelings or not wishing to show that he had no clue as to the meaning of any of the numbers being presented. He knew that the development director had been hired because of her expertise in direct mail, and he and the other board members, with equal parts hope, assumption, and denial, felt that everything would work out eventually. The organization had embarked on what was, for them, an enormously expensive effort to build membership. They were using direct mail very effectively, but forgetting that they also need to do other kinds of fundraising in order to keep their budget balanced.

THE PURPOSE OF ACQUISITION

Acquiring new donors is the first step in building a fundraising program. Clearly, if you can't get people to give once, you are not going to be able to ask them to renew or upgrade their gifts. Further, a broad base of donors gives groups stability as well as political power. (See box on page 124, "Reasons for Being Supported by a Broad Range of Donors.") However, many groups forget that acquisition is just the first step in a series of steps we will take with donors, and that, in fact, if a group is not willing or able to conduct an active renewal program and an effective major gifts program, it might as well not acquire donors at all. Why? Let's step back and look at the whole fundraising picture for a moment.

To support our organizations, we don't just want to raise money now — we want to raise money year after year after year, more and more money. And we shouldn't have to work harder and harder to do it. In fact, in a successful fundraising program, fundraising costs become smaller as a percentage of money raised, and the same number of people working the same amount of time should be able to raise more and more money each year.

To have a successful fundraising program requires developing a broad base of people who believe in our work and give us resources. They give money themselves, they ask their friends, service club, house of worship to give, they get the business, foundation, or corporation where they work to give, and so on. When a person gives for the first time, whether $1 for a raffle ticket, $25 for a membership, or $100 for a major gift, they have been "acquired" as a donor. Our goal is then to invite them to give again and again, and to invite them to give more and more — including not just money, but time, advice, contacts, and so on. The purpose of fundraising is to build relationships — relationships that raise money, volunteers, goodwill, power, and so on.

By seeing your donors as friends of the organization, you set up your fundraising program to relate to them as friends. Like all friends, some donors will do more with the group, like volunteer and serve on the board, and some will do less. But people will do more only if they are asked to do more and if they are treated like friends and not impersonations of an ATM.

In designing an acquisition program, then, a group needs to figure out how many donors it needs to acquire. Knowing that, on average, about two-thirds of donors who give in one year will give the next year (expressed in fundraising lingo, we call that a 66% retention rate) allows a group to figure out how many new donors it will need to acquire just to stay the same size. If a group wants to grow, it needs to replace the donors it lost and add new donors. If a group wanted to double its membership, for example, it would need a 133% increase in members to do so — 33% to replace the lost members and 100% to double. If your retention rate is greater than 66%, you will need to recruit fewer donors. If you have a retention rate far lower than 66%, before you acquire a new round of donors you will want to analyze why people give only once or twice and not again.

TIME IS NOT EXPANDABLE

All fundraising takes time, and grassroots organizations always have to choose among strategies. They are rarely in a position to pursue all the fundraising strategies they would like, so when they choose to focus largely on acquisition for a year or two, they will probably have to pay less attention to major gifts. Heavy investment of time and resources on a large special event (for example, to celebrate an anniversary) may mean less attention to direct mail or phone canvassing.

Ideally, a group balances its focus so that, while each year one strategy may be emphasized over another, over the course of two or three years, everything balances out. New organizations, or organizations building a donor base for the first time, must focus on acquisition for the first year or two of their existence. Groups with a lot of donors but no major donor program are foolish to keep acquiring new donors when they should be trying to get a cross-section of current donors to give larger gifts.

Organizations that want financial stability often seek it by establishing reserve funds or endowments. While that is certainly appropriate, groups should understand that donors are like an endowment — if treated properly, they can be counted on to yield a certain amount of money every year, and they are likely to fluctuate less than the stock market.

HOW TO ACQUIRE NEW DONORS

There are a few methods that an organization can employ to acquire new donors. Each of them has different costs, success rates, and implications for the financial future of the group, and each of them is more or less appropriate and useful depending on an organization's financial situation.

Direct Mail

Direct mail, used exclusively by the development director in the example above, is a good method of potentially increasing membership by several dozen — or even several thousand — members at a time. However, it is initially one of the most costly ways to acquire new donors. Because of the expenses of renting mailing lists and writing, designing, printing, and mailing an appeal package, it is highly unusual for a group to make a profit on direct mail until the donors acquired by it begin to give extra gifts or renew their membership. Usually donors acquired in the first year of a direct mail program do not provide net income until the second year of their membership.

In fact, a group may not even break even on their direct mail program during its first year; instead, they may have to spend more money than they take in just to acquire the new donors who will add to their income in following years. Thus a direct mail strategy can be a deficit line in a budget for the first year it is implemented and still be successful because of the number of donors that were brought in.

Going back to our opening story, let's see how this is so. The development director's extremely ambitious plan called for mailing 200,000 pieces over the course of a year. By the end of the year, the typical 1% response rate for direct mail had led them to acquire 2,000 new donors. The cost of the campaign, including the lists, printing, mailing house, postage, and so on — but not including staff time — was $100,000. These 2,000 donors mostly gave $35 (a basic membership). Of course some gave less and some more, including a few who gave $1,000. Overall, the gross income for this mailing was an impressive $80,000.

In other words, the group spent $20,000 to acquire 2,000 donors (or $10 per donor — inexpensive in direct mail terms) who could then be approached over and over. It will now take about a year for additional donations and renewals from those new donors — beyond their initial membership gift — to make up that $20,000. If two-thirds of them renew with the mode gift being $35, the group will earn $70,000; the renewal mailing might cost them $1,500 at most, for a profit of $68,500. This will pay back the $20,000 and give them $48,500 toward program or other fundraising expenses. This is great if you have $20,000 that you can "loan" to your fundraising program for a year; however, this group did not have this luxury.

In order to launch the program, the development director had secured a no-interest loan of $100,000 from a foundation with an agreement to pay it back by the end of the first year. They were able to pay back the $80,000 that had come in from the mailing, but the remaining $20,000 became projected as deficit. Thus, this group acquired a deficit along with a lot of new members. This happened because they failed to take into account a few details:

1. They didn't account for the fact that they would have to wait more than a year to see profit from the mail program.

2. Although the cost of the development director's salary was in the budget, the board had counted on the income from the mailing to pay at least part of her salary and the executive director had hoped that another foundation grant would pay the rest of her salary. Neither of these assumptions panned out, so the group incurred more of a deficit every month the development director worked.

3. Given such a big direct mail program, the development director had no time to do any other fundraising, leaving all remaining fundraising coordination in the hands of the executive director. This was just what he was trying to get away from by hiring a development director.

4. The group did not have a clear reason for needing so many new members. If they had spent less time and money acquiring people, they could have worked with current donors to get renewals and major gifts.

Fortunately, this group solved its problems fairly easily. They began using other acquisition strategies besides direct mail, cutting back the development director's time on that strategy, and refocusing her energy into retaining and upgrading existing donors. By asking donors who had been giving the same amount for three years or more to double their gift, they were able to raise $37,000. About half of those asked doubled their gift; of the group that didn't double, about half increased their gift somewhat. This money more than paid for the development director's salary. Next, the development director negotiated with the foundation to pay back the last $20,000 of their loan at the end of the second year of the direct mail program. Finally, the group stepped back to take a look at its overall fundraising plan.

OTHER ACQUISITION STRATEGIES

Personal Contact

Personal contact is a very successful acquisition strategy, even though it is more often used for upgrading donors and seeking major gifts. In one version of personal contact for acquisition, board members, staff, and volunteers brainstorm a list of all the people who have never given before and who they think might be interested in joining or helping the organization with a gift. The development director drafts a letter that each person can then personalize for their contacts. In the letter, they promise to follow up with a phone call to answer questions and get a response. A week after the letters are mailed, each person calls their contacts.

Personal letters from board members and volunteers to 10 or 20 friends each will often yield a 10% response (compared to the 1% to 2% that is excellent for direct mail). If letters are indeed followed up by a phone call, response can be increased to 20%. Here is a comparison of the costs of a personal letter effort and direct mail:

PERSONAL LETTER EFFORT AND DIRECT MAIL:

Personal letter

10 board members send 20 letters each to friends = 200 letters

10% response = 20 donations

If donations average $35, then gross income = $700

Cost of mailing = $75

Net income = $625

Direct mail

2,000 letters yield a 1% response = 20 donations

If donations average $35, then gross income = $700

Cost of mailing (includes renting lists, printing, paying mail house) = $750–$1,000

Net income = minus $50–$300

Special Events

Special events are good for both acquisition and retention of donors, and certain kinds of events, for upgrading gifts. Events that are going to be used to acquire donors have to be constructed with that end in mind, however. Current donors, friends, board members, staff, and volunteers need to be encouraged to bring new people to the event. The event needs to be interesting or fun for a new person. Lectures, comedians, movie benefits, house tours, festivals, art openings, and awards lend themselves well to this type of acquisition event.

Anniversaries, celebrations of work accomplished, holiday parties, or any event where a lot of the people will know each other and will want to talk with each other, and where a lot of the presentation will be in-jokes or stories people can only appreciate if they know who's being talked about, do not lend themselves to bringing in new people and ought to be planned and seen as retention strategies.

At an acquisition event, some people in the organization do the job of meeting and greeting new people and making them feel welcome. These volunteers circulate and introduce themselves to people they don't recognize. Sometimes, people who are new to the organization are asked to stand or to wear a name tag of a certain color.

The work of the group is explained in some detail — detail that will be very familiar to people close to the organization. There is a way to capture the names and addresses of new people, either through a door prize drawing or a circulated mailing list. As people leave the event, they are thanked warmly for coming and they leave feeling, "This is a very friendly group." (See also, "Don't Just Stand There, *Say Something!*" by Kim Klein.)

Afterwards, the new people are sent a letter that thanks them again for coming and for supporting the organization. Shortly after that, they are invited to become members or to give more money.

House Parties

House parties are another form of personal contact and are often a good way to acquire new donors. For this strategy, a donor, usually a board member, opens their home to their friends and colleagues, inviting them to hear a brief presentation about the organization. Refreshments are served, the host introduces someone from the organization who describes the need for the group's work and its successes and momentum, and the host makes a fundraising pitch inviting his or her guests to contribute, providing a way for them to do so on the spot. (See "Putting on a House Party" by Kim Klein.)

A house party strategy works best if several board members agree to host such gatherings, as doing so builds wider interest in the group and provides a sense of shared involvement among board members. Also, while one house party may only generate a few new members or donations, the cumulative effect of a dozen house parties with 10 to 20 new donors per party can make this a successful strategy in terms of numbers as well as money.

Canvass

For groups working on local issues, a neighborhood-by-neighborhood, or precinct-by-precinct, all-volunteer canvass can be a great acquisition strategy. A canvass works best if a group has an issue that can be easily explained in a brief encounter: "Hi, I'm with People Urging Utility Rate Reform — PUURR. You may have seen our big cat logo in front of the gas company. I want to talk to you about how you can lower your heating bills, if you have a minute." With a willing listener, the canvasser explains how joining the group can help regulate gas and electric costs, or insure that low-income people and seniors have subsidized heating, or whatever the group is doing on this issue. One or two minutes into the rap, the canvasser should be saying, "So, I am hoping you will join PUURR with a gift of $25." Each house might take five minutes to visit.

A canvass is labor intensive. It requires a lot of volunteers to be successful, with training required ahead of time so that volunteers can answer questions and give information, and so the group has clear message control. People have to be given the option to give much less money — $2–$3 even — and still be made to feel appreciated.

A big mistake that canvasses traditionally make is not thanking people by mail who have made their gift at the door. Without this critical step, a canvass may acquire a lot of people, but their renewal rate will be very low.

WHAT TO HAVE IN PLACE WHEN ACQUIRING NEW DONORS

Organizations that are acquiring new donors, especially many new donors at once, need to have a certain infrastructure in place to deal with their new donors. They should ask themselves the following questions:

- Is there a system for writing and sending thank-you notes within 72 hours of receiving a gift?

- Who will enter information about each donor in the database, and is the database adequate to the task and easy to use?

- Does the group have a newsletter to keep donors informed about its work and does the newsletter come out regularly?

- Finally, is there a plan for working with donors once you acquire them? Since building relationships with donors is the true task of a fundraising program, methods for renewing and upgrading donors, and just plain keeping in contact with them, must be in place.

LESSONS

The first lesson to be learned from examining acquisition strategies is that there are several more inexpensive ways of getting new donors than direct mail. Personal contact, house parties, events, and canvassing are all less cost-intensive ways of acquiring new donors.

The second lesson is that a group needs to set a goal of how many new donors it wants to recruit. If a group wants several thousand new donors in one year, direct mail is a good way to get them, but the group has to understand the time lag between the investment in the mailing and the positive cash flow it will eventually generate, and it must have systems in place to deal with the donors it acquires.

The third lesson is that donors will respond to personal attention. The majority of donors to most groups will relate to the group through the mail (or increasingly by e-mail). They will get appeals and respond; they will get newsletters and thank-you notes and feel good about the group. The more personal your communication with your donors, the more they are likely to respond with extra gifts.

Some of your donors will even like your group the best of all the groups they give to. Maybe they think you do the best work, or that your issue is most important, or they admire someone in the group. If asked, these donors will give you the most money they can possibly afford. Your job is to figure out who these donors are, to help create more of them by doing high-quality, visible work, and to ask them to give more. Upwards of 10% of your donor base will give you about 60% of your income. To get these donors you must acquire them, and then work with them once they are giving, inviting them to give bigger gifts. Acquisition is a critical part of a larger fundraising plan, but is not an end in itself.

2001

Reasons for Being Supported by a Broad Range of Donors

Adapted from *Fundraising for the Long Haul,* by Kim Klein (Chardon Press, 2000).

PHILOSOPHICAL REASONS

1. We wish to be mission driven. We want to do what needs to be done and say what needs to be said to those who need to be told, without fearing financial repercussions. We recognize the difference between being mission driven and being donor driven, staff driven, or foundation driven.

2. We wish to belong to the community we serve, and we are interested in knowing what people who share our beliefs think about our work.

3. We believe that financial support from a wide variety of people is one test of the validity of our work.

4. We believe that maintaining a broad base of donors is the most responsible and fiscally prudent way to finance our organization.

5. We believe that maintaining a broad base of donors furthers our educational, organizing, and advocacy goals. This group of people can be called on to come to demonstrations, write letters, or engage in other needed actions in addition to giving money.

It is also helpful to consider the practical reasons that an organization would want to seek support from a broad base of individuals. Some of these are embedded in the philosophical tenets above, and I hasten to add that I believe philosophy is practical. However, without a deep belief in the importance of doing fundraising this way, practicality degenerates into cynical opportunism or an effort reluctantly and badly done.

PRACTICAL REASONS

1. The vast majority of money given away in the United States (and in every country where giving has been studied) comes from individuals. The majority of that money comes from middle-class, working-class, and poor people — in other words, most people. So, if you really want access to money, you will raise it from the people who give it, which fortunately happens to be the majority of people.

2. Financial stability depends on diversity — both in the sources of money and in the number and types of people raising this money.

3. Many of the strategies for raising money apply only or mainly to raising money from individuals — canvassing, direct mail, special events, planned giving.

4. If you want to engage in any kind of electoral politics or want to influence the outcome of legislation, you will have to raise most of your money from individuals. (You will also have to work with a different tax status than a 501(c)(3) designation.)

Making the Most of Your Anniversary

By LUCY GRUGETT and STEPHANIE ROTH

The Center for Anti-Violence Education is a 22-year-old institution in Brooklyn, New York, that works to end violence against women and children on both individual and institutional levels, primarily through community education programs, self-defense courses, and martial arts training. The hard work of our 3.5 paid staff people is greatly enhanced by the dedicated efforts of close to 50 volunteers.

Historically the organization has raised 35% to 45% of its income from fees, which gives it a distinct advantage over grassroots organizations without services to sell. But due to its unusual combination of martial arts training and a social justice approach to antiviolence work, other sources of support — particularly from foundations — have been hard to come by.

In 1993, we had 266 individual donors (separate from students, who pay monthly class fees), who contributed a total of $13,270. Events brought in $11,500 more. As 1994 approached, we realized there was an ideal opportunity to use the milestone of our 20th anniversary as a way to increase the visibility of the organization, expand our fundraising capacity, and bring in new donors. We also saw the need to take risks in our fundraising activities in order to make a leap in our individual donor fundraising.

As we wanted to maximize the fundraising potential of the anniversary, we planned to celebrate the occasion over the course of the entire year with a variety of activities, described below. For this 20th anniversary year, we decided to set the rather ambitious goal of raising $100,000 from individual contributions.

With the small paid staff already overextended in programmatic, administrative, and fundraising work, we decided to take what felt like a great financial risk: We hired a 20th anniversary year coordinator to work one-half to one full day a week for the year. She helped us develop a plan for the anniversary year, implement some

components of the plan, and solve various problems along the way. We also hired an event coordinator half-time for six months to help organize the gala event that took place at the end of the anniversary year.

At the end of a very full year of activities and celebrations, the center had raised close to $80,000. Though this was short of our original goal, we felt good about what we had achieved. For one thing, this amount was more than three times the amount we had raised the previous year from individual donors. We also increased our donor base from 266 to 483 donors, the largest growth in any previous single year. We now have a stronger base from which to expand and raise more money in the years to come.

As you'll read below, we did not have great success with every strategy, but we pushed ourselves to think big, take risks, and move forward with the momentum that a significant anniversary can provide.

PROJECTS OF THE ANNIVERSARY YEAR

1. The 20th Anniversary Committee. Recognizing that our board of directors was small and not very well connected in the larger community, we decided to establish a 20th Anniversary Committee. Our idea was to identify and solicit the participation of women who could help broaden our reach to new constituencies. We brainstormed a list of about 75 women, and ultimately recruited 35 to join the committee.

We first approached committee prospects with a letter, which presented a short history of the center and its work, gave preliminary plans for the anniversary year, and described the responsibilities of committee members. We asked that each member of the committee attend three or four meetings during the year to generate ideas and build energy, join either the Major Donor Campaign or Gala Event Committee, and share skills and knowledge in areas such as graphic design, public relations, or connections with other community organizations. We also stated our expectation that committee members would take the lead by making their own financial contribution to the organization.

Follow-up calls were made to each committee prospect by the executive director, the event coordinator, or in a few cases by a board member. Because of time constraints, we did not interview prospects in person, but spent time on the phone answering questions and determining their interest and ability to make a commitment.

The actual participation of committee members was mixed. Some were extraordinarily generous in giving of their time, energy, and money; some hardly participated at all. But most did make a financial contribution, attend at least one meeting, and help to get the word out about the end-of-the-year gala. Moreover, the impressive roster of committee members on our letterhead was definitely noticed by foundation and corporate funders whom we solicited for support that year.

The Anniversary Committee brought new women from the community into the work of the center. We have made important new friends, several of whom have continued to help us since the committee disbanded. We learned that having a formal relationship with people inspired support and, as a result, we plan to start an Advisory Council. Committee members also introduced us to new prospects for our board of directors.

2. The 20th Anniversary Report. Like many small nonprofits, the center does not produce an annual report, and we had no single piece of promotional material that encompassed our mission, programs, and history. We felt that a well-designed, nicely produced booklet with lots of pictures and limited text would be useful for both fundraising and promotional activities. We hired an outside writer for the first time, assuming it would speed up and streamline the process. We learned, however, that because of our desire to "get it right" and solicit feedback from several key people in the organization, we needed much more time than we had originally anticipated. We hoped we could write, design, and print the booklet in a couple of months, but it ended up taking more than four months to complete. If we had known to plan for several drafts going back and forth, it would have saved us much frustration. In the end, however, we were pleased with the final product. It gave us a concise vehicle with which to introduce our work, and we benefited from the experience of putting together a more upscale and ambitious fundraising document than we had previously published.

3. The Kickoff Event. We launched the 20th anniversary with a reception, which took place on a weeknight from 5 to 7 P.M. We used it as an opportunity to reach out to current donors, potential supporters, and friends of the center, and to begin to solidify the participation of the 20th Anniversary Committee. The program included a short demonstration of kids doing safety/self-defense skits, a reading from a new novel about young women and violence by a local author and friend of the center, and food and drink. No admission was charged, and a fundraising pitch was made by none other than Kim Klein, an old friend of the organization. More than 100 people attended, and we raised approximately $3,500.

We did not plan the kickoff as a major fundraising event, but used it to bring people together who would be involved in activities throughout the year and to build excitement and interest. A lot of goodwill from that event translated into contributions, both monetary and otherwise, during the rest of the year.

4. The Major Donor Campaign. The center had run annual major donor campaigns with limited success for the previous three years. This was mostly due to our difficulty finding people willing to participate (including board members), and the fact that we have a small donor base to draw from. For the anniversary year, the critical difference was having a larger number of people involved in asking, and therefore, a larger pool of prospects. A Major Donor Committee was formed, made up of 20th Anniversary Committee members, students from the center, and staff and board members. We ran an extended campaign through the spring, fall, and winter. We solicited our current donor list as well as new prospects for contributions of $100 or more.

The campaign was far more successful than in past years, raising $31,735. Although we did not reach our goal of $50,000, we were pleased with the growth. We are beginning to understand that building a donor base takes time, patience, and persistence. Even with a larger committee, the center's executive director and the anniversary coordinator made the bulk of the asks. Our largest individual gift, $5,000, was raised by the executive director, but contact with the prospect was made with the assistance of a 20th Anniversary Committee member.

5. The Children's Poster Campaign. Young people make up almost half the membership of the center through the Children's Empowerment Project. For the anniversary, we invited the children to participate in an art project: Children's Visions of Peace and Safety. An artist donated her time to supervise two sessions (divided by age) and furnished vividly colored paper for them to make collages, which she told us generally reproduced better than drawings. Working with the center staff, the artist first led a discussion with the young participants about the kinds of images that represented safety and nonviolence to each of them: a favorite relative's house, the beach, being in bed at home, playing with friends, a tree house, walking a dog, and abstract images as well.

The children created artwork that was evocative and powerful. In keeping with our noncompetitive educational philosophy, we exhibited all the collages at a local university and at the gala celebration later in the year. Three that would reproduce well were chosen to be part of a striking four-color poster (see illustration), designed by another volunteer. We were able to get a local politician to underwrite the cost of printing, which totaled $2,500.

The Children's Visions of Peace and Safety Poster is a beautiful and tangible souvenir of the 20th anniversary and embodies the spirit of the center's antiviolence work. We gave copies of the poster as thank yous to committee members and major donors. We also sold a few at the gala celebration and through our newsletter.

6. The Neighborhood Collection Can Campaign. To increase our visibility in the center's immediate Brooklyn neighborhood and, of course, to raise money, we launched a canister solicitation campaign. Volunteers approached neighborhood stores and many agreed to let us place a can on their counter. Some merchants also made cash donations. Some turned us down because they said the canisters would be stolen and, alas, several canisters *were* taken. Since then, we've noticed that other organizations chain their receptacles down! We also made up "palm cards" that were left next to each canister for folks to take, with safety tips, information about the center's programs, and resource numbers for rape crisis centers, battered women's shelters, incest hotlines, and other support services.

A disappointing $305 came from this campaign; although we didn't really know what to expect, we had hoped to bring in $2,000–$3,000.

7. The 20th Anniversary Gala Celebration. The culmination of more than a year's activities, the gala celebration

was the most ambitious event the center had ever produced. We honored five individuals and organizations who had made important contributions to antiviolence work. Each awardee gave a short presentation about something that had inspired their work. It made for a very moving and powerful evening. A reception after the event gave the more than 300 people who attended a chance to mingle and partake of food and drink.

To increase the income from the event beyond ticket sales, we solicited sponsorships from individuals and businesses several months in advance of the event. More than 1,100 invitations were sent by the center and committee members asking people to sponsor the event at different levels of giving. Basic admission was $35, and sponsorship levels ranged from $75 to $5,000. This was the first time the center used this standard fundraising device, and it was quite successful. We know that many people contributed at the $125 and $250 levels who would not have responded to non-event solicitations with that size of contribution. Corporate contributions totaled $7,000, and contributions overall totaled $25,829. A commemorative journal grossed nearly $5,000.

The 20th anniversary was certainly the most ambitious fundraising the center has ever attempted. It required an enormous amount of time and organizational energy, and would not have been possible without the assistance of our part-time consultants and our core of volunteers. Knowing this ahead of time is important. We would not have had the success in terms of money raised, donors acquired, and community members involved if we had tried to do it with our limited staff time. Ultimately, it was successful in pushing us past our comfort level in asking for large gifts, making the necessary long-term commitment to building our individual donor base, and sowing the seeds for a stronger, healthier organization. We're looking forward to celebrating another 20 years!

1996

How to Produce (and Raise Money from) an Ad Journal

By STEPHANIE ROTH

A good way to increase your income from a special event, raise money from local community businesses, mark an important anniversary, and/or promote your organization's work is through the production of an ad journal. An ad journal is a pamphlet or booklet that is essentially a PR piece for your organization produced for a specific occasion. Although it contains information about your organization, it is made up primarily of advertisements that you have sold. The goal is to raise more money through ad sales than it costs to produce, print, and distribute the ad journal.

BENEFITS OF AD JOURNALS

There are both tangible and intangible benefits to producing an ad journal. On the tangible side are increased financial contributions; on the intangible side are increased involvement from businesses and volunteers.

- Ad journals can be very profitable, since they need not cost a lot to produce. A page of ads is typically sold at a rate that is five to ten times more than the cost to produce it, depending on a number of factors, including total number of pages of the ad journal, quality of paper, and costs of design, production, and printing.

- Small business owners will sometimes spend more money for an ad than they would for a contribution because it is a way to promote their business to a very targeted audience. Businesses have advertising budgets from which to purchase ad space in your journal even if they do not allocate money for charitable contributions.

- Ad journals can generate support from individuals and businesses that might not be as likely to respond to a request for a direct contribution. Those who do not yet have a strong connection to your cause can be sold on the idea of the exposure that advertising will give them.

- Members of your organization who are still reluctant to ask for money often find it easier to sell ads. This experience may be the first step in people being willing to ask for individual contributions.

As is true with special events, the first time you produce an ad journal is the hardest. By doing the journal on an annual basis, however, you will develop a body of advertisers that are likely to renew their ads, so your job gets easier each year. For the same amount of time spent, or less, your journal will make more and more money as you increase the number of advertisers and get better at the mechanics of production.

Including copy in the journal that is interesting and appealing to your constituency will make it easier to sell ads. Non-ad copy in the journal depends on the occasion for which you are producing it. The Astraea National Lesbian Action Foundation, for example, produces an ad journal for their annual Lesbian Writers' Fund Gala. In addition to ads, their journal includes poetry and short fiction by writers who are receiving an award at the gala, a list of individuals and businesses that are sponsors of the event, statements from the executive director and board chair, photographs of people involved in the writers' fund, and information about the Astraea Foundation.

Having an occasion at which to distribute the ad journal also ensures a specific audience who will see — and, we hope, look through — the publication, something advertisers will care about.

PITCHING THE ADS

Selling ad space can be a challenge, however, particularly if your organization is not well known in your community. Advertisers generally know that they will not get the kind of exposure through your journal that they would in a local newspaper. Do not be surprised if prospective advertisers complain that they never get any business from ads they place in nonprofit organizations' journals. There are several things you can say to counter this complaint:

- Their ad lets the reader know that this business cares about your issues and is willing to support you. In many communities, people like to support businesses that they perceive as being responsive to them. Environmentalists will be more likely to do business with someone who supports an environmental organization. Women may prefer to do business with women-owned companies. Even if customers don't specifically tie their patronage to the ad, chances are it is drawing some business.

- Advertisers will be reaching a potentially new constituency for a reasonable cost.

- It is a commonly accepted advertising principle that people need to see the name of a product at least three times before they purchase it. This makes it difficult to measure response to any single advertisement. (You can point out one way to measure response is to include a coupon in the ad offering readers a discount for the product or services.) Although the readers of your journal may not go out the next day and call the accountant who advertised there, the next time they are looking for someone to do their taxes, they may remember his or her name when they see it in the yellow pages.

Most important in your pitch, however, is to sell your cause to a group of prospects you have good reason to think might support you. This goal is the same as for a solicitation for a gift of any kind. And, like most successful campaigns, most of the ads you sell will be to people known to someone in the organization or to local businesses that know the important work your organization does in the community.

SHOULD YOU DO AN AD JOURNAL?

In considering whether or not to produce an ad journal, think about the following issues:

Do you have enough volunteers to work on it? Producing an ad journal is labor intensive and requires an enormous amount of follow-up and attention to detail. If you are producing an ad journal as part of a special event, you should create a separate committee of at least three volunteers who work exclusively on the ad journal.

Do you have enough lead time to produce the journal? Ideally you need four months, particularly if you are doing it for the first time, to put your ad journal together, including selling ads and completing the design and production work. Although this will vary greatly with the size and fundraising goals of your ad journal, your committee should plan to spend a total of 6 to 10 hours a week for the first month, and up to 15 or 20 hours a week after that.

Have you defined the audience or constituency for the journal? Prospective advertisers will want to know who will see their ads. A special event gives you a specific time, place, and audience. Otherwise you need to be prepared to let advertisers know who they can expect will see their ads.

Do you know who your potential advertisers are? See below for ideas on developing a fundraising goal that will determine how many prospects you need, developing a good prospects list, and determining if you have enough prospects to reach your goal. Assuming that for first-time requests made either in person or by letter with a follow-up phone call, 20% – 30% will say yes. You will need at least 100 prospects to sell 30 ads.

Is your community deluged with ad journals already? If Gina's Pizza Parlor is asked to buy ads in a dozen journals each year from local community organizations, Gina may be reluctant to buy yet another ad from your group.

STEPS IN PRODUCING AN AD JOURNAL

Once you've decided to go forward with an ad journal, here are the steps to follow for the greatest success.

1. Determine Your Fundraising Goal

How much money do you want to make from the ad journal? If you have produced a journal for your organization in the past, use that experience as a starting point for estimating an achievable goal. Assuming that factors such as the state of the economy in your community, public awareness of your organization, and competition from other nonprofits haven't changed dramatically since your last ad journal, you can assume that for the same amount of effort and time, you will raise more and more money every year.

If this is your first ad journal, your fundraising goal will be made based on the lists of potential advertisers you can generate: Are they strong prospects? That is, do they know about your organization? Do they support similar kinds of organizations? Assume that with a strong prospect list you can expect to sell one ad for every three names on your list.

2. Develop a Budget

Complete a detailed income and expense projection for the project. Expenses will include

DESIGN AND PRODUCTION

Have a designer create a template for the journal, including pages for ad and non-ad copy. Keep in mind that it is most cost effective to print pages that are a standard size — either 8.5" × 11" or 5.5" × 8.5". You may find a volunteer within your organization who knows how to use a desktop publishing program such as PageMaker or QuarkXPress, but you may need to hire a graphic designer to do this part of the job.

PRINTING

There are two types of materials to be printed:

Materials used to solicit ads, such as a letter, sample page layout, reply form, and other information about your organization. (Unless you're sending a large quantity of solicitation materials, these are usually photocopied in-house.)

The journal itself. Printing costs will depend on the total number of pages of the journal, the quality of the paper you use, and whether or not you are using photographs. Printing can be as much as 60–70% of the entire cost of producing the journal.

Postage. Include the costs of sending out the journal to your advertisers when it is completed, as well as the cost of sending solicitation letters.

Telephone. Be sure to figure in this expense if solicitations are to be made to businesses outside of your local calling area.

Staff time. This is a separate area from the people you hire for the technical aspects of producing the journal and includes any staff time used for getting materials together, soliciting ads, and working with volunteer ad salespeople, the designer, and the printer. Because the cost of salaried staff's time is not an out-of-pocket expense, many organizations choose not to include it in their budget. However, you will have a much clearer picture of the resources it takes to produce the journal if you track the amount of time staff spends.

Income will come, of course, from ad sales. In order to do a projection of income, you need to set prices for the ads and decide on the number of pages your ad journal will have. If this is your first journal, see if you can find out what other organizations in your community charge for ads. An example of a price range used by a midsized nonprofit organization in New York City in 1994 for an ad journal with pages measuring 8.5" × 11" was the following:

One-line greeting (or listing of name): $50

Eighth-page (or business-card size): $100

Quarter-page: $175

Half-page: $325

Full page: $600

Inside front and back covers: $700

The prices for ads should be set so as to give an incentive to place larger ads. For example, a half-page should cost less than twice the amount of a quarter-page ad.

3. Develop prospect lists

Like any fundraising strategy, your best prospects are people you and the folks in your organization already know. Here's a place to start:

- Vendors that your organization does business with or has relationships with, e.g., office supply store, printers, landlord, neighborhood deli.

- Businesses that your members use or work for.

- People who want to be known to your community, including self-employed individuals, such as therapists, chiropractors, real estate agents, and accountants who serve the community in which you operate; businesses that have advertised in ad journals of similar organizations in your community; and nonprofit organizations that you work closely with.

As in any kind of fundraising strategy, you will first want to approach people who are most likely to say yes and later solicit less likely prospects. When you then begin to ask prospects who are not as close to the organization, you can indicate that a number of ads have already been sold so that they know they are part of a larger group of people who support your work.

As part of the process of developing a prospect list for selling ads, ask your members to make up a list of all the businesses they come into contact with, using the following checklist to generate ideas:

Where you shop for groceries _____

Your local dry cleaner _____

Your hairdresser/barber_____

Companies you or your friends and family members work for _____

Restaurants you go to _____

Your dentist, doctor, chiropractor, therapist, or other health care practitioner _____

In addition to your members' contacts, some have found it useful to look through the ad journals of similar kinds of organizations in your community. The Astraea Foundation developed part of their prospect list from the ad journals of several lesbian and gay organizations in New York City. Because they knew that advertisers in these journals were lesbian- or gay-owned businesses or at least lesbian/gay friendly, there was good reason to think they would at least consider placing an ad in Astraea's ad journal.

Compile the lists from your members into a master list of prospects that can be assigned to the volunteers working on the ad journal. If members are willing, it's preferable to have them solicit ads from their own prospects.

4. Develop a Packet and Send to Prospects

A packet should include the following:

- A solicitation letter explaining the purpose of the ad journal, what the money is being raised for, the audience or market for the ads (who will receive the journal), the good publicity it will give the businesses that support your work, and what non-ad copy will be part of the publication.

- An ad-rate sheet that explains the prices for different sizes of ads, deadlines for submitting ad copy, and a tear-off to send back an agreement to place the ad.

- A diagram or sample page showing ad sizes, proportions, and layout possibilities. This visual aid is particularly useful to people who are not accustomed to placing display advertising.

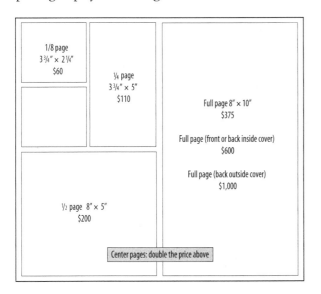

- Clear instructions about the format ads should be in. Increasingly, designers prefer electronic files, rather than hard copy for ads. Such files can be e-mailed to your designer. Electronic files of ads that have photographs or logos may need to come in special format, such as TIFF or EPS; your designer should make these specifications clear in the instructions.

Send the packets out to your prospect list at least one month before ad copy is due. This gives businesses or individuals the time to put together an ad if they don't have one available.

At this point, you need to decide whether you're willing to design ads for people who don't have easy access to design resources — or who won't take the time to design their own. For these people, add a design fee to the cost of placing an ad in your journal and set the deadline for getting that ad copy in a couple of weeks earlier than the deadline for designed ads.

5. Make Follow-up Calls

This is the most critical step in the entire process. A committee of volunteers should make follow-up calls to those who received the solicitation package. The purpose of the calls is to obtain commitments from people and then actually get the ad copy in. Those who have contacts with the businesses and individuals being solicited should as much as possible be enlisted to make the follow-up calls.

Often the most time-consuming part of this process is getting the ad copy in hand after someone has agreed to place an ad in your journal.

Here is a scenario that can happen with any number of potential advertisers:

March 1 — You send a solicitation packet to the attention of Rochelle, your sales rep at Office Helper, the local office supply store with which you do a lot of business.

March 10 — You follow up with a phone call to Rochelle. She isn't available, so you leave a message.

March 13 — You call again. Rochelle doesn't remember receiving the packet, so you explain that your organization is putting together an ad journal and would like Office Helper to place an ad. She asks you to send another copy of the materials and says she'll have to talk to the store manager. You send another packet out that day, indicating that you'll call back again in a couple of days.

March 16 — You call back and Rochelle says that she showed the letter to her manager who is now thinking about it and will let you know within the week.

March 23 — You haven't heard anything from Rochelle, so you call again. She's gone on vacation for the week and the manager is not available to speak to you.

March 30 — Rochelle calls you and says the store will take out a half-page ad and will get the copy to you by the following week (which happens to be the deadline, fortunately).

April 8 — Ad copy from Office Helper has not arrived, so you call Rochelle to find out what happened. She said their ad designer was out sick and they need another couple of days. She also tells you that they realized they had overspent their advertising and contributions budget this year, so will have to take out a smaller, one-quarter page ad.

April 15 — You go to Office Helper personally to pick up the ad so that your designer can get the ad in time for it to appear in the ad journal.

This is not a particularly unusual scenario, and many other things can happen, such as the ad copy arrives in a program your designer can't open, or the ad copy needs to be designed even though camera-ready copy had been promised.

Like special events, there is no way to anticipate all the

glitches, setbacks, and delays that can happen in producing an ad journal. It is therefore very important to give yourself plenty of time to deal with them and to try to hold people to deadlines as much as you possibly can.

6. Produce the Journal

Production of the ad journal involves making design decisions (such as the typeface for non-ad copy, the look of borders around pages or ads) and production decisions, including the order in which the pages will appear in the finished booklet and the total number of pages the journal will consist of.

Keep in mind that it is much easier for your designer if he or she gets *all of* the copy at once. Giving her ads and other copy as they trickle in will cause delays and frustration on all sides.

It's most cost effective for printing if your journal is a standard size, such as 8.5" × 11" or 5.5" × 8.5". Remember, too, that the total number of pages must be a multiple of four, because a book or pamphlet is printed on both sides of a piece of paper that is then folded in half or in quarters. Thus the total number of pages will be 4, 8, 12, 16, etc.

Allow plenty of time for the production phase, and even more if a volunteer is producing the journal. Plan for at least two weeks for the design phase and two more weeks for printing.

SPECIAL TERMS

For people new to producing publications of this kind, it may be useful to know a few of the technical terms that designers and printers may use as though they were part of your everyday vocabulary. Your best resource, however, is your printer. Check with them about any technical issues that arise.

Halftones are photographs converted by the printer into a series of dots using a screening process. They may be made by the printer from original black-and-white glossy photos or from images scanned into an electronic file according to your designer's instructions.

Screen tint is a way of setting off or calling attention to a section of a page by creating a block of gray (or if using color, a paler density of the color) "behind" the type.

Line Screen tells you the number of lines (or dots) per inch at which the screens used for halftones and tints will be printed. The higher the number, the crisper the quality.

Linotronic or lino print is a higher quality print than a laser printer can produce. A laser printer produces 300 (or 600) dots per inch (dpi) for text, compared to linotronic

output, which ranges from 1,200 to 2,400 dpi. If any of your advertisers are unable to submit their ad electronically, they can have a lino produced at a special photo lab. These high-quality prints can be expensive — $10 or more per page.

You may not need to know these terms at all to handle the production of your ad journal. However, I once had the experience of being asked by a potential advertiser what line screen we were using. Not knowing what that meant, I called our designer, who told me that the line screen was 53. I called the advertiser back and she said "53! That's strange." I still didn't understand what the problem was and wished I knew more of the technical language of the printing business.

TIMELINE FOR PRODUCING AN AD JOURNAL

Here is a typical timeline for a four-month schedule for producing an ad journal from start to finish.

Weeks 1–3: Planning phase: Determine size of the ad journal, ad rates, prospect lists, recruit committee of volunteer solicitors, write solicitation letter, meet with designer, making sure that you and she agree on what the final product should look like.

Week 4: Send solicitation packet to prospects.

Weeks 5–7: Conduct follow-up calls.

Week 7: Published deadline for ads, including copy for ads you will be designing

Week 9: Deadline for all non-ad copy

Week 10: Real deadline: The time by which you absolutely have to have all the ad copy in hand. Do not let people know that you are working with this deadline. It is only meant to give you time to track down ads from people who can't meet the stated deadline.

Weeks 11: Designer delivers first draft to you.

Week 12: Two people proofread journal. Don't leave out this critical step!

Week 13: Journal is back with designer for corrections and comes back to you for final proofreading.

Week 14: Journal goes to printer.

Week 16: Journal is delivered from printer.

If you begin to incorporate ad journals as an annual fundraising activity, you will develop systems, prospects, and a timeline that work best for you and may speed up the process by a week or two. However, always give yourself an extra week for each deadline that you set to accommodate crises and unforeseen delays. You will be much less stressed and have a better product as a result.

1994

How to Do a Raffle

By KIM KLEIN

A common, easy, and fun way to raise almost any amount of money is a raffle. Almost everyone is familiar with raffles, having bought tickets for them, perhaps even won a prize in one. Because raffles are so common, most people don't realize that they can be complicated. When organizing a raffle, you can make your life more difficult by not paying attention to the myriad details that a raffle involves.

The first fact to keep in mind is that raffles have to be organized carefully so that they don't violate gambling laws. Although laws against raffles are rarely enforced, it is important to organize your raffle so that you are within the bounds of the law. In addition to federal and state laws, you need to find out the laws in your own community. Sometimes you will need to register with the sheriff's department, and in some towns laws against raffles are strictly enforced and you simply will not be able to do one. We will discuss how to set up your raffle so that you will be within the laws of most states. Ironically, states with their own lottery tend to be more likely to stop a raffle from taking place than states without a lottery.

Raffles basically appeal to people's desire to get something for less than it is worth. Here's how they work: Your organization gets some gifts donated, which are used as the prizes. These gifts can vary and may include cash, services such as child care for an evening or having your windows washed, or trips, microwaves, VCRs, and so forth. Generally, there are five to ten prizes, one of which is a grand prize. Tickets are sold for somewhere between $1 and $10 each. Many more tickets are sold than prizes available, so a person's chances of winning are relatively small. At an appointed day and time, all the tickets are put into a barrel or other container, stirred up, and an uninvolved person (such as a child) draws out the winning tickets.

The organization makes money from the number of tickets sold. There is no other source of income in a raffle. The costs can be kept low; ideally, the only costs are printing the tickets and getting the prizes to the winners. As a result, most of the income is profit.

There are three parts to a successful raffle, each requiring three steps. These are described in detail in the rest of this article.

ORGANIZING THE RAFFLE

Step One: Get the Prizes

Bring together a small committee (two or three people) to decide when the raffle will be held and what the prizes will be. It is helpful if the prizes have a theme, such as "vacations," "services," "household," or "restaurants." Make a list of all the vendors who might give you a prize, and list specifically what you want from them, such as dinner for two, a weekend cabin, etc. Remember that people who own small businesses, particularly storefronts, frequently get asked to donate raffle prizes. They may have policies against doing it; they may have donated to five other charities and are not taking on anymore; they may be having a hard time in their business and not be inclined to give you anything. Have at least twice as many potential sources of prizes as prizes needed.

The small committee goes out and solicits the prizes. They stress to each merchant how many people will see the tickets, how much other publicity you are going to do, how you will not ask for another item this year, or whatever is true for you. Merchants must think about how giving your organization an item is good for their business, and you must help them in that thinking.

Step Two: Get the Workers

While you are soliciting prizes, start calling your volunteers to ask how many tickets they are willing to handle. Some people hate raffles — don't push them into taking tickets; they will resent it and probably won't sell their tickets. Give the tickets to people who work in large office buildings or unions, or who have large families or a large circle of friends. Offer a prize for the person who brings in the most money selling tickets.

Keep track of who said they would distribute tickets. Raffles are a good opportunity to get some peripheral people involved, so don't just go to your reliable volunteers who already do everything else. Ask each person if they know someone who would be good at getting people to buy tickets. People's spouses or lovers, neighbors, business partners, etc., can be recruited for this effort.

Step Three: Get the Tickets

Once they have the prizes, the committee decides which will be the grand prize, the second prize, and so on. They decide on the date of the raffle drawing. Raffle ticket sales should go on for at least a month, and can continue for up to six months without losing momentum. The ideal time period for a raffle is two to three months.

Printing the tickets requires attention to detail. (See illustration for the points discussed.) First of all, it is with the tickets that groups usually run afoul with the law. This is because raffle tickets cannot actually be "sold." We speak of "selling" tickets but actually what we should say is that the ticket is free and a donation of $1 (or whatever the amount determined) is requested. Technically, someone can ask for a free ticket and not give you any money. If you were to turn down that request, it would be clear that you are selling the ticket and that is against the law. In this article, we refer to "selling" the tickets because that is the common shorthand; however, keep in mind that we are not truly selling anything.

You must print on the ticket how a person can get a free ticket and that a list of winners will be available and supplied on request. This is to help ensure that the prizes are actually awarded. To increase sales, also indicate on the ticket that the donor doesn't have to be present to win.

The tickets must be numbered so that they are easy to keep track of. Although it costs more for the printer to number the tickets, it is worth it. Many organizations try to save money by not having numbered tickets or by numbering the tickets themselves. This is an unwise savings of money or a foolish use of time. It is also critical that the ticket stub be perforated so it can be easily separated from the body of the ticket. Don't save money by printing

cheap raffle tickets. Your volunteers will not distribute them as easily and donors will be reluctant to give their money when the ticket does not appear properly done.

Because of the need for numbering and perforation, not all printers can print raffle tickets. Find a printer who can, even if you cannot use your regular printer. Needless to say, seek to have the printing donated, but don't scrimp on print costs. They should be your only cost.

Notice in the illustration that the seller is asked to sign his or her name on the ticket stub. This is another incentive that you can build in to your raffle: giving a prize to any person who sold winning tickets. A person is obviously more likely to win such a prize if they have sold a lot of tickets.

To promote the organization, also include a box for the purchaser to check to get more information about the group's work. If you do make such an offer, be sure you go through all the tickets, pull out those with checked boxes, and send the information in a timely manner.

To know how many tickets to print, add up how many tickets the volunteer workers are willing to take and note what your goal is for the raffle. Always print at least 200 more tickets than your financial goal, because some tickets are bound to be lost or mutilated.

One final word concerning the law: Many groups send raffle tickets to potential donors through the mail. This is against postal law and, if caught, your letters will be sent back. If you send tickets by bulk mail, you risk having your bulk mail permit revoked.

In any case, raffles are not mail appeals. If you want to use the mail to raise money, do so, but do not combine raffles and mail appeals.

TICKET "SALES"

Step Four: Distribute and Keep Track of the Tickets

Make a list of everyone selling tickets and the numbers on the tickets they take. Keep track of the tickets as they are returned. Have a date by which all ticket stubs and donations are to be turned in. Call volunteers with unsold tickets to remind them of this deadline.

Step Five: Encourage the Workers

Call your volunteers at least once a week to see how they are doing with their tickets. Remind them of the deadline and to send in their stubs and cash. To encourage competition, tell them who is winning the "most sold" prize so far.

The job of the small committee is not to sell tickets, but to keep other people selling them. A raffle works best when organized like a pyramid, with the most tickets being sold by a large number of workers, and the smaller number of workers distributing the tickets to others. Raffles fail when there are not enough people selling tickets, or when the people who take tickets don't sell them. Be sure to have a lot of people selling tickets, and keep reminding them of due dates, praising those who are doing their job and encouraging those who aren't.

Every volunteer ought to be able to sell a minimum of 25 tickets. Most people who live in a town or city can sell 50 tickets in two or three weeks with no difficulty. Some people will be able to sell 100 to 500 in one or two months.

Step Six: Set Up the Drawing

The drawing is held on the date printed on the ticket. Some organizations hold the raffle drawing as part of another event, such as a dance or auction. Using a raffle as a part of another event increases your profit (and may sell more tickets right up to the moment of the drawing), but it involves organizing the other event as well. However, you don't need to have another event — it is fine to have a small party for all those who worked on the raffle and sold tickets and do the drawing there. If you have good food and drink, the drawing is then a celebration and a reward for a job well done, as well as a way to ensure that all the sold tickets are turned in on time.

Step Seven: Round Up the Tickets

Surprisingly, most people find the most difficult task in a raffle lies not in getting the prizes and not in getting the workers, but in getting the tickets and the cash back.

Some volunteers will be careless with their ticket stubs, or return stubs and promise cash later, or claim to have sold tickets when they really haven't. If you have encouraged people to turn in money and stubs as they go along, you will have less difficulty than if you wait to collect all the stubs and proceeds until just before the drawing. Final submission of stubs and cash should be due at least three days, and preferably five days, before the drawing. That way, you can ensure that you have all the tickets accounted for well ahead of time. People should turn in unsold tickets as well so that all numbers are accounted for.

The problem with a raffle is that all the transactions are in small amounts of cash. Someone sells three tickets to a co-worker, puts the stubs and dollar bills into their wallet, then goes to lunch and uses that cash for lunch without thinking. Later, they turn in more stubs than cash. Without a careful recordkeeping system, this error might not be caught.

Another advantage of getting ticket stubs in well ahead of time is that some people try to make their stub into the winning one by bending down a corner, sticking something on the back, or tearing it nearly in half and then taping it together. Workers will sometimes fold ticket stubs or spill stuff on them. These stubs cannot be used, and new stubs must be written. This is, in part, the use of the 200 or so extra tickets. For the drawing, the stubs must be as uniform as possible.

THE DRAWING AND BEYOND

Step Eight: Hold the Drawing

Get a big box or barrel for the ticket stubs. Be sure to mix and remix the stubs thoroughly after each prize is drawn. Start with the bottom prize and work up to the grand prize. Have a blindfolded adult or child do the actual drawing to guarantee neutrality.

After the prizes are drawn, announce the prizes for top salespeople and award these. Many organizations give several prizes to their salespeople. In addition to the person who sold the most tickets, they award a prize to the person who got the most prizes donated, to the person who got the most other people to sell tickets, to the person who sold the most tickets in a week or to a single person, and so on. Having a lot of prizes for salespeople is a good motivator for those who are competitive during the selling process and a nice reward at the end.

After the drawing, sort through the tickets to find those where people checked that they were interested in getting more information about your group.

Many organizations also use the ticket stubs to get names and addresses for a mail appeal later. It can be labor intensive to sort through the ticket stubs, eliminating current members' names and making sure that you only have one ticket stub for each person, even if they bought 20 tickets. However, this is a productive way to build a good mailing list.

Step Nine: Send Out the Prizes, Thank Yous, and Evaluate

Arrange for the winners to get their prizes, either by picking them up at your office or receiving them in the mail.

Send thank-you notes to each person who sold tickets and to all the merchants and others who donated prizes.

Count your money. Note how many tickets were unsold, where the problems were with the workers, the merchants, the tickets themselves, etc. Make a file with all the information about the raffle, including a list of winners, a list of people donating items, a list of volunteers, and notes about timing and other issues. The next year, it will be much simpler to do the raffle if a committee can pull out the file and benefit from the previous year's experience.

1987

Selling Social Change:
How to Earn Money from Your Mission

By ANDY ROBINSON

I have a confession to make: I don't trust capitalism. In fact, I've spent most of my professional life dealing with the messes created or abetted by our market economy — poverty, inequity, militarism, and environmental troubles, to name a few. So what I'm about to write surprises even me.

Capitalism — at least the small-scale, neighborhood-grown variety — can be an instrument for social change. Dozens of progressive organizations across the country are developing and selling goods and services that support and extend their missions. Ironically, many of these groups are anticapitalist — actively challenging the economic assumptions that drive our society — yet they have also found ways to earn significant income from sales. In doing so, they are discovering new strategies for educating their communities, activating their constituents, and expanding their budgets.

These nonprofits have gone way beyond T-shirts and coffee mugs, earning 10–40% of their revenue from mission-related sales. Some provide services: investment research, self-defense training, ecotourism, curriculum development. Others publish books and reports about their issues and programs. Still others sell goods ranging from traditional garden seeds to music CDs. All products are designed to support organizational goals; the fact that they generate income is an added benefit.

WHY EARNED INCOME?

The reasons for creating and selling goods and services are as varied as the nonprofits that do it. Among the most important are the following:

1. Funding diversity. Having a broad and diverse funding base — especially money raised from your community — is the most effective way to ensure the survival and good health of your organization. Sales income can be an important part of the mix.

2. Expand donor base. Sales, like fundraising, is built on relationships. Customers are good prospects for additional donations because 1) they know your work firsthand, 2) they believe in your mission, and 3) they've already written a check to your group. The inverse is also true: With modest effort, members/donors can be converted to buyers, which means they write you several checks each year.

3. Less reliance on grants. Grants are problematic for at least three reasons. Foundations and corporations combined provide only 12% of the private-sector money given to U.S. charities, so groups that rely on funding from these sources are chasing a small piece of a very large pie. Furthermore, fewer than 15% of all proposals submitted are actually funded, which makes for lousy odds. Finally, grants are known as "soft money" because they are seldom renewable. By developing a range of grassroots fundraising strategies, including earned income, nonprofits can have more control over their destiny, instead of relying on luck and the goodwill of grants officers. (Ironically, a diverse funding base makes it easier to get grants, since most grantmakers prefer to invest in successful groups that have broad support.)

4. Publicity and advocacy opportunities. The creation of goods and services provides "handles" for promoting your cause, as well as your products. With creativity and persistence, you can get a lot of free publicity from the news media.

5. Skill building and leadership development. To do this work successfully, your group will need expertise in market research, graphic design, advertising, promotions, accounting, customer service — it's a long list. Since you need most of these skills anyway to run any sort of non-profit, the process of developing and selling products can have a positive ripple effect throughout the organization. Along the way, you'll discover (or create) new opportunities to challenge, involve, and train your staff, board, and key volunteers.

DANGER: ROUGH ROAD AHEAD

If this sounds too good to be true, it probably is. Here are five reasons that an earned-income strategy might not be appropriate for your organization.

1. They add work. Accountant and trainer Terry Miller, who has advised many organizations, is wary of most earned-income strategies. When clients consider what he calls "venturesome activities," he often counsels against it. "Nonprofits are rarely managed well enough to run their regular projects," he says. By adding more work, he contends, they tend to divert management time and energy away from their main programs. Because of the potential for overload and burnout, he concludes, "most groups are not good candidates to add any sort of business venture."

2. Mission creep. Do you know what happens when you start shifting your goals and programs to take advantage of funding opportunities? If you're not careful, the tail (the need for money) starts wagging the dog (your mission). While this problem is most evident in the search for grant money, it can also arise through the sales of goods and services.

3. Up-front costs. You've heard it before: You have to spend money to make money. If you don't have start-up capital, nothing happens. You might identify a grantmaker or major donor who will subsidize the venture — either as an outright gift or a "program-related investment," through which a limited number of foundations provide funds at a low interest rate — but the research and application process will take at least six months. After all the work and waiting, your odds of getting funded are not good.

4. Potential tax liability. Even tax-exempt charities are liable for federal taxes on net income from sales of items or other business ventures unrelated to their mission. It's known as the Unrelated Business Income Tax, or UBIT. State and local taxes are also added in many areas. How can you determine what is "mission-related" and what isn't? Terry Miller offers a hypothetical example: A nonprofit day care center decides to publish and sell a baby-sitting guide, which includes educational games, tips on keeping kids entertained, food suggestions, emergency phone numbers, and so on. If the center's purpose, as

outlined in its articles of incorporation and application for tax exemption, is to provide day care, net income from the baby-sitting guide would be taxable. If, on the other hand, the organizing documents include language about child care education for parents and other caregivers, the net proceeds would be related to the exempt purpose, and therefore not taxable.

When he raises this example, Miller says, "most organizations scurry back to look at their founding documents." In other words, the decision about what constitutes "mission-related" may have been inadvertently made by your organization's founders when they filed for incorporation. This decision cannot be easily amended by rewriting the mission statement — the IRS looks at the founding documents, not the latest version. To allow for future flexibility, creators of new organizations would be wise to use broad language when defining the purpose of their groups.

5. Sometimes they lose money. Even the best ideas are not always profitable. Every earned-income strategy involves risk. How much risk can your organization handle? Stated another way, how much time and money can you afford to lose? Since both are precious, it pays to be cautious.

Now that you understand the pros and cons of earned income, let's see how this strategy works in practice.

NATIVE SEEDS/SEARCH

Native Seeds/SEARCH works to conserve the traditional crops, seeds, and farming methods that have sustained native peoples throughout the U.S. Southwest and northern Mexico. The organization, with offices in Tucson and Albuquerque, manages a seed bank with 1,800 crop varieties, including corn, beans, squash, chiles, sunflowers, melons, and gourds. More than 250 varieties are offered for sale to gardeners (and free to Native Americans living in the region). Since many of these crops are rare or endangered, one of the organization's goals is to distribute them widely to ensure their survival. By selling seeds, they support and promote their mission.

Four seasonal catalogs, mailed to 22,000 households, also feature traditional Southwestern foods, gardening books, native crafts, regional cookbooks, and gift baskets. Mail-order income, combined with walk-in sales, accounted for 38% of the group's $500,000 annual budget in 1996.

In deciding which items to include, executive director Angelo Joaquin, Jr., says, "If it helps indigenous farmers to stay on the land and keep farming, we should sell it." Joaquin, a member of the Tohono O'odham Nation, adds, "We educate the public about how native people think about life in this region. In that sense, we promote cultural diversity through the products we choose." Distribution manager Junie Hostetler adds three more criteria: quality, sales potential, and origin. "We're about to offer soup mixes and dried tomatoes from San Juan Pueblo in New Mexico," she says. "Whenever we buy directly from a Native American community, we're helping to fulfill our mission."

Native Seeds/SEARCH runs a diabetes education program targeting Native Americans, who face an epidemic of the disease. This program promotes the consumption of nutritious desert foods, which historically protected local peoples from diabetes. Many of these foods — tepary beans, chia and psyllium seeds, nopalitos (cactus pads) — are offered through the catalog and discounted to Native Americans. Joaquin is most excited about the recent availability of mesquite meal — ground from the seeds and pods of the mesquite tree — which consumers have been requesting for years.

In 1996, Native Seeds/SEARCH served more than 4,000 customers. Thirty percent were members of the organization, paying annual dues of at least $20 per year. Sales receipts make evident that these people were also the most generous and committed: The average member/customer spent 60% more on purchases than the average nonmember/customer. The organization encourages all shoppers to join through a special annual appeal. Last year, 10% were converted to members.

Over the next three to five years, Native Seeds/SEARCH plans to increase earned income to 50% of the organization's budget. Joaquin is banking on a new retail location in Tucson, which has exceeded projections during its first months of operation. He remains cautious about what goes into the store, however. "We could probably make a lot of money selling tourist-type things," he says, "but we're not driven by money. We have to convey respect for these seeds and the people who grow them. We are simply caretakers."

DATACENTER

DataCenter, which is based in Oakland, California, provides tactical research services to community organizations, labor unions, investigative journalists, and others. The organization was founded in 1976, with its mission "to give activists a strategic advantage through the power of information," says managing director Ruth Bukowiecki. Today, 25% of its $625,000 budget comes from client services fees, subscriptions, and other earned income; the balance is raised from donations and grants.

DataCenter services include customized research; a public access library; "current awareness" services to track press coverage of specific issues, people, or events; a computerized listing of plant closures and layoffs; Information Services Latin America (ISLA), a press reprint service covering developments in Latin America; and Culture-Watch, a monthly newsletter profiling activities of the religious right wing. The organization serves about 1,000 clients each year, including the American Civil Liberties Union, Greenpeace, Hotel Employees and Restaurant Employees International Union, and the Silicon Valley Toxics Coalition.

Immigration attorneys needing human rights documentation for their clients contract with DataCenter, which has a long history with Latin American issues and sources. Journalists often hire the organization for investigative research. An emerging customer base is socially responsible investment firms, which seek information on corporate labor practices, minority hiring, human rights records, environmental policies, etc. For example, the California employee pension program recently hired DataCenter to review layoff announcements of companies in its stock portfolio.

Unfortunately, many clients — especially grassroots groups — cannot afford research services, which cost $85 to $140 per hour. So DataCenter offers a sliding-scale fee. While few nonprofits pay full rate, Bukowiecki says, "most pay something." To make up the difference, the organization aggressively seeks full-charge customers and solicits foundation grants for its pro bono program.

Prospective customers — even those who can pay — have to meet the DataCenter profile before they are accepted. Says Bukowiecki, "We have turned down corporate clients who want marketing information on Latin America, such as Nike, because we don't agree with their practices."

To find new clients, and to keep tabs on the needs of social change groups, staff have begun traveling to conferences to lead workshops on doing research. The group is building stronger ties to the labor movement — a big prospective client — and also working with foundations to identify grantee organizations that would benefit from research assistance.

One thing that Bukowiecki does not want is lots of coverage in the general-interest media. "If you're in the news daily," she warns, "95% of your calls will be inappropriate." She cites the example of students looking for help with their research papers. Her message: Target your outreach to the customers you most want to serve. Everything else is wasted effort.

SOUTHWEST ORGANIZING PROJECT

SouthWest Organizing Project, or SWOP, is a multi-racial community organization in Albuquerque. SWOP works to promote racial and gender equality, and social and economic justice, by promoting self-determination for disenfranchised communities. The group is involved in a variety of issues: fighting corporate welfare, promoting fair pay and improved conditions for farmworkers, stopping toxic waste dumping in poor neighborhoods, and resisting Albuquerque's expansion into Native American sacred sites, to name a few.

As part of its community education strategy, SouthWest Organizing Project has an active publications program. One of the titles SWOP has published is *500 Years of Chicano History,* a 240-page book with 800 pictures, which builds on an earlier edition published in 1976 by the Chicano Communications Center. All told, more than 22,000 copies have been distributed.

To promote the book, SWOP mails flyers to school districts, individual teachers, and bilingual education associations. They sell directly to bookstores and distributors — Barnes & Noble, Borders, Baker & Taylor — and feature *500 Years* in their newsletter, *Voces Unidas,* which has a circulation of 11,000 households. The group also offers an annual discount to encourage holiday gift buyers.

According to Louis Head, SWOP's development coordinator, Chicano youth are consistently good customers, which means the organization is reaching its number one target market. To reach well-to-do progressives, the organization put ordering information about the book on the Internet. But, Head says, "the biggest response came from Chicano students."

SWOP also distributes an accompanying curriculum guide and an English-language video, *¡Viva la Causa! 500 Years of Chicano History,* with narration, archival footage, and lively music ranging from traditional corridos to rap. Three hundred copies of the "teaching packet" — book, curriculum guide, and video — have sold at $114 each. A Spanish-language version of the video will be available this fall. (This is a terrific example of how to augment successful products, and increase income, by creating new products that appeal to the same consumers.)

SouthWest Organizing Project also publishes *Intel Inside New Mexico: A Case Study of Environmental and Economic Injustice.* When it opened a plant in the Albuquerque area, Intel received large tax subsidies, permits to draw water from the local aquifer, streamlined air-emissions regulations, and a host of other concessions in exchange for the promise of local jobs. This report documents SWOP's long-running campaign to make the semiconductor manufacturer more accountable to the public. The report is being purchased by government agencies, city councils, community organizations, and socially responsible investors who are monitoring the high-tech industry in their own communities. "As the level of understanding about this industry starts to change," says Head, "more and more people are asking for our materials."

From all of its products, SWOP will earn $40,000–$45,000 from sales this year, or 15% of its budget. "People who understand the funding diversity issue," says Head, "get excited when we tell them about our sales income."

CAN IT WORK FOR YOUR GROUP?

There you have it, the promise, the pitfalls, and three successful examples. If you're ready to explore potential earned-income strategies for your organization, you'll need to do some basic market research. Consider the following points.

1. What do you now offer — products, services, expertise — that someone might buy? Would any current clients — people or organizations you serve for free — be willing to pay for your work? If so, how much would they pay? How can you best convert them from clients to customers? How will you identify and recruit new customers?

2. What's your niche — how is your work unique? How can you differentiate your products and/or services from others that are also available?

3. What resources — time, money, skills — can you apply to developing and marketing your goods and services? How much will this effort cost, and when will you need the money? How will you develop and/or hire the skills you lack? How much time and money can you afford to spend before your earned-income strategies actually earn income?

4. How will your proposed activities affect your tax status and tax liability?

5. Who are your role models? Which organizations in your field or your community generate earned income, and how do they do it? Which groups have tried and failed? What can you learn from their experiences?

6. Any other potential obstacles? How will you anticipate and address these problems?

If you're baffled by any of these questions, you would be wise to back off, reevaluate, conduct more research, redesign, or perhaps abandon your earned-income fantasies. On the other hand, if you can answer them all with confidence, you might be ready to launch your new venture. Good luck!

1998

A Small Town Tackles a Big Project

By SHIRLEY WILCOX

On September 28, 1990, just two weeks after Roann, Indiana's annual Covered Bridge Festival, someone set the historic bridge afire. Although firefighters from eight departments responded, flames shot high into the evening sky and the bridge was left a charred, smoking hulk. A landmark built in 1877, Roann Covered Bridge is on the National Register of Historic Places.

Over the years, this small rural community had lost its school, its merchants, and its major enterprises to larger towns. Losing the bridge was a big blow. It was, as local citizen Ann Mullenix said, "almost like losing a member of your family."

When stunned citizens gathered the next morning, their meeting amounted to a wake. But about ten days later, they met again to consider what could be done.

THE TOWN TAKES HEART

The meeting began on a doubtful, downbeat note, voices negative, faces gloomy. Repairs that might take years and cost a million dollars seemed impossible for a rural village of 500 to pay for.

That's where Amos Schwartz came in. A contractor from Geneva, Indiana, Schwartz chided the people of Roann for being faint of heart. In his slight Swiss accent, he said not only should the bridge be saved, but the job could be done for $250,000 to $300,000. Says townsperson Henry Becker, "Schwartz was just the man we needed. A sense of purpose seized us." Everybody in town began to believe the bridge could be reconstructed.

And everyone cared. That's where the town's strength lay.

Townsfolk formed the Roann Covered Bridge Association and began to consider how to proceed. If they were going to do anything, there was no time to waste. The Historic Landmarks Foundation of Indiana had a grant available, but only about four days were left in which to apply. To qualify, they had to raise $10,000 in matching funds.

Volunteers went door-to-door, and within those four days $8,000 funneled in. "It was a good cause. We didn't have to explain or sell," one solicitor noted. A couple of $1,000 donations put them over the top and the grant was theirs.

That made a big $20,000 boost toward the Roann Covered Bridge Association's next effort — an auction held the day after Thanksgiving. As word went around, auction items came in by the truckload — things that might ordinarily have gone into a spate of garage sales. When the last "Sold!" sounded, $17,700 had been raised. Best of all, no cash outlay had been necessary. Everything from several Exercycles to the services of the auctioneer and his crew had been donated.

SMALL EVENTS ADD UP

Bridge repair estimates had now been finalized at $320,000. Meeting each Thursday to brainstorm where the remaining funds would come from, townspeople came up with a potpourri of fundraisers. No idea was too small to be considered, and many small enterprises brought in money that brought up the total raised.

In conjunction with the November auction, a craft and bake sale had gone well. They held another bake sale. Canisters placed in stores in surrounding towns brought in more than $3,000 for the fund. Softball games cleared $500.

Indiana is well known for basketball fervor. What is not so well known is that after graduation, Hoosier players form community, factory, and church teams and continue playing for fun. The fundraising group decided to use them, setting up a tournament to which teams from nearby towns were invited. Henry Becker, now treasurer for the bridge fund, was able to bank another $2,100 from the basketball tourney. "They played pretty good ball, too," said Becker.

Aluminum collection stations, set up at convenient spots on nearby highways, brought in nearly $3,500, thanks to the generosity of the local aluminum company, which gave a 20-cent premium for each can collected.

The group's biggest single moneymaker, however, was a 300-page cookbook, put together by Louella Krom. All recipes were donated. As first and second printings of 1,500 quickly sold out, 3,000 more copies were ordered and they, too, sold well. The cookbook cleared $24,000.

Wabash County originally had five covered bridges. Local artist Gladys Schuman had sketched all five. Her sketches, donated by her son, Philip Fawley, were reproduced in miniature to make unique note paper. Sales of these added to the cause.

Many other small projects sprang up. A donation of $2 lit a colored bulb on the community Christmas tree, each light in honor of friend or family. The tree came to glowing life, and credits listed in the weekly *Bridge Bulletin* sparked interest.

The *Bridge Bulletin* was another project that grew from the association's Thursdays night brainstorming sessions. Published weekly by association member Ann Mullenix, the *Bulletin* kept interest high and information current. Copies were left on post office counters, distributed through stores and businesses, and rested beside the salt, pepper, and ketchup on each table in Roann's sole restaurant. Not only did the *Bulletin* increase turnout for fundraising activities, but weekly updates of funds raised won over early disbelievers.

Some fundraisers sprang up as private projects. Jim Huffman bought Rubbermaid bird feeders in the shape of a covered bridge. Painting these barn red, Huffman attached a miniature "Roann Covered Bridge" sign and a price tag of $25. In all, 80 were sold, and, after the first 5 that Huffman bought to decorate, the rest were donated, 25 of them by the Rubbermaid Company.

Jim's brother Chuck crafted and sold bridge belt buckles, clocks with a woodburned bridge design, and sweatshirts printed with a picture of the Roann Covered Bridge. All proceeds went into the fund.

Several people had had the presence of mind to photograph the bridge in flames, and one of these dramatic photos went onto a brochure. When businesses enclosed these with client or vendor correspondence, come sizeable donations drifted in — $75, $100. Eventually, corporate donations totaled $5,200, even without an organized industrial drive. The bridge association felt businesses already got asked too often.

County schoolteachers, who saw the covered bridge fire as an opportunity to enliven history lessons, also pitched in. One roomful of children at O. J. Neighbors School in Wabash, Indiana, raffled toys donated by Toys-R-Us, adding $80 to the bridge fund. Responding to letters from teachers of Metro North Elementary School, schoolchildren from elementary schools all over Indiana sent small amounts. Their contributions totaled $2,740.

The Roann Covered Bridge Association's Thursday sessions were open to any and all ideas. However, realizing that a small fundraising base hasn't room for long odds, they turned down things like a book of coupons usable in local stores that would return only $1 for every $29 worth of sales. As their fund grew, the bridge association could proudly say that for every dollar collected, approximately 96 cents stayed in the fund.

The effort was run on a businesslike basis, with month-to-month reports of contributions, expenses, and banking activities printed out for committee meetings. Cannily invested in interest-bearing accounts, the fund also grew of itself. As contributions were deposited, interest income mounted to $3,500, and continued to grow until all the money was spent for construction costs.

MINIMAL EXPENSES

The biggest fundraising plus for this group may have been in keeping advertising and other expenses to a minimum. Merchants sponsored ads for basketball games, auctions, suppers, and other projects. Printing costs of the *Bridge Bulletin* were underwritten by anonymous donors. Volunteers contributed many hours and few turned in requests for reimbursement of expenses.

Little or no financial layout was required for a spring street festival, with games, dunk tank, and the like staffed by volunteers. Farmers donated nine hogs for the sausage and pancake breakfast and the hog roast supper, and the festival cleared $4,200 from these events.

Suppers put on by volunteers were also a smash success. This was partly because everyone in town reachable by telephone received a personal invitation. Callers divided up the local phone book — "You take the A's and B's; I'll take the C's and D's" — and telephoned every household. For the chili supper, more supplies had to be rushed in — twice. Fresher chili was never served.

GOVERNMENT AGENCIES TAKE NOTICE

In the midst of these efforts, Wabash County commissioners, taking notice of the unique value of a covered bridge, voted $35,000 for its repair. That, and a grant of $219,000 from the Indiana Department of Commerce, put Roann Covered Bridge Association's fundraising over the top.

At the beginning of their undertaking, the group had no idea that such a large grant was available. When they learned about it, they didn't much care for the idea of hiring professionals to process an application. However, as amateurs in the ways of government, they may not have secured this grant without help. Certainly, they would not have received it so quickly.

The firm from Fort Wayne that was hired to handle the application also administered the grant. "They charge a lot," said a committee member, "$2,800 to apply, $9,500 to administer the grant. We didn't really like that, but it seemed necessary to have someone who knew the ropes." Recommended by a representative from the Department of Commerce, the firm secured the grant from the department in three months. By now, Roann Covered Bridge Association had raised $65,000, and this favorable percentage of local money seemed to impress the grant committee.

Thus, only six short, busy months after their bridge burned, the village of Roann raised the final dollar needed for its repair. The town celebrated.

GRACE NOTES

The town's fundraising effort has ended on a grace note — in fact, more than one. At the 1991 annual bridge festival, Roann Covered Bridge Association sponsored wagon rides and a tour of the old river mill, closed to tour groups for several years, as a small return for the town's outpouring of goodwill and funds.

Amos Schwartz, the contractor, videotaped reconstruction of the bridge, which began December 1, 1991, and donated copies of the tape to schools as a public service. Spliced into tapes of the bridge burning, this video has become a vivid reminder of the lasting damage carelessness and vandalism can inflict.

The aluminum recycling effort begun to raise bridge funds continued as an antilittering conservation project.

Meanwhile, based on the momentum they created raising funds to repair the bridge, members of Roann Covered Bridge Association raised an additional $32,000 to install a sprinkler system in the repaired bridge. The sprinklers were installed in 1992.

Thanks to a potpourri of fundraising ideas and many willing volunteers, a continuing place on the map has been ensured for this gutsy Indiana village and its unique bridge.

Large numbers of people from all over the United States now visit the bridge. Although they could drive across the bridge, most visitors prefer to walk across. Joggers, hikers, and bikers are its main traffic, while automobiles zip across Eel River on an adjacent concrete span erected by Indiana's Department of Transportation.

Because a wooden structure is in need of regular maintenance, fundraising efforts continue. Louella Krom's cookbook has been reissued. Funds raised from its sale will go to repaint the bridge.

1992

Organizational &
Board Development

The Board and Fundraising

By KIM KLEIN

The broad purpose of a board of directors is to run the organization effectively. To do so, board members are bound to ensure that an organization is operating within state and federal laws, earning its money honestly and spending it responsibly, and adopting programs and procedures most conducive to carrying out its mission. Among the responsibilities that board members must assume in carrying out the board's purpose is responsibility for the continued funding and financial health of the organization. In this respect, board members have two tasks: to give money and to raise money. More often than not, however, board members are hesitant to embrace these two activities.

The resistance to giving money is often expressed with the argument, "Time is money." Board members often feel that because they give time they should not be called on to give money.

The reluctance of board members to take responsibility for raising money can usually be traced to three sources: 1) Board members don't understand the importance of taking a leadership role in fundraising, 2) they are afraid to ask for money, and 3) if an organization has paid staff, board members may feel that it is the staff's job to fundraise.

Let's look at each of these problems more closely.

TIME IS NOT MONEY

While a person's time is valuable to them, it is not the same as money. You cannot go to the telephone company and offer to run its switchboard in order to pay your phone bill. You cannot pay your staff or buy your office supplies with your time. And whereas everyone has the same amount of time in a day, people have vastly unequal amounts of money.

Comparing time and money is like comparing apples and asphalt. Board members must understand that contributions of time and money are very different, although equally important, parts of their role.

BOARD LEADERSHIP IN FUNDRAISING

The reason that board members must take a leadership role in fundraising is simple: They own the organization. They are responsible for the well-being of the organization and for its successes. Furthermore, the organization's supporters and potential supporters see board members as the people most committed and dedicated to the organization. If they, who care the most about the group, will not take a lead role in fundraising, why should anyone else support the group?

When the board does take the lead, its members and the staff approaching individuals, corporations, and foundations for funds can say, "We have 100% commitment from our board. All board members give money and raise money." This position strengthens their fundraising case a great deal. More and more, sophisticated individuals and foundations are asking organizations about the role of the board in fundraising and taking a more positive look at groups whose boards play an active part.

However, when it comes to asking people for money, even board members who willingly donate may be reluctant to ask others to do so. This sometimes seems ironic in light of the fact that most people are rarely nervous to ask someone for their time, even though, unlike money, time is a nonrenewable resource.

In training, I often use this example: "If a board member is assigned to call three people and tell them about a meeting on Wednesday night, he or she will most likely do it. If two people can come to the meeting and one can't, the board member does not take this personally and feel like a failure. However, if this same board member is assigned to ask these same three people for $100 each, he or she will probably be very uncomfortable without training in how to ask for money."

Asking for money is a skill and thus can be learned. All board members should have the opportunity to attend a training session on asking for money, as many fundraising strategies require board members to make face-to-face solicitations.

Not Everyone Has to Ask for Money All the Time

In a diversified fundraising plan, however, some board members can participate in fundraising strategies that do not require asking for money directly. While some can solicit large gifts, others can plan special events, write mail appeals, market products for sale, write thank-you notes, stuff envelopes, enter information into a database, etc. Everyone's interests and skills can be used.

Board members inexperienced in fundraising can start with an easy assignment ("Sell these 20 raffle tickets") and then move on to more difficult assignments ("Ask this person for $1,000"). Some fundraising strategies will use all the board members (selling tickets to the dance), whereas others will require the work of only one or two people (speaking to service clubs or writing mail appeals).

PAID STAFF CANNOT DO IT ALL

Paid staff also have specific roles in fundraising. These are to help plan fundraising strategies, coordinate fundraising activities, keep records, take care of routine fundraising tasks such as renewal appeals, and assist board members by writing letters for them, form fundraising plans with them, and accompany them to solicitation meetings.

Fundraising staff provide all the backup needed for effective fundraising. It is clearly impossible, however, for one person or even several people to do all the work necessary in a diversified fundraising plan. Just as it is foolish for an organization to depend on one or two sources of funding, it is equally unwise for it to depend on one or two people to do fundraising.

SHARING THE WORK AND THE POWER

The final reason for all board members to participate in fundraising is to ensure that the work is evenly shared. Fundraising is rarely anyone's favorite task, so it is impor-

tant that each board member knows that the other members are doing their share. If a few members do all the fundraising, resentments are bound to arise.

The same resentments will surface if some board members give money and others don't. Those who give may feel that their donation "buys" them out of some work or that their money entitles them to more power. Those who do not give money may feel that they do all the work or that those who give money have more power.

When board members know that everyone is giving their best effort to fundraising according to their abilities, the board will function most smoothly and all members will be more willing to take on fundraising tasks.

"I Don't Know Anyone with Money"

In the August, 1985 *Grassroots Fundraising Journal* article "Major Donor Prospecting," Kim Klein wrote, "Someone should write a song with 'I don't know anyone with money' as the chorus." Margaret Becker, a consultant in nonprofit management and fundraising, did just that.

Sung to the tune of *"Side by Side"*
Board Member stands and faces the rest of the group, singing:

> I don't know anybody with money!
> Maybe you think I'm being funny
> But it's perfectly true
> There's nothin' I can do
> Fellow Board Members.
>
> No one ever told me the truth here
> "Bout Board Members raising money this year
> I'm just a volunteer
> Can't you see my fear?
> Fellow Board Members.

Refrain:

> > Let the staff do it!
> > Let the staff volunteer.
> > As long as we love the program
> > Maybe the money'll appear.
>
> When they've all had their flops
> And quit trying
> We'll cut the budget and buyin'
> And our programs will cease
> With me still at peace,
> Fellow Board Members.

1997

When Board Members Wriggle Out of Fundraising

By KIM KLEIN

A friend called me recently with a problem I have been hearing rather often lately. She is the director of a five-year-old grassroots community organizing project in a big city. Each board member was carefully screened and oriented. They knew that fundraising would be a major part of their board work, and they were told that fact as many times as possible. I have trained that board myself in how to ask for money and have reviewed the organization's fundraising plans, written materials, prospect lists, and so on.

The board members are honorable, decent, hard working people. They have good politics and they span a broad cross-section of the community. There are eight women and seven men, half are people of color, three are disabled, two are lesbians, and one is a gay man. They are from a range of class backgrounds. From a social justice perspective and from an organizational development viewpoint, it is almost a perfect board. They were recruited properly, trained well and thoroughly, they are committed to the work of the organization, and they are very effective in everything except fundraising.

This is the problem of my friend, the director. Here's what she told me:

Our six-week campaign ended three months ago. People took their prospect names and then didn't do the work. Each person had a reasonable excuse such as, "My mother is sick," "I had a root canal and couldn't talk," "My names were stolen along with the radio out of my car," and so on. As a result, we extended the campaign another month. Then more awful things happened to everybody, like falling down the stairs, pressure at work, ear infection, dog died, and so on. We had raised only $1,000 toward a goal of $15,000! Only two people had done their work. Everyone felt bad, so we extended the campaign another two weeks.

Now people are saying that they have called their prospects, or they have tried to call many times, or the prospect said that he or she would send money. But very few prospects have sent money, and when I have run into prospects at parties or around town, some have said, "I haven't heard from your group in a long time." I hate to say it, but I think my board members are lying to me about their fundraising.

I hate to say it, but I think she's right. In fact, the lying started with the number of crises that affected every board member the day the campaign started. Probably two or three people did have legitimate reasons for not getting to their work, and everyone else realized how good that sounded. Since only the most accident-prone, bad-luck person can keep having a new crisis each week the campaign is extended, some people are now forced to say that they have done their work but they don't know why their people aren't responding. Three months after the end of a six-week $15,000 campaign, this group has $2,500 and a demoralized board.

Each group that is experiencing the phenomenon of having set up a thoughtful structure, brought on wonderful and carefully screened board members, trained them, prepared them, and then sent them off to do their fundraising with little result is different in some ways, but there are some similarities. The following are possibilities of what may have happened. Not all will apply to any one group, and no single possibility will entirely explain what happened. But each can provide some insight and suggest opportunities for change.

WHO CLEANS THE COOP

In every case I have heard of, the director of the organization was raising money along with the board, and the director actually was bringing money in. Thus, the organization could keep running without the board members doing their work, at least for the time being. In several cases, the director finally took the prospect lists from each board member and did the fundraising themselves. Board members were spared any consequences of their actions, and the message from the director was clear: If you don't do your work, I'll do it for you.

This situation reminds me of a friend who grew up on a farm. One of her jobs was cleaning out the chicken coop, which she hated and loathed and which made her slightly nauseated. She would put it off so long that her mother would finally do it. My friend would be grounded for a week, severely chastised, and would feel bad that her already overworked mother had to take on this extra task, but no matter what happened to her, it was better than actually cleaning out the chicken coop.

There are two solutions to this problem: one, the "tough love" response, which is "Let the chickens live in dirt and die that way," which, in fundraising translates to, "Let the group not get this money." In some ways this is ideal, because it makes immediately clear what happens when the board doesn't do its work. However, it also drags some innocent parties into the fray. In the case of an organization, the staff might not get paid or the clients might go unserved — an expensive way to make a point.

Another possibility is to acknowledge what has happened and redefine the campaign. In our case study, the first step would be to end the campaign when it was due to end. The campaign was not successful. Extending it merely put good time after bad into it. If it had ended the day it was supposed to, the board would have had to decide how to raise the $14,000 that the campaign didn't. Freed of the tasks they had not accomplished during the campaign, each person would have been able to say what was true for them such as, "I can only ask for money from people I don't know. I can't ask my friends." Or, "I need to go on somebody else's call with them a few times. I just can't imagine how this works." They can admit to the real reasons for not doing their work. Each person's needs can now be accommodated.

THE GAME GOES ON

Social change organizations, and nonprofits in general, try to reflect compassion and understanding in how they do their work, as well as in the work itself. We are all aware that process and product are not separable. Thus, when anyone has a crisis, we tend to be understanding and supportive. This is good and should not be changed. However, in the organizations that have contacted me because board members were not doing their fundraising, people were given a lot of time at board meetings to discuss whatever crisis was hanging them up. Although some people were experiencing true problems, the real crisis was that everyone was praying for a disaster so they wouldn't have to do their fundraising. It quickly became in style to be in crisis, and people who were managing to do their fundraising constituted a small minority.

Fundraising campaigns must be run so that at all times it appears that most people are getting their work done, and not the reverse. Every letter written, every phone call made, every tiny piece of work is reported and acknowledged, and reasons for not doing work, regardless of how legitimate, are played down. For a person in genuine crisis, the board chair or development staff will confer privately and remove their tasks until the person can take them on again. Like a player injured in a football game, that person is "benched" and the rest of the team plays without him or her. The game goes on. It lasts the same amount of time and the rules are the same.

DO IT TOGETHER

Fundraising staff need to be proactive in order to lessen frustration and reach solutions more quickly. There are several common reasons that board members won't actually go ask for money, even after dozens of training sessions and hours of preparation. One reason is that the board member is afraid to go alone. The staff person can offer to go with them if asked, but the board member has to admit vulnerability in order to ask. Instead, the staff person can try calling a board member who seems reluctant and say, "I have an appointment with Robin Rolling next week. Can you come with me? I think Robin would really like to meet one of our board members." Now the board member can do you a favor and also see how a solicitation works.

A second reason is that board members feel the process is going to take too long. The bulk of time, of course, is spent agonizing over the process. To get past this problem, build two weekday evening get-togethers into the campaign. The first evening everyone comes to the office and writes their letters to potential major donors. The second evening, everyone comes and makes their phone calls requesting an appointment. This creates both peer pressure and peer support, and it also adds deadlines to the campaign. The campaign begins on a certain day, by another date all letters are written, by a third date all phone calls are made, and by a fourth date all visits are set up.

TRY HONESTY

If all else fails, try honesty. Privately say to a board member, "It seems like this is really hard for you. What can I do to make it better?" Cutting to the crux of the problem will let the board member admit what is going on. You can then decide how to solve the problem.

Building a fundraising board takes more time than it should. Over the years I have realized that while everything we print in the *Journal* works, it doesn't work all the time. Sometimes the board simply doesn't come together around fundraising. When that happens, you need to bring on new board members, bring in other volunteers to help — anything to create a different dynamic in the group. The group has a personality that is bigger and different from the individual personalities in the group. Constantly assessing what kind of "corporate culture" you are creating will allow you to intercept unproductive dynamics before they take over.

1989

How to Get Your Board to Raise Money: Plan X

By KIM KLEIN

As longtime *Journal* readers know, we have offered dozens of ideas over the years about ways to get board members to raise money. We have outlined the rationale for board members to be involved in fundraising and tried to shame, cajole, reward, threaten, coax, or badger board members into raising money. We have suggested dozens of different ways board members can be involved in fundraising without directly asking for money. In fact, we have written so many articles on this topic that we have compiled the best of them into a very popular booklet called *The Board of Directors*. Judging from sales of that booklet and repeated requests for training on the subject, we flatter ourselves that we have been helpful.

However, over the years it has struck me that part of the problem of getting board members to raise money is the structure of the board's fundraising committee. People have tried to make that structure work in various ways, which is why this article is called "Plan X" — we have gone through Plans A–W already.

Plan X promotes the possibly shocking idea of getting rid of your fundraising committee. The existence of the fundraising committee may be one of the main reasons that board members don't raise money. The committee is often made up of some combination of people who weren't at the meeting when the committees were formed, the newest board members, and people who have been on the committee for a long time and are burned out. This collection of people is not particularly effective as a committee.

Even if everyone on the committee has chosen to be there, they will be coming to fundraising from very different viewpoints. One person will suggest doing an event in order to raise the organization's visibility. Another will argue that an event is too much work for too little money. That person will make a compelling case for a major donor campaign. A third will say that the problem is that the group doesn't reach out to people enough and will suggest a phone or direct mail campaign to bring in a lot of new donors. The group will debate the pros and cons of each idea without realizing that the organization should probably engage in all three strategies.

Sometimes people are recruited onto the fundraising committee with the promise that their job is to coordinate the fundraising work of the rest of the board. The committee members develop a plan and what each board member's role should be and then spend their time resenting the other board members for not doing the work that has been assigned to them. Board members not on the fundraising committee resent the work assignments because they are serving on other committees, and some of them went to great lengths not to be on the fundraising committee because they don't want to do fundraising.

TWO OPTIONS FOR REPLACING THE FUNDRAISING COMMITTEE

This article outlines two options for reorganizing the way fundraising is divided among your board members. These options offer a way to structure fundraising along more logical lines and should be seen as a way to implement the fundraising efforts you are probably already making.

Option One: Go from One Committee to Four

Replace the single fundraising committee with four committees which are named after and do the work implied in the three functions of fundraising — acquisition, retention, and upgrade.

The acquisition committee is in charge of all efforts to get people to become donors: direct mail, special events, media, speaking engagements — any effort whose main or sole purpose is to recruit new donors who have not given before. The acquisition committee's success is measured by how many donors it brings in rather than how much money it raises. This measure is valid because acquisition strategies are the costliest to implement, and sometimes even successful acquisition efforts lose money. This is the perfect committee for board members who are willing to ask friends to join, or those members who like speaking at Rotary Clubs, churches, synagogues, neighborhood meetings, and so on, or those people who like mingling at events with people they have never met.

The retention committee does all the work that goes into getting people to renew their gift. They supervise or even put out the newsletter, oversee the database, send out extra appeals for money, and conduct the yearly phone-a-thon to members. Some special events, especially open houses or the annual general meeting in membership organizations, fall under the purview of this committee.

This is the perfect committee for people who are willing to talk to people who are known to be supportive of your group. Their goals relate to retaining both money and people. This committee keeps track of your retention rate and makes sure it is what it should be. (An organization's retention rate is the percentage of donors giving one year who give the next. A good retention rate is about 66% — in other words, of all the people who gave one year, two-thirds of that group gave again the next year. Higher retention rates usually indicate that the group has a weak acquisition program — not enough donors are being brought in. Lower retention rates probably indicate that donors are not being asked for money often enough.)

The upgrade committee (more traditionally known as the major gifts committee) has two somewhat different tasks. First, they identify people who could give large gifts (a major gift is defined by the organization, but is generally any gift over $100). Most of these people will come from the existing list of donors, but this committee may also invite people to become first-time donors to the organization with a large gift. Second, the upgrade committee works with the top 10% of the donors to ask them to renew or increase their giving. (In an organization with a successful program of individual donors, the top 10% should be supplying 60% of the money the organization raises from individuals.) Because this committee works closely with a smaller number of donors, their success is measured in large part by how much money they raise.

The upgrade committee will oversee or implement the major donor drives, possibly the pledge system, cultivation events, special mailings to major donors, and the like. This committee is for board members comfortable with asking for money in person and those who want to raise the most money for their fundraising efforts.

One member from each committee is assigned to an oversight committee (a more true fundraising committee) so that the acquisitions, retention, and upgrade committees coordinate their work and have a clear division of tasks. Sometimes one or two of the committees may work together on a strategy, such as an event aimed at both new and old donors.

The amount of work and even the kind of work each committee does depends in large part on how many paid staff are involved in fundraising. If the organization has a full-time development director, that person will do much of the coordination and overall planning. She or he may handle all the mailings and the newsletter. Each organization can work this out, so that everyone's efforts are being used in the most effective way. The acquisition and retention committees understand that their work is in part to move people to the next level — from prospect to new donor, new donor to continuing donor, from continuing donor to major donor.

Organizations that are building an endowment or planning for a capital campaign will have to create committees for those fundraising activities as well. Many organizations that have gone to this system have also brought people who are not board members onto each of the committees to augment the work of the board members.

Everyone on the board is on one of these committees, so there is no ducking out of fundraising. However, each committee requires different skills, and this structure allows the organization to play to each board member's strength.

Several groups I have worked with have converted to this structure. Some have really liked it, others are still deciding how they like it. However, none of the groups has gone back to the old style of a single fundraising committee because, with this system, each group has experienced more involvement from more board members.

Option Two: Move from Standing Committees to Ad Hoc Committees

Option Two argues against having any standing committees. Many boards are using this idea already with functions like nominating, hiring, or strategic planning. The committees are formed, do their work, and dissolve. Finance, personnel, and fundraising have not lent themselves to this structure as easily because they are ongoing functions. However, there is a way to organize your fundraising on this ad hoc basis. To do so, your fundraising plan needs to be structured so that as many strategies as possible are time-limited activities and as little as possible is ongoing. When the plan is put on a calendar, at any given time no more than two strategies are being actively pursued. Then committees are formed for each strategy. The following sample calendar shows how this ad hoc committee structure could work:

JANUARY 5–MARCH 1: MEMBERSHIP DRIVE

Goal: 250 new members; income goals to be determined.

Strategies: Mail; one-day all-volunteer canvass; Annual General Meeting March 1.

Membership Committee: Ten people: three oversee acquisition mailing, three recruit and train current members to carry out canvass, and four plan Annual General Meeting.

Budget: To be determined with Development Director.

MARCH 15–APRIL 15: RENEWAL CAMPAIGN

Goal: 400 renewals with a median gift of $50 = $20,000 minimum.

Strategies: Send out renewal mailing, with follow-up phone call at phone-a-thon evenings of April 2–3.

Renewal committee: Three people plus volunteers for phone-a-thon.

Budget: $500 for mailing and snacks at phone-a-thon.

MAY 1–AUGUST 1: HOUSE PARTIES

Goal: ten house parties raising $1,000 each = $10,000 from 200 new or upgraded donors.

Strategy: Find ten people to host house parties they think could bring in $1,000. Create generic invitation each host can use with house party packet. Help hosts figure out how many people to invite, when to have it, and who should speak.

House Party Committee: Two people plus ten hosts plus three speakers who can cover all ten parties. The two people on the committee may also be hosts or speakers.

Budget: $1,000 for invitations and materials to give out at parties.

SEPTEMBER 10–OCTOBER 30: MAJOR DONOR CAMPAIGN

Goal: $50,000 raised from 200 donors.

Strategy: Combination of personal letters, follow-up phone calls and visits to current high-end donors.

Major Donor Committee: Five people to coordinate plus 15 more to help with prospect identification, letters, calls, and visits.

Budget: $1,500 for training major gifts committee, materials for committee members and for donors.

NOVEMBER 10–DECEMBER 15: YEAR-END WRAP-UP

Goal: Ask everyone to renew who hasn't already done so; make sure all major donors have received proper follow-up; send out year-end appeal to current donors; hold open house.

Strategies: Mail, phone, personal letters and personal phone calls, open house.

Year-End Wrap-Up Committee: Three people plus the rest of board and staff for discrete projects.

Goals and Budget: To be determined depending on outcome of previous strategies.

Notice that there are about two weeks between the end of one fundraising period and the beginning of the next. Designing fundraising this way will depend on having a full-time development director, as a lot of coordination, preparation, and follow-up are required to make this work. However, this is a great way to get board members involved because they only have to work on one strategy plus be available for the year-end wrap-up. Once they have finished house parties or the phone-a-thon, they do not need to think about fundraising until that strategy comes around the next year.

Organizations that have used this option report great success or great failure with it, depending on the experience of the development director with all these strategies and his or her ability to work well with a constantly changing set of volunteers. The other variable is having enough people to call on for specific tasks. This option will definitely fail if the same people are making the calls at the phone-a-thon, then hosting a house party, followed by asking for money in person and then helping with the year-end wrap-up. That is a formula for certain burnout.

CONCLUSION

I believe that the options presented here provide a lot of flexibility and room for creativity, yet offer enough structure so that you do not drown in possibilities of how to organize your fundraising. As with all volunteer work, the premise we are operating from is that the volunteers (in this case, board members) know and accept their responsibility with regard to fundraising and are willing (they don't have to love it) to carry out the tasks that they commit to.

We are also assuming that the paid staff wants to have a lot of volunteers involved. This would mean that staff have to be willing to take the advice of board members and the suggestions of volunteers and work as a team. This is quite different from the "sole proprietor" approach that is popular among staff who believe they can do everything better and easier themselves and that using volunteers takes too much effort.

Organizations that want to last encourage people to know how to do many jobs. Theaters have understudies for key roles, sports teams have players ready to replace those who are injured, successful businesses have people who can handle a variety of jobs. This flexibility requires practice and systematically providing learning opportunities. Just as it is obvious that an organization with one or two sources of funding is not on its way to self-sufficiency, the same is true of an organization with two or three people who raise all the money.

Whatever structure you choose for fundraising, make sure it involves the maximum number of people you can possibly manage, so that as many people as possible have as much experience as possible in all the strategies for fundraising your organization uses.

Board Member Involvement Pays Off

By SHELDON RAMPTON

Money was one of the main topics at my first board meeting when I joined the board in 1986. Our organization, the Wisconsin Coordinating Council on Nicaragua (WCCN), was spending more than we were taking in. We were borrowing from project funds to pay our administrative costs, and our executive director was deferring her salary.

After the meeting I approached John, our staff "fundraising consultant," with some admittedly half-baked fundraising ideas. With what I've learned since, his response now seems symptomatic of the reasons that we were having financial difficulty.

"Fundraising? Don't worry about it," he said. "There are other board members with more fundraising contacts than you have. Leave it to them. Besides, I've got some grant proposals in the works, and we should be getting some foundation support within a couple of months."

Today, nobody tells anybody on the WCCN board "not to worry" about fundraising. We have worked to recruit and train board members who take fundraising seriously. It's been a real learning experience, and many of our best lessons have come from the school of hard knocks.

In June of 1987, our board chairperson sent an emergency appeal to our members, warning that "we are facing a summer cash shortfall of $15,000. WCCN has enough money to operate for just six more weeks until we would be forced to begin staff layoffs."

WCCN staff — who at that time were doing most of our fundraising — realized that we needed greater board involvement. Instead of telling board members "not to worry about it," John began to admonish us at every meeting that we needed to "do something." This provoked a certain amount of tension between staff and board. "He's always telling us that we need to wake up and smell the coffee, but he isn't telling us how to *do* the fundraising," complained one board member.

In reality, staff at the time were probably giving the board too much advice. At one meeting, staff presented the board with a detailed plan for a fundraising phone-a-thon. The problem was, only two members of the board were able to participate on the weekend that staff had designated. Discussion quickly shifted away from the board's role in fundraising to whether we should hire additional fundraising staff.

A FIRST CAMPAIGN

June of 1988 saw the WCCN board's first attempt to carry out a major donor phone campaign. Our goal was to raise $5,000. With tensions around fundraising high, staff did everything they could to lighten the board's burden. They prepared personalized letters and gave each board member a list of potential donors and a phone script to use in calling them. The only thing that board members had to do was sign and mail the letters and make an average of five phone calls apiece.

"We wanted to make the June 1998 campaign as painless as possible for board members," recalled our executive director. In reality, staff had made it so painless that most of us barely noticed it was happening.

Recently, I had occasion to go through our records for the 1988 campaign. I was surprised to find my name on file next to a list of seven donors that I had been assigned to contact. I didn't remember having even *seen* that list previously. In fact, I only recognized two the names on it, and I'm sure I never called those two. Unfortunately, my non-participation was typical of the level of board involvement in out 1988 campaign, which raised a total of $445.

Despite the shortcomings of this campaign, it laid the groundwork for future success. Here are the mistakes we realized we had made:

- Lack of board participation in planning the campaign
- No campaign kickoff meeting or training to get everyone on board and rolling
- Nobody pushing the board to make their calls
- Choosing summer to kick off the campaign

DOING IT RIGHT

In May of 1989, WCCN established a development committee composed of active board members and began planning a campaign that would rectify past mistakes.

This time, instead of presenting board members with lists of assigned names, members of the development committee met personally with each board member and went over our entire donor list, asking them to select the names that they would be most willing to contact. Various board members had different ideas for how they wanted to go about contacting their donors. We tried to give them flexible options, while stressing the importance of contacting each donor personally — by telephone if not face-to-face.

We kicked off the campaign in October with a special weekend board training session, and members of the development committee periodically phoned other board members to check on their progress. We also set a definite closing date for the campaign by scheduling a post-campaign party in November. Not all board members completed all of their calls by the closing date, but most did.

The result? The 1989 campaign raised a total of $33,409. Nothing in our experience prior to that campaign would have suggested that we could expect that level of success. We proved to ourselves that our board *could* do effective fundraising.

A MORE DIFFICULT CAMPAIGN

During our most recent campaign, in the fall of 1990, we faced a much more difficult situation politically. The Sandinistas had been defeated in Nicaragua's elections, and by the time our campaign kicked off, fears of war in the Middle East had become more pressing in many people's minds that the situation in Central America.

Our 1990 campaign was even better organized than the one in 1989. We refined our campaign materials, our timeline, and our process for involving board members, and we saw a higher level of board participation. We brought in slightly under $30,000.

In light of the political situation, I consider the 1990 campaign *more* successful than the 1989 campaign, even though it raised less money. It took place at a time when long-standing Nicaraguan solidarity groups were facing funding setbacks and, in some cases, disbanding. For us, the experience that we had accumulated paid off in the form of continued financial stability, despite circumstances that might have forced us out of existence a couple of years previously.

MAIN LESSONS

Overall, the main lessons we have learned about major donor fundraising have been the following:

- Major donor campaigns *do* work.
- Participation of volunteers and/or board members is essential to the success of fundraising. It's infinitely easier to persuade volunteers to participate in the work of fundraising if they've participated in the planning.
- Major donor campaigns don't always work the first time. If you haven't tried a major donor campaign before, be prepared to make some mistakes. Don't get discouraged. Learn from those mistakes. Try and try again until you get it right.

1991

How Does Your Board Measure Up?

By STEPHANIE ROTH

Want a quick and simple way to evaluate the strengths and weaknesses of your board? The chart that follows is a useful tool for identifying areas where your board's structure and functioning may need improvement.

There is no magic formula to a high-functioning board, and you do not necessarily have serious problems if your board is not structured or organized as the items on this chart suggest. Nevertheless, the exercise of completing this chart as part of a larger board evaluation process can be extremely useful in determining areas that most need attention, development, and/or reorganization. The scoring gives you a way to place your board on a scale that ranges from most to least effective.

Keep in mind that boards change when the board members themselves are clear about the need to do so. More real progress results when board members can see for themselves how they measure up than when they are told by the executive director or an outside consultant. This chart is a guide by which your board can decide for itself what needs to change.

Remember too that board members are volunteers, with busy lives apart from the time they serve on the board. Progress may be slow, but as long as it is steady, you will experience positive outcomes.

The work of developing a board is ongoing for the life of your organization. Though you will face different challenges at different stages, there is never a point at which you will have a "perfect" board. Like relationships, families, and communities, the board is a part of an evolving and changing organism. With luck, the challenges will not overwhelm or discourage you, but provide keys to new ways of moving forward.

Using the Chart

1. Schedule a board meeting at which you can focus the entire meeting on the process, or make it part of a longer board retreat.

2. Distribute a copy of the chart to each board member to fill out so that everyone has the opportunity to express their opinion about how the board is functioning.

3. Use the group's responses as a guide to the areas it most wants to work on now. If more than a couple of areas need attention, choose the top two or three that can be the focus of the board's work for the next six months. There will always be things that need improvement; you will make more progress biting off smaller rather than larger pieces at one time.

(Please see chart on next page.)

How Does Your Board Measure Up?

Rate your board using the following scale:

0—No, this doesn't exist on our board   **1**— We're working on it   **2**— Yes, we're in great shape on this item

A. SELECTION & COMPOSITION	RATING
1. The board is composed of persons vitally interested in the work of the organization.	
2. The board is representative of its constituency with regard to race, class, gender, and sexual orientation.	
3. There is a balance of new and experienced board members to guarantee both continuity and new thinking.	
4. Board members have the combination of skills (e.g. fundraising, management, legal, fiscal, etc.) necessary to carry out their work.	
5. There is a limit to the number of consecutive terms a member can serve on the board. (No life terms!)	
6. The organization has a pool of potential board members identified for the future.	
7. The organization develops future board members through the use of volunteers on committees.	
8. New board members are recruited and selected using a thorough review process.	
SUBTOTAL	

B. ORIENTATION & TRAINING	
9. There is a statement of agreement outlining the duties and responsibilities of board members that all board members sign.	
10. The board understands its legal liability.	
11. The organization provides an orientation for new board members.	
12. The organization supplies a board manual to all board members that includes, but is not limited to, descriptions of current programs, a list of board members, budget and funding information, by-laws, and personnel policies.	
13. The organization makes training opportunities available for board members to increase skills related to their board responsibilities.	
SUBTOTAL	

C. STRUCTURE & ORGANIZATION OF THE BOARD	
14. The board has a simple, concise set of by-laws that describes the duties of board members and officers, as well as the procedures by which the board conducts its business.	
15. The board has a mechanism (such as an executive committee) for handling matters that must be addressed between meetings.	
16. The board elects a chairperson (or cochairs) to provide leadership and coordinate the ongoing work of the board and its committees.	
17. The board has active committees (e.g., fundraising, personnel, nominating, long-range planning) with specific assignments and responsibilities.	
18. Committee assignments are reviewed and evaluated periodically.	
19. Working relations between the board chairperson(s) and the executive director are strong and productive.	
20. Board and staff members are clear about their respective duties and responsibilities.	
21. Working relations between the staff and board are characterized by mutual respect and rapport.	
SUBTOTAL	

D. THE BOARD AT WORK

22. There are regularly scheduled board meetings at least four times a year.	
23. Meetings begin and end on time as per agreed-upon schedule.	
24. There is adequate preparation and distribution of material, including agendas, study documents, etc., in advance of board meetings.	
25. Board meetings are characterized by open discussion, creative thinking, and active participation together.	
26. Board meetings deal primarily with policy formulation; program, financial, and long-range planning; financial review; and evaluating the work of the organization.	
27. Minutes of board and committee meetings are written and circulated to the members.	
28. Committees are active and complete assigned tasks in a timely manner.	
29. The board is aware of matters of community, state, and nationwide concern within the field of service of the organization.	
30. Individual members of the board accept and carry out assignments within the area of their talents and expertise.	
31. Board members follow through on their commitments in a timely manner.	
32. Board members make a generous financial contribution (self-defined) to the organization on an annual basis.	
33. All board members are involved in some aspect of fundraising for the organization.	
34. The board conducts an annual review of its own organization and work.	
35. New leadership is emerging consistently from the board and its committees.	
SUBTOTAL	

ADD UP YOUR TOTAL SCORE

If your score is

58–70: You're in great shape. You have a healthy board with good working relationships. You should consider sharing some of your secrets with the rest of us! (One of your secrets is that you realize that the work of developing an effective board is a lifelong process.)

46–57: You're on the way to a strong, effective board; pay attention to your weak spots, and involve the entire board in developing solutions.

30–45: You have lots of room for improvement. The board needs to prioritize areas to work on—both in the short and long term—make a plan, and work the plan!

Under 30: You're probably experiencing problems already. Now is the time to devote serious attention to ways to strengthen the structure, composition, and functioning of the board. If not, your programs, and ultimately the entire organization, will suffer.

1998

Contracts with Board Members:
A Working Model

By OCTAVIA MORGAN

Herding cats doesn't begin to describe what it can be like to coordinate board fundraising. To me, it often feels like trying to simultaneously herd cats, birds, and fish toward the same corral, all of them moving at different speeds and with varying levels of interest and motivation. On any given nonprofit board of directors, you might find people with no experience in fundraising and people who do it for a living. Some board members will have lots of time, others are extremely busy. During the five years that I served as the Development Director for the International Gay and Lesbian Human Rights Commission (IGLHRC), the organization used three strategies to successfully maintain 100% board-member participation in fundraising.

1. THE PLEDGE FORM

The pledge form was my opportunity to get a specific and concrete commitment from board members. I developed the form with the executive director and some members of the board. The form evolved from a very simple document with one blank for a personal giving pledge to the more complex version shown here. We altered the form over time for two main reasons: to show the full range of the types of contributions board members could make and to concertize their annual commitments.

The form was designed to assist board members in thinking carefully and realistically about the various commitments they could make to the organization during the year. I encouraged people to promise only what they could really do and not to be overambitious. I found it to be essential to have people sign and date the form to reinforce the seriousness of their commitment.

The version of the form shown here reflects one of the most important things I learned — to have full board participation in fundraising there must be a range of ways for people to participate. Board members have vastly different levels of expertise and interest, and the time they have to do fundraising varies from year to year as their lives change. Some people will do a great job with getting friends to attend a house party, others are savvy about ask-ing for major gifts. If board members self-select the types of fundraising that they feel they can do, they are more likely to keep their promises.

2. A SUPPORTIVE ENVIRONMENT

An atmosphere on the board that supports fundraising is just as important as having a good pledge form. When people joined the IGLHRC board, they acknowledged in writing that they understood that one of their duties was fundraising. The pledge forms were filled out during the first board meeting of the fiscal year and at this time the board co-chairs would encourage everyone to push themselves in both raising and giving funds. We made an effort to conduct fundraising trainings about once a year during board meetings, and sometimes we held discussions where people could speak about the successes and pitfalls of their fundraising efforts. The leaders of the board talked openly about their own pledges and gave other members verbal encouragement throughout the year. Board members who were less experienced in fundraising could choose to pair with a more experienced person to learn how to do donor solicitations.

As the development director, I tried to provide as much logistical support as I could for board fundraising. This included providing template letters for those who were soliciting funds from their friends and colleagues by mail, doing the actual mailing if they didn't have time, and coordinating most of the logistics of house parties they were hosting (creating and mailing invitations, setting up a host committee, etc.). I also developed handouts on how to write a fundraising letter, how to give a pitch at a house party, and how to solicit donors verbally. At the beginning of each fiscal year, the development department would update the Frequently Asked Questions document so that board members would always have fresh information about the organization's work at their fingertips. If there were particular themes that we wanted to emphasize in fundraising during a certain time, we would also put those in writing.

3. FOLLOW-UP

Even those who make promises with the best of intentions sometimes require nudging to fulfill them. While board members' individual pledges were confidential, I made a written and verbal report at each board meeting that detailed progress made toward the board's total giving and raising goals. At the meetings, I found it useful to give members a copy of their own pledge form, since there were always some people who would forget the commitments they had made. I would encourage board members to specify exactly when they planned to do their fundraising activities and would do my best to start nudging them by e-mail and phone in the months and weeks prior to that time to give them enough time to prepare and plan properly. Finally, each person on the board development committee was assigned a few board members with whom they kept in regular touch throughout the year. This connection was designed both to remind board members of the work they had pledged to do and to support them in their fundraising efforts.

In the end, what really matters is that each member of the board is participating in fundraising in some way, both by donating money themselves and by asking others for money. As the coordinator of board fundraising, my goals were to help board members stretch themselves as fundraisers and as donors, and to give them concrete tools to make fundraising easier and less intimidating than they might imagine it. The pledge form is an invaluable tool in facilitating successful board fundraising.

Board Pledge Form — Confidential

FISCAL YEAR _____ **: OCTOBER 1 – SEPTEMBER 30TH**

BOARD MEMBER NAME: _____

International Gay and Lesbian Human Rights Commission recognizes the many and diverse contributions and skills that its board members give to the organization, including time, knowledge, connections, staff support, ideas, and perspectives, to name a few. The organization encourages creative forms of contributions and sees them as essential to its growth and health. In addition, IGLHRC recognizes the importance of board participation in fundraising.

My commitment to IGLHRC consists of the following pledge:

1) **PERSONAL GIFT** — Board members may make a personal gift to IGLHRC by being on the host committee for one of our two major events and/or by giving separate from these events.

☐ I will personally donate $ _____ in the following installments: ☐ monthly ☐ quarterly ☐ yearly

☐ I pledge $_____ to be on the host committee for the annual fundraising event to be held in June.
(The minimum host committee pledge for last year was $500.)

☐ I pledge $_____ to be on the host committee for the annual fundraising event in September. (The minimum host committee pledge for last year was $100.)

TOTAL personal pledge: $_____ (sum of three amounts above)

2) **RAISING MONEY** — My goal is to raise $_____ (beyond my own personal donation) in the following ways:
Please note: This pledge means that you actually ask the donor or funder for the money, or that you actively lobby for the money. If you introduced IGLHRC to a source of money in the past but are no longer involved in asking or lobbying for the funds, please do not include this source.

House Party
☐ I will host a fundraising party at my home. ☐ I will organize such a party at someone else's home.
Month(s) in which I would like to do the party: _____ City _____

Donor Solicitation — Existing Donors
☐ I will visit donors to ask them for a gift. Number of visits I will make _____
I will make visits in the following geographical area(s). (Will you be traveling this year? Use other side if necessary)

_____

☐ If possible, I would like to do one or two visits with an experienced solicitor.

☐ I will call _____ (number) existing donors to ask them to renew their pledge.

I understand that I may need to call each donor several times in an attempt to have a conversation with them.

continued

Donor Solicitation—New Donors

My goal is to bring in _____ new donors.   ☐ I will solicit people I know personally who are not already IGLHRC donors.

Names of people I'd like to solicit: _____

_____

I will solicit these people through: ☐ a personal letter   ☐ meetings   ☐ calls

☐ I have access to the following prospective lists to which the organization could possibly do a mailing (such as clubs, spiritual groups, subscribers to publications): _____

Foundation Contacts

☐ I will write letters of support to foundations where I have contacts.   ☐ I will meet with foundations officers I know.

My contacts at foundations include the following: (please list even if you think we already know) _____

_____

Corporate Contacts

I have contacts with the following corporations: _____

_____

3) IN-KIND DONATIONS — I will make the following in-kind donations (frequent flyer miles are very useful if you have them):

_____

4) ASSISTING WITH MAJOR EVENTS — I would like to be involved in one of IGLHRC's major events. I'm interested in the following event(s):

☐ Felipa de Souza Awards, June, New York City   ☐ Celebration of Courage, September, San Francisco

I'm interested in getting involved by:

☐ Serving on the planning committee   ☐ Soliciting corporate sponsors   ☐ Helping with set-up the day of the event
☐ Recruiting host committee members   ☐ Other: _____

5) COMMITTEE WORK — I will serve on the following committees:

Standing: ☐ Nominations   ☐ Development/Visibility   ☐ Research and Advocacy   ☐ Executive
Ad Hoc: ☐ Retreat Planning Committee

6) TRAINING

☐ I am interested in offering trainings to the board and/or staff in the following area(s): _____

_____

☐ I am in interesting in participating in training in the following area(s): _____

_____

7) MEDIA WORK AND CONTACTS

☐ I know mainstream, GLBT, or other alternative press reporters, editors, or producers whom I would be willing to contact to place IGLHRC stories.

☐ I have academic contacts who might be helpful placing stories for IGLHRC.

☐ I am willing to write letters to the editor for IGLHRC in conjunction with staff.

☐ I am willing to write an article (500 words) for IGLHRC's newsletter.

8) PROGRAM SUPPORT/CONTACTS — I will offer my expertise and/or contacts to IGLHRC staff in the following areas (including expertise with particular countries or issues, language skills, writing an article for the newsletter, etc.):

_____

9) OTHER — I would like also to contribute to and/or benefit from IGLHRC in the following way(s):

_____

SIGNATURE: _____   DATE: _____

These commitments will be reviewed during the fiscal year with the Board Co-Chairs or the Chair of the Development and Visibility Committee

1998

Membership Pays:
The Role of Members in Grassroots Fundraising

By SARA MERSHA

Grassroots organizations know the importance of having and developing membership to build leadership and power. We also know, at least theoretically, the importance of doing grassroots fundraising so that we can be directed not by foundation trends, but by our goals to fundamentally transform social systems of oppression and exploitation. The experience of DARE — Direct Action for Rights and Equality — shows the benefits of linking these two activities by involving members in grassroots fundraising. DARE is a multiracial, multilingual grassroots community organization in Providence, Rhode Island, whose mission is to organize low-income families in communities of color for social, economic, and political justice.

Membership involvement in fundraising not only brings in more money for our crucial work, it also builds the organization by deepening members' commitment, developing leadership skills beyond a core group, building connections and teamwork among members, and expanding members' ability to drive the organization's work.

DEEPENING COMMITMENT: MEMBERSHIP DUES

Since DARE was founded in 1986 — by five people around a kitchen table, as the story goes — dues have been a key component in defining membership. Dues contribute only a small percentage of the organization's budget; in recent years, DARE has raised $2,500 to $3,000 in membership dues. In an overall organizational budget of about $300,000, this may seem like a drop in the bucket. Why then, with a membership of low-income families in communities of color would DARE consider a person's decision to contribute money a determining factor? Simply put, requiring dues money to the organization raises the stakes,

forcing people to take their commitment to the organization more seriously. The noticeable trend is that those who pay dues are more likely to show up and take more of a role in building both campaigns and committees. Furthermore, members are willing to make this commitment because of the benefits of being a part of the organization.

Mary Kay Harris has been a DARE member since her son was assaulted by the police more than three years ago. She joined because she saw that DARE was working in a larger way on police relations and could help her address her son's case. After being a member for a year or two, she became co-chair of the Committee for Police Accountability. Today she is on staff as the Membership Coordinator. "When I was asked to join and pay membership dues," recalls Mary Kay, "I had to think about it. Once I made that commitment, I was happy to pay the dues, because it gave me a sense of belonging to something, a sense of ownership. By paying the dues, I knew my voice was just as important as the voice of anyone else in the organization. Honestly, if dues weren't a requirement and I hadn't paid, I wouldn't be here now. I follow my money — wherever it goes, I go."

Melvin Carter joined DARE almost two years ago, when he heard that DARE had won a policy to turn over city-owned vacant lots to neighbors for $1. "I saw direct benefits to paying dues to DARE," reports Mel. "Before I walked through that door, I was by myself, no one was helping me and I had no power. DARE helped me fight to get one of those lots for my community to use." Mel is now active in two DARE initiatives: Project GREEN and Behind the Walls, a new campaign against the criminal injustice system. When asked why he is still a dues-paying member, he responds, "I have a son in prison. In 1995, I came close to being in prison myself. I know that at any moment, someone could look at me and accuse me of a crime and because of my skin color, that might be enough to put me away. But since I'm a part of DARE, I feel that I'm not alone. I always believe that if people unite together, we have a voice and power."

Two years ago, DARE's membership voted to increase dues from $24 to $30 a year — the first dues increase in 12 years. A year later, what used to be DARE's Home Daycare Justice Committee became its own organization, the Daycare Justice Co-op. In an example of what they took with them from DARE membership, the co-op's membership of more than 75 family child care providers voted to set their dues at $100 per year. Nurys Medina, the current co-op chairperson, recalls, "We were all at a meeting and everyone there agreed to pay the $100, because we wanted to have enough money to do what we need in the co-op." The providers are low income — after expenses, they make just over $3 an hour from the state. However, Nurys says, "It's fair to give this much money, because it is to something that we benefit from; because of the co-op, we've been able to fight to get health insurance and one week of vacation. It's something that we care a lot about, so we're willing to pay the dues."

Dues collection systems can be a challenge — many members pay portions at a time, and it takes work to get everyone's payments up-to-date. DARE sends reminders in the mail quarterly, asks people for dues at each membership meeting, and has a Membership Outreach Committee to do one-on-one asks with members. Though the rates of payment are not 100%, Mary Kay Harris reports, "Since I became Membership Coordinator, members chase me down to pay dues. They want to do it because they see the work DARE does, see that together we are getting the job done and taking a stand."

DEVELOPING LEADERSHIP AND TEAMWORK: THE ADBOOK

One of DARE's most successful grassroots fundraisers, both in total money raised and in levels of membership participation, is the annual adbook. DARE members and staff ask neighborhood businesses, ally organizations, elected officials, and other DARE supporters to purchase an advertisement to go into a book. The book is then distributed throughout DARE's circles. Those who purchase ads get recognition from DARE members and supporters, and DARE brings in significant contributions.

Gladys Gould, a DARE community organizer, is this year's staff coordinator of the adbook, working closely with the members on the Adbook Committee to make sure that all the work gets done. She explains that a crucial component in making the adbook a successful fundraiser is setting goals, both individually and as a group: "Last year, I was a member of the Adbook Committee, and we each had our own goals for how much money we would sell in ads. It was hard to reach my goal, but I remember that we got most excited about reaching our overall goal for the organization together, and we did!" The process of having a group goal — and a group reward of a trip to Six Flags Amusement Park when the goal was reached — brought people together in an exciting way. Last year, DARE members and staff brought in more than $26,000 from ad sales, and this year's Adbook Committee set the goal even higher, at $30,000.

Shannah Kurland, Executive Director of DARE, reflects that part of the success of involving members in adbook sales comes from the fact that everyone can participate. "Everybody has some kind of contact they can ask," she comments, "because everybody has connections with some kind of institution in the community, whether it's the gas company, the local grocery store, an elected official from their neighborhood, a union or other organization of which they are a part."

Another important factor in the adbook's success is the tradition of it. People know how to do it because they have been doing it for years, and they teach new generations of DARE members through example and a structured buddy system. Thus, the adbook project provides an excellent opportunity to bring members together who do not know each other well. Black and Latino members are often enthusiastic about being paired up together, so that they can have the advantage of working with someone who speaks another language and therefore have access to more prospects.

Furthermore, the buddy system is a great structure for leadership development. Two years ago, Maxine Anderson was new to adselling and insisted that she could not sell ads. Shakira Abdullah, a longtime DARE leader, became her buddy. Shakira helped Maxine identify prospects and went out with her when she went to sell ads, giving her feedback on what she did well and what she could do better. The next year, Maxine was DARE's top member adseller, raising more than $1,000 in ads!

DRIVING THE WORK: CONNECTIONS BETWEEN MEMBER FUNDRAISING AND ORGANIZING

Fundraising alone can do a lot for an organization, but it is even more meaningful when it reflects and connects to the organization's actual work. This connection can be inherent in the type of fundraising activity or it may come out of individual members' high levels of commitment.

DARE special events have never brought in large amounts of money, but because they reflect and build on the community and culture of the organization, members wish to invest time in them. One special event that developed out of the organization's strategic planning process was a Millennium Vision Party. This party brought together members, allies, and other DARE supporters in a celebration where they reconnected with the organization and its purposes. Though not as successful a fundraising event as we had hoped, it nevertheless brought out a lot of volunteers and boosted organizational spirit. Pattie Horton, DARE's Administrative Coordinator, organized the event. "The Vision Party brought in more volunteers than I've ever seen work on an event! People wanted to be a part of it, to be a part of creating this vision, and they gave their time and other in-kind donations to make this happen," she said. From fixing up the building and donating and preparing food to sharing their vision for the organization at the event itself, members played a key role in putting the event together.

The Multicultural Extravaganza is a fundraiser DARE has run for the past four years, bringing a variety of talent and food together in a festive atmosphere. The first two years, DARE staff coordinated the event. For the past two years, however, Rayna Lopez, a DARE member who helped with the event during its first years, has coordinated everything. She handles many of the tasks personally, from recruiting talent to doing outreach that boosts ticket sales. Additionally, she recruits members to help her with specific tasks, such as soliciting food donations, cooking, helping with auditions, and of course, selling tickets. This year was the most successful Multicultural Extravaganza ever, with more than 500 people attending and more than $2,000 net brought into the organization. And all this occurred through an event that now requires minimal levels of staff time! Shakira Abdullah, now DARE Treasurer, explains that DARE members put so much into this event "because this is our gift to ourselves and to the community — we're celebrating ourselves, what we love and enjoy in life!"

Though fundraising events may be seen as isolated activities, DARE has found that members' involvement in fundraising is highly connected to their commitment to the work of the organization. Juan Gallardo joined DARE a year ago and connected immediately to the Jobs with Dignity campaign, a project to win passage of a city ordinance mandating good jobs that are accessible to the community and pay a living wage. As a school bus driver, Juan currently receives no benefits; he is deeply connected to the campaign both through self-interest and because he believes what it proposes is right. Two weeks before the Multicultural Extravaganza event, he turned in $140 in cash from ticket sales, and added even more money at the event, bringing his ticket sales alone near $200. Juan has since joined the Adbook Committee, continuing his dedication to making DARE's fundraising a success.

Monique Williams is another prime example of the way that commitment to the organizing work can drive members' fundraising involvement. Monique is chair of DARE's Police Accountability Committee and worked with other members to run it without much staff support for two years. A recent victory reinvigorated the committee, and Monique started talking with other committee members about how to build the campaign further. They decided that having a part-time organizer would be key. Monique knew that the organization would need to raise a significant amount of money to be able to hire another staff person, but she did not let that stop her. She met with DARE's executive director to brainstorm possible funding sources, then worked closely with staff and other committee members to raise $25,000 for the campaign through a successful grant proposal! Monique had a vision for what she wanted the committee to be able to do, and then found a way to fundraise to accomplish her goals.

DARE is now working to expand its members' involvement in fundraising by focusing on increasing their participation in developing the organization's overall fundraising plan. The first step is to build a fundraising committee of members that will work closely with the organization's finance committee. Shannah Kurland explains, "This new focus will build members' power in the organization. It is an opportunity for members to make decisions on what they want to spend money on and then figure out how to use fundraising to make this happen."

2000

A Few Words on Better Board Meetings

By KIM KLEIN

Few things are likely to be as frustrating to paid staff as when board members come unprepared for meetings. Staff are especially frustrated if they have diligently prepared for a board meeting and carefully sent out essential material in plenty of time for board members to read it so that they can make intelligent choices on the actions to be taken. Too often, a quarter of the board members don't come to the meeting, another quarter forget to bring their board packets, and no one shows evidence of having actually read any of the conscientiously prepared materials.

"My board members are so thoughtless," reported one exasperated director, "that they will sit down at the meeting and open up the envelope of stuff I sent them for the first time — and they do it right in front of me!"

These experiences highlight the fact that board members and paid staff are operating from two entirely different frameworks. Board members work for an organization in their "spare" time or "free" time. Staff people work for the same organization using their "paid" time. For all their thoroughness, staff people often do not take the board member's frame of reference into account, which is the source of staff frustration. No matter how well-meaning, dedicated, sophisticated, compulsive, or responsible board members are, they simply will not expend the amount of time and effort required to balance the time and effort a paid staff person has put in on behalf of helping the board run the organization.

This is an inherent, unresolvable inequality. However, it can be mitigated by using certain techniques, built on principles of human nature, to increase board members' participation. This article explores two points at which staff can work to narrow the gap: before the board meeting and at the board meeting.

BEFORE THE BOARD MEETING

1. Use the installment plan. Most staff people realize that it is essential for board members to be familiar with the background, complexities, and options involved in decisions they will need to make at the meeting. Having materials ahead of time gives board members a chance to read them in advance, make notes, and understand what is being asked of them. However, most staff know that board members often do not read material sent in advance. The secret is to send the materials in "chapters." Imagine that you are serializing your advance reading for the board meeting. First, you send the minutes from the previous meeting immediately after that meeting. Two weeks before the next board meeting, you send a budget report. A few days after that, you send an annotated agenda. One or two days before the meeting, you send another piece of information. Some board members will complain that they want all the materials sent at once. Others will grumble about the postage cost of these piecemeal mailings. But each of them will have read at least some of the materials and many will have read all of them.

2. Be personal. Remember the direct mail adage that people love to read about themselves? Whenever you can, add a personal note to a mailing, but not always on the front page of the information. For example, in a summary of two choices for an ongoing campaign, one staff person wrote a note on page 2 to two board members ("Really think about this — your comments will sway the group"), a note to one member in the middle of page 3 ("I think this was your idea, wasn't it?") and notes at the beginning and end of the documents to the other two board members. When the board meeting came, each board member had read the whole document. (If you don't think board members will look inside for personal notes, add a Post-it to the front of the document that will direct them to look inside: "See page 2.")

This is also a useful strategy when developing the materials themselves. For example, a report on the fundraising committee's plans — even if a staff person wrote it — ought to be sent to the chair of the fundraising committee for his or her signature before it goes out to the rest of the board. Since most people will not sign something they haven't read, staff will know that the chair read the material. Committee reports can refer to members of the committee by name, such as, "At the suggestion of Peggy R., we decided to move the mail appeal from October to September," or "Gene P. solved our rug problem by agreeing to ask Joe's Carpets and Floor Coverings to donate one." When people notice that their names will appear in material sent for advance reading, they will be more likely to take the time to read it.

3. Invite action. Whenever possible, without being artificial, require some action from board members prior to the meeting that will cause them to read the material. This can be stated in a personal note, "George, I am assuming you will give the Personnel Committee report. Call me if you need more information than is in here." Or, "Penny, can you speak to Lorraine and make sure we are using Johnson Park Activity Center for our annual meeting? Then we can announce that at the board meeting. I'll call you later about the schedule for the invitations."

Another option is sending a form that board members must return:

Memo

TO: Board of Directors
FROM: Sonia Alvarado, Board Chair
RE: Your fundraising assignments

Please check below the things you have been able to do with regard to your prospects and return this to me by Sept. 22 so I can report overall progress to the board at our meeting.

☐ I got the material you sent.
☐ I have called ____ (#) people.
☐ I have set up ____ (#) of meetings with prospects.
☐ I haven't been able to reach anybody.
☐ I need more
    ☐ Brochures
    ☐ Envelopes
    ☐ Sample letters
☐ I would like someone to go with me when meeting prospects.

HERE'S A SAMPLE FOR REGIONAL OR NATIONAL BOARDS:

TO: Board of Directors

Please fill out the form below letting me know your arrival time, whether you need a place to stay, child care, etc. Send this to me no later than _____ (date).

4. Reach out. Finally, three or four days before the board meeting, each board member should be called and asked if he or she is coming to the meeting and whether the materials sent ahead were clear. For board members who often don't read anything in advance, specific questions can be asked, such as, "Did the budget report make clear that we are buying a computer over the next year, which means we will be buying it in two fiscal years instead of just one as was recommended at the last meeting?"

These calls should ideally be done by board members. For instance, the chair of the board ought to call anyone who is supposed to give a report at the meeting. As staff, you would call the chair to go over the list of people who should give reports and ask the chair to call them.

Saying to the chairperson, "Sarah, when you call Titus, will you ask him if the stuff about the coalition meeting makes sense to someone who wasn't at the last board meeting? I'm afraid I may have been too terse," will cause both Sarah and Titus to read the information about the coalition meeting without ever implying that you thought they might not have done so.

The purpose of this advance work is to show the board that each of their opinions is important and counts with you. Board members are choosing to carry out their responsibilities in a sea of conflicting demands for their time and the time will go to the highest bidder — the person who gives the most back for the time put in. Board members most often don't do their job because their experience on other boards has been that their work is not valued.

AT THE BOARD MEETING

1. Have coffee, tea, cookies, fruit, or other snacks available.

2. Hold the board meeting in a reasonably pleasant place that is easy to find. If your office is overcrowded and messy, don't have your board meeting there. Board members often volunteer to have meetings at their homes, but homes can be hard to find and people then feel that they are a guest in someone's house rather than a board member at a meeting. In most communities it should be possible to reserve a neutral assembly space, such as a room in a bank, church, or community center, without charge.

3. Have the chair agree to start the meeting on time, even if only two or three board members are there. If the chair is late, ask one of the other board members to step in until the chair arrives. You will only need to do this once to show that board meetings start promptly. Have a similar agreement to end on time.

4. Make sure the agenda builds in a short time for people to review material. Even those who have read it in advance may not remember it thoroughly.

5. Be sure that everyone knows each other. This is particularly important for boards that meet infrequently, when board members come from far away, or when there are new board members. Spend time greeting people, introducing people again, etc. As each person comes into the room, say, "Hello, [Name]," in a fairly loud voice so that anyone who didn't remember that person will be reminded of who they are. Always use board members' names to them and about them, even if your sentence would work without doing that. For example, say "Carmen, how are you?" rather than just "How are you?" or, "I was just saying to Loretta that it hasn't rained in two weeks," instead of "I was just saying that it hadn't rained ..." In situations where there are a lot of new people, name tags are important.

6. Have an alarm clock or wall clock visible to the whole group so that everyone becomes somewhat conscious of time.

7. For meetings that are scheduled to exceed two hours, be sure the agenda builds in 15-minute breaks after every second hour.

8. Make sure that the person facilitating the meeting is skilled in basic facilitation techniques. This may mean working with her or him ahead of time to be sure that everything runs smoothly.

9. Remember that people are often afraid to ask for clarification of points they may feel they ought to know. For example, at a meeting of a new grassroots organization, a board member did not know the meaning of the 501(c)(3) status that was being discussed. She thought people were talking about Levi's 501 jeans. As board members debated whether to get "501(c)(3) status" she retreated in puzzle-

ment. Board members can't be expected to remember every current acronym either. While staff are completely familiar with the BEB Coalition and the SEH Network, along with ASPI, SECU, etc., board members can be lost. Take time for definitions. Do not ask, "Does everyone know what SEIU is?" People who don't will not be comfortable raising their hands. Simply say, "People will remember that SEIU is the Service Employees International Union and we are working with them on the health care initiative, which we sometimes refer to as PCP."

10. For every major decision, coach the chair to make sure everyone is heard from. The chair should look at each person and ask their opinion: "Rosa, what do you think?" "Gary, we haven't heard from you." This technique will ensure that no one feels left out.

11. Have a few extra copies of all the materials you sent ahead, but not enough that people think you assumed they would forget them. In a board of 12 people, two extra copies of everything shows that you realize someone's mail could have gotten lost, but that basically you trust board members to bring their materials.

12. Make sure the chair ends the meeting formally. She can say something like, "This meeting is adjourned," or, "That's all for today. See you on the 12th," or, "Thanks for coming and working so hard." As staff, you can try to say goodbye to everyone individually on their way out.

In summary, board members will generally rise to the occasion. As staff, it is your job to keep creating the occasion.

1996

Reflections from a Board Member

By STEPHANIE ROTH

I have experienced the complexities of boards from many angles and perspectives — as a staff member, board member, and consultant/trainer. Although I've probably spent as much time over the past 20 years consulting with organizations on how to strengthen their boards as I have serving on them, it is my experiences as a board member that have led me to write this article.

Most people involved with nonprofits know how difficult it is to find a well-functioning board. An exercise I've borrowed from consultant/trainer Burke Keegan asks participants to brainstorm qualities of "the board from hell." Whether the group I'm working with is made up primarily of staff people *or* board members, this exercise never fails to get a laugh as well as produce pages of problems they've experienced with their organization's board.

More and more people in nonprofit organizations are starting to question the very structure of boards, whereby a group of volunteers who do not have day-to-day involvement with the work of an organization nevertheless have ultimate legal responsibility for what it does. But until a new and better model is created, we need to figure out ways to make the experience of being on a board of directors a more fruitful and satisfying — not to mention useful — one.

Over all my years working with them, I have tried to convince both board and staff people that fundraising is an essential part of a board member's responsibilities. When people have said to me, "But we're not a fundraising board," my response has been, "Then you're not a very effective one either, because fundraising is an important responsibility of any nonprofit board." I say this not just because the money itself is critical to the survival of the organization, but also because of the close relationship between fundraising and other programmatic work. Fundraising, like program work, builds new constituencies and involves members, volunteers, and leaders in making the work more visible, as well as recruiting new interest in and sources of support for the organization. When board members ask their friends, family, colleagues, and neighbors to make a contribution, attend a special event, or purchase a raffle ticket, they are bringing in potential new allies and activists to the cause.

While I still believe that there is a vital connection between fundraising and program work, I've also seen situations where board members feel that fundraising is the *only* thing the staff wants them to work on, and have felt that their role in program, governance, and strategic thinking and planning is not considered essential or even particularly desirable. This attitude reinforces a dangerous separation of fundraising from programmatic work, hindering everybody's efforts on behalf of the organization. Ideally, everyone should be involved in both fundraising and programmatic work as the way to best advance the goals of the organization. Board members are far more effective in raising money if they are committed, passionate, and *involved* with the organization's work.

As a professional fundraising consultant, I was surprised to find myself on a board where the staff had high expectations of my work raising money for the organization, but did not want me to ask any questions about fundraising strategies, the financial growth of the organization, or how decisions about budget and fundraising were made. I realized that without being involved in developing the fundraising plan and in analyzing the effectiveness of past efforts, I was not as motivated to carry out fundraising tasks. Also, in order to maintain my enthusiasm for asking people for money, I needed to be part of the discussions about how our programs were making a difference in the world — how effective they were at stopping sexism, or challenging racism, or ending violence against gay men and lesbians, or halting environmental devastation from corporate polluters.

I realize that my background in fundraising and non-profit management is not the typical board member's experience, and I'm happy to bring my experience in those areas to causes I care most about. But, like other people, I join boards to learn something new and to gain new skills as well as to use my existing ones. Board members want to engage in the analysis that will inform how the organization does business this year and in the years to come. They want to have opportunities to participate in national conferences and other activities to learn more about the issues and, ultimately, to become stronger advocates for the organization and its cause.

Because of experiences like mine, board members are becoming frustrated with the problems of serving on a board. One board member complained to me that the actual work of being on the board was totally different from what he had expected, and that he didn't like it very much. Most of his time was spent talking about personnel matters, by-law revisions, recruitment of new board members, and fundraising. His enthusiasm about the actual work of the organization had waned as his input or involvement on a programmatic level was discouraged by the executive director and limited to staff reports given at board meetings.

People join boards because they care about the cause and want to give their time and money to something they believe in deeply. Too often, however, their actual experience of being on the board consists of long meetings devoted mainly to administrative details, crisis management around personnel or funding problems, and being told endlessly that they aren't raising enough money.

On the other side of the board/staff dynamic, staff people often view board meetings as a necessary downside to their job responsibilities. From their vantage point, the meetings take a lot of time to prepare for and only lead to more work from the demands that board members make of them. I recently met with the executive director of an organization on whose board I had previously served. She wanted my advice about how she could strengthen the board and develop a better working relationship with its members. At one point in the meeting I said, "Please be

completely honest with me. Do you find the board of directors to be mostly a burden, a group you have endless obligation to, but that you get very little back from?" She confessed that was how she felt much of the time.

A CHALLENGE

I'd like to pose a challenge to my colleagues who serve on the boards of organizations they care deeply about, and to the staff members we work closely with: Let's create ways to have a true partnership where each member of an organization — staff, board, client/consumer, member — has an important role to play in furthering the mission.

It's true that some board members may become too involved in what is appropriately the work of the staff and fail to recognize when they have begun to try to micro-manage these activities. Most board members, however, have neither the time nor inclination to work at this intimate a level. Nevertheless, an organization must guard against micromanaging by board members by clarifying the difference between the job of the board members and that of staff. For any organization, the exact responsibilities of board and staff will depend on the size of the organization, its stage of development, number of staff people, and other factors. At the same time, staff and board members must find meaningful and appropriate ways to involve board members in an organization's programmatic work. Without an appreciation for their desire and ability to be more than fundraising machines, crisis managers, and names on a letterhead, organizations will have a harder and harder time finding committed, skilled, and enthusiastic people to serve on boards.

HOW CAN WE BEGIN?

The reality of running a nonprofit organization is that everyone — board members, executive directors, and other management staff — feels beleaguered by having to do too much administrative and fundraising work. They resent how little time is left for the work that drew them to the organization in the first place. But it costs more to run a nonprofit today than a decade ago because of more expensive technology (computers, fax machines, etc.) and increased competition for less funding. Government cutbacks since 1980 have meant less money from those funding sources while competition grows from an expanding number of nonprofits for private-sector funds. While more money in absolute dollars is being donated by the private sector every year, this growth has not made up for the loss of funds from government sources.

I have two suggestions for ways to cope with this very real problem. First, be clear with *all* members of the organization that fundraising *is* part of the work, not some thankless task that allows others to do the "real" work. Through fundraising we involve people who are vitally interested in the mission of our organizations; and fundraising gives us the chance to have interesting, even challenging conversations with a broad range of people who want to make the world a better place through their financial support of our work.

Second, *all* members of the organization need to participate in serious discussions about what's happening in the field, how our organizations should respond to changes in the larger society that affect our work, and even what kinds of new program areas the organization should consider. These discussions should welcome the perspectives of board, staff, volunteers, and other constituents.

One way is for organizations to hold an annual board-staff retreat to give themselves the time to have more open-ended and thoughtful discussions. Another way is to schedule time at each board meeting to reflect on these issues. Don't let the "business" part of the work overwhelm the commitment people have to the mission of your organization.

Being a board member can be a thankless job if it does not offer the right balance of hard work (including fundraising), productive and meaningful discussions about important issues, and respect for board members' varied contributions. When this balance is achieved, being a board member can produce huge rewards for both the organization and the individual.

1997

When Money Isn't the Problem

By KIM KLEIN

Most nonprofit organizations need more money than they have. To increase their funds, they either seek new strategies for raising money or they strive to upgrade their existing strategies. However, a significant number of nonprofit organizations that think they need more money actually have any number of other problems that must be solved before their fundraising efforts can improve. In fact, these organizations sometimes have an effective fundraising program in place but their other problems obscure its success.

Because almost every organizational problem will show up eventually — if not first — as a lack of money, organizations are quick to blame their fundraising efforts for their lack of funds. But just as a rash can be a symptom of a number of illnesses that may have nothing to do with your skin, so a lack of money may point to a number of problems that have nothing to do with money. Rarely is lack of fundraising effort the main problem and never is it the only problem.

This article presents several short case studies to explore four of the most common organizational problems. In each case, the problem appeared to be a lack of money and the solution appeared to be more or different fundraising activities. In fact, when the problem was properly identified, the solution chosen by the group was unrelated to fundraising. Other solutions were also possible, but you will see that the creativity applied in these instances generally resulted in positive solutions.

PROBLEM AREA ONE: UNREALISTIC GOALS

Example A:

A sexual assault prevention project faced a $14,000 shortfall in their community-based fundraising efforts.

When describing this deficit, they explained that they "always fall short of their fundraising goals." Their paid fundraising coordinator was disheartened, feeling that no amount of work made any difference. Here's what their fundraising plans and past performance looked like:

SOURCE	YEAR 1 ACTUAL INCOME	YEAR 2 ACTUAL INCOME	YEAR 3 GOAL	YEAR 3 ACTUAL INCOME
Raffle	$2,500	$3,000	$10,000	$6,000
Membership	$1,500	$2,000	$12,000	$8,000
Major Gifts	$5,000	$8,000	$20,000	$13,000
Volunteer Canvass	$3,000	$3,500	$8,000	$5,000
TOTAL	$12,000	$16,500	$50,000	$32,000

Real Problem: The real problem is easy to see. Having showed steady financial growth for two years, the group decided to hire a fundraising staff person to increase their income even more significantly so that they could expand their program. They then set goals that required raising two or three times more than they ever had. The effect of the staff person was clear: Income in every category had gone up and total income to date was nearly double that of the previous year. However, the goals that had been set were unrealistic.

Solution: The group revised their goals downward and postponed the beginning of the new program until the following year. Far from feeling discouraged about their fundraising, they realized that their decision to hire a fundraiser was a good one, and that their efforts really were paying off.

Example B:

A reproductive rights group planned and organized an event to protest threats to a woman's right to choose. A demonstration was to be followed by a small concert in a park featuring a local bluegrass band. Admission to the concert was set at $10. They hoped to attract 500 people, making their projected gross income $5,000 and their net income about $3,000. They planned to raise even more money by selling drinks and food at the concert.

Because they were so caught up in the preparations for the demonstration, they decided not to advertise the concert widely, but to try to attract most of the demonstrators to the concert. The demonstration went well. About 2,000 people came, the press gave it good coverage, and there were no problems with police or bystanders. The concert, however, did not go as well. Though the concert was mentioned several times during the day and flyers about it were distributed, only 200 people came. With the sale of drinks and food, the concert netted about $750, less than one-third of the hoped-for total. The problem was blamed on poor publicity.

Real Problem: The real problem here is again an unrealistic goal. This organization, with only one part-time staff person, set itself up for failure by planning a major demonstration and a major fundraising event for the same day. They saw the demonstration and the concert as related events that would naturally flow into each other. In fact, this was not the case. Having spent their afternoon at a demonstration that ended at 5:00 P.M., most people were not interested in going to a concert that began at 7:00 P.M.

Solution: The solution here is for the group to identify what they want from their special events. When money is a primary goal, they must give the moneymaking event enough time for proper advertising and coordination.

When a good time for the demonstrators as well as publicity for the group is the primary goal, then the concert needs to be part of the rally at the end of the demonstration. The demonstrators could march down Main Street, rally at City Park, then be entertained by the bluegrass band and go home.

PROBLEM AREA TWO: INCOMPETENT OR UNQUALIFIED STAFF

Example A:

An environmental organization needs an accountant. With money coming in from many sources, including foundation funding for several projects, they need someone who can keep careful track of both project funds and operating costs. The brother of a board member needs a job and a change of pace. A car mechanic by training, he has recently been the manager of a gas station. No one on the hiring committee has accounting skills and, needing

an accountant quickly, they decide to offer the board member's brother the job. Reasoning that he can add and subtract and has small-business experience, they foresee no problems.

During the annual audit, the organization learns that foundation money designated for a special project has been used to pay other bills. The cash flow generated by this grant has disguised the lack of money coming in from other sources. The project to be completed with this grant now does not have the cash it needs.

The board members decide that they have slacked off in their fundraising efforts and resolve to make up this deficit.

Real Problem: While the board's decision to increase fundraising is certainly commendable, they will find themselves in this situation or worse until they deal with the fact that they have hired an unqualified person as their accountant. Generally, it is not a good idea to spend money designated for one program on something else. If you are going to use grant money specifically designated for one program to fund other things, you need to have a plan for making up that money.

Solution: The accountant is happy in the job and everyone likes him. The organization chooses to pay his way to attend night classes in accounting and to hire a consultant to set up the books and supervise the staff person for a few months. Although these were extra expenditures for the group, they felt it was worthwhile to retain what is basically a good employee. The board's extra efforts in fundraising make up the money needed for the project, which is finished on time.

Example B:

A dynamic and capable leader was executive director of a group advocating for senior citizens in a small city for ten years. With three other people, she was one of the founders of this highly respected organization. Last year she developed a debilitating kidney disease that left her exhausted much of the time and affected her short-term memory. The disease is progressive, and she will eventually lose her kidney function and require dialysis. She cut back from her more-than-full-time schedule to three-quarter time, but even so could usually work only three or four hours a day. Her memory loss caused her to miss important meetings and some appointments with donors.

The director insisted that she was fine, just tired, and that her missed meetings were the result of having too much on her mind. No one wanted to talk honestly with her about her illness, so the other two staff members tried to do parts of her job as well as their own. Everyone had a "wait and see" attitude. One board member summed up the situation: "I suppose someday something serious is going to happen, but we will cross that bridge when we come to it." Meanwhile, fundraising efforts began to fall off, as the director's lack of energy made it impossible for her to keep up with the fundraising aspects of her work.

Real Problem: Here is a classic problem that most often occurs with substance abuse, but can occur with any serious illness — everyone, including the ill person, participates in denying the effects of the illness, hoping against hope that it will all work out. This is a misplaced sense of kindness. There is, in fact, nothing kind about standing by and watching the organization this woman has been instrumental in building slowly fall apart because she can't continue to do her work. Further, board members fail in their responsibility to act in the best interests of the organization by not dealing with the situation.

Solution: Two of the director's closest friends, who were also the other co-founders of the group, spent an afternoon with the director and a therapist who specializes in the needs of people with debilitating or terminal illnesses. During this session, the director was able to admit that she feared she was indispensable and also that she was having difficulty adjusting to her disease. In addition, she explained that she needed her salary to pay the increasing costs related to her illness, such as special food and a housecleaner.

A solution to all these problems was fairly simple. The director qualified for disability insurance and could cut back to work half-time without any loss of income. Another staff person was promoted to fill in the other half of the director position. The current director began bringing other people to her meetings with funders and donors. It was imperative that this organization have more people doing fundraising so that the task did not fall solely on the director. With this decrease in both work and worry, chances were good that the director would be able to stay with the organization as long she was able to work.

In these two examples and dozens of others, people are given or retained in jobs for reasons that have nothing to do with the job and that ignore the health of the organization. "He's in therapy." "Her relationship just broke up." "He's a single father." "Her mother has cancer." These are serious issues for which we must have compassion, but they are not job qualifications. Obviously, social change groups want to be more humane than corporations or businesses seem to be. But giving people too much latitude is neither good for the organization nor kind to the person. The crises brought on by these and other situations usually show up in lack of money. More money will only buy time and extend the crisis for more months.

PROBLEM AREA THREE: POOR RECORDKEEPING

Example A:

A women's health organization had a mailing list of 1,000 names. To be a member and stay on the mailing list, one paid organizational dues of $20 per year. Every September, the volunteer fundraising committee sent out a renewal letter to the entire list. For the next 12 weeks, committee members took turns coming in to the office to write thank-you notes to the donors and add to or correct addresses on the mailing list. The mailing list was kept on a simple database that could record donors' names and addresses but did not have room for the date or amount of their gift. Over the past three years, income from the membership list had dropped while the cost of maintaining the list had risen. The committee's solution was to recruit more paying members, and they planned to launch a large direct mail campaign.

Real Problem: The volunteers who sent the mailing and maintain the list had no agreed-upon system for recording information. Some volunteers sending thank-you notes added everyone to the list without checking to see if they were already on it, creating duplicate listings. In two years, no name had been removed from the list because no one looked for lapsed members. The renewal sent in September went to everyone, even if they had just joined the organization the month before. Angry or puzzled letters from members were filed away in an envelope marked "To be answered."

Solution: Before this group recruited any more members, it dealt with its infrastructure and organizational problems. First, it bought a fundraising database that could hold more information than simply name and address. Then, the volunteers created and then agreed on a system for keeping track of information. They reviewed the list of donors and eliminated duplicate addresses and deleted names of long-lapsed donors. They began to keep track of how much money members sent and when. They created a quarterly renewal system, so that people were sent renewal letters during the quarter that they previously gave. This made the renewal system much more manageable and accurate. One volunteer took on the task of answering letters, phone calls, or e-mails from disgruntled members. Having done these tasks, they were in a position to launch a larger direct mail campaign, as well as to work with their current donors to ask them for more money.

Example B:

A legal aid organization published three different booklets on various aspects of legal rights. The books were priced to realize a slight profit, and an excellent marketing strategy was implemented. The booklets sold much better than expected and the job of fulfillment fell on the organization's secretary. The secretary could not keep up with the orders along with the rest of her work and became resentful that this job was simply thrown to her. She delayed filling the orders until her other work was done, which meant long waits in receiving booklets for those who ordered them. There was no system for keeping track of orders. Once she filled an order, the secretary simply threw away the order form. Checks were often not cashed for three or four months, and the wait for booklets stretched to four weeks, then six weeks, and then three months, resulting in a number of complaints. Because there was no inventory system, the group would run out of a title before ordering more. This added weeks to a customer's wait. Given all these problems, the executive director decided the sales were not worth the effort and suspended the marketing plan. "It will be easier to get the money from a foundation and give the books away for free," he said.

Real Problem: Here the director decided to abandon a successful fundraising strategy and community service because neither he nor the secretary knew how to put proper fulfillment procedures in place. Giving the books away for free won't solve this problem, as people will still have to wait and will still be frustrated.

Solution: A board member who runs a retail store intervened. She helped the secretary set up an inventory control system on her computer, which showed the remaining number of booklets on hand each time an order was entered. That way, the secretary could always tell when to order more. Further, once the name and address were entered, the program allowed the secretary to print out a label, saving her the previously tedious task of handwriting labels for mailing. She also got permission from the director to hire a work-study student three hours a week to handle fulfillment. The group retained its income, continued to distribute valuable information, and the secretary was able to do her work.

PROBLEM AREA FOUR:
INTOLERABLE WORKING CONDITIONS

Almost all low-budget organizations make do with less than adequate working space — conditions are often too crowded, too noisy, too dirty, too cold in the winter, and too warm in the summer. But some make do with conditions that rival the garment industry of the 19th century or the living conditions of many migrant workers of today. Ironically, activists will work in conditions they would protest vociferously if they found them among workers in other industries.

Example A:

A tenants' rights organization with two staff people operated from a prefab storage unit in the back of a block of stores. The unit measured 9' × 12' and had no running water. (They used the bathroom of a nearby gas station and brought in drinking water in gallon jugs.) Heat was provided by a hastily installed woodstove at one end of the unit. Light came from one bare bulb; the electrical outlets needed to operate the computer and fax machines were provided by a sympathetic store owner through a series of extension cords. In the winter, a staff person came in early, built a fire and went home for an hour while the office warmed up. The workers and many of the board members felt that the office should be located in the neighborhood it served and should not be fancier than the living conditions of the tenants who were the constituents of the organization. They proudly brought potential donors to their office to show that no extra money was spent on frills and felt that their limited success in raising money was due to donor bias against poor tenants.

Real Problem: Here the problem was one of assumptions. The first assumption was that any office situation better than near squalor would call the organization's sincerity into question. The second was that donors were biased against them so their chances of raising money, particularly major gifts, were slim. A compounding problem was time lost in heating the space and in staff absenteeism for almost constant colds and flu during the winter. The organization was finally forced to face the problem when the fire department declared the woodstove unsafe and ordered the landlord to fix it. He refused, explaining that the space was a storage facility and not designed to be an office. He felt he had been doing the group a favor to let them have this space . The organization was forced to move.

Solution: The organization moved to a small office in a neighborhood church. There they paid little rent, as the pastor of the church was sympathetic to the work of the organization and many of the congregants were tenants the group worked with. At the church the group had access to a photocopy machine and a conference room for meetings. They were warm in the winter and cool in the summer. At the same time, they maintained their goal of staying in the neighborhood and not living better than the tenants they serve. Some of the potential donors who visited their old office started giving them money, explaining that their new location seemed much more appropriate. One donor said that he had wondered if they were on the "up and up" when he saw their storage-unit office. Another said she couldn't see giving to an organization to work for tenants' rights that didn't seem to have a clue how to get decent space for themselves. The tenant leaders of the organization were the most supportive of all, and many of them began to volunteer in the office.

Example B:

A child care center operated its program in a very large restored barn. The barn had been converted into a wonderful, if somewhat noisy, classroom and play area. In the back of the barn several of the former horse stalls made great storage areas. One was used as a small art room. The remaining horse stall served as the program's office but did not convert into great office space. The noise from the children was deafening for the administrator, so she normally came in late and worked well into the evening after the children had gone home. Her office was overcrowded, and because it could not be locked, she sometimes found that children had been playing in it. Although she asked the board several times for an office away from the facility, they felt it was an unnecessary extravagance and that all extra funds should go to the children's program.

As time went on, the administrator missed funding deadlines and almost lost a major block of funds from the state because her reports were tardy. The administrator complained of overwork and having no time to do fundraising. She felt tired all the time. The board proposed hiring someone part-time to help her. This person would share her office.

Real Problem: This administrator may have been overworked, but there was no way to know how many of her problems were due to her working conditions. She worked mostly in the evenings, and she resented the effects on her personal life, and she was more tired than if she had been able to work during the day. Because she often could not be reached during normal business hours, she had frustrated and annoyed funders, government officials, and donors. Ultimately, she felt isolated and unsupported.

Solution: Finally realizing that the good of the children would be best served by making it possible for the administrator to do her job, the board agreed to take the money they were prepared to use for an assistant to rent an office space away from the facility. They and the administrator would now be able to assess if she truly had too much work.

SUMMARY

Groups often find it liberating to learn that their problem is not money related and can be solved through means other than simply raising more funds. It is sobering to realize that when the problem is not related to money, no amount of money will solve it.

All organizational problems must be examined from a variety of angles, both to analyze the problem accurately and to be sure that all solutions are being considered so that the best one can be chosen.

1993

Organizational Development:
The Seven Deadly Sins

By ANDREA AYVAZIAN

What is organizational development? Organizational development means self-consciously dealing with issues concerning the structure and management of your organization. These issues affect groups whether or not we talk about or deal with them directly. For each organization, therefore, the time comes to look at and address the issues honestly, in a way that will cause the group to grow and strengthen.

Organizational development issues are internal. They are either helping you in or hindering you from meeting the goals that you have put before you.

Organizations, like people, go through life changes and life cycles. And, like people, organizations mature over time. As we age we become different from the infants we were so many years ago. We have grown and changed. Even so, some things about our characters and our personalities remain with us. The same is true for groups. They mature over time, changing as they need to while keeping their basic character and "personality."

Many social change groups have been formed in the last 20 years, and many more are in various stages of development today. For new groups that have moved beyond those initial meetings around kitchen tables and in church basements, it is now time to take a good look at internal organizational issues. This process of self-analysis can help pinpoint weaknesses in a group's organizational structure that may be preventing the good work from getting done.

In my travels to social change groups around the country, I repeatedly hear about obstacles arising from internal issues that are keeping groups limited and less effective than they might be. What I present here are the seven most common obstacles I see that are keeping groups stuck in some of their program work and impeding positive organizational development. There's no order to these seven. The first is not the most common or the most serious and the seventh is not the least common or the least serious.

1. FOUNDERS' DISEASE

The first problem is something that has been called "Founders' Disease." One aspect of Founders' Disease is when the original people in your group cling to the way things have always been. "That's not the way to do it," people say in response to new ideas. "Oh, yes, we tried that two years ago, but that doesn't work." "That plan's not a good one. We tossed that out three years ago." These original people have made themselves indispensable and are absolutely attached to the way things have always been.

Ironically, the founders or that original core group frequently are saying at the same time, "We want new blood. We want new members. We need to broaden our base." Though they are saying they want new people in the group, they are giving mixed messages when new people do come. They say, "Come to our meetings. We have refreshments. We're planning programs. We want your input." Once new people get there, however, the founders often talk mostly to each other, make plans with an interchange and a dynamic that leaves new people out. They may welcome new people but not give them meaningful tasks to do. There are often an in-group jargon and a sense of who has been there a long time. When these dynamics are in place, new people often feel they don't know how to plug in.

For those of us working in social change, there's a sharp irony here. We talk about empowering the world, empowering our community, empowering congregations, and everyone else, but we disempower new people who come to our meetings. First we say, "We're glad you came," and then we unwittingly do things to discourage them from coming back. As much as we do not want to convey a sense of elitism or exclusiveness, we are creating it.

If the symptoms of Founders' Disease sound familiar to you, raise it as an issue in your group. Have a meeting with just the founders and say, "We may be saying we want new members, but we're not acting that way."

How to Help

One way to cure Founders' Disease is to institute a buddy system. A "veteran" becomes the buddy of a new person at a meeting and is required to have contact with the new person before the next meeting. During this contact, she or he should ask the new person how they are doing with the group: "Did the meeting make sense? What were your impressions? Did you understand how we were making decisions? Was the agenda clear? What thoughts did you have?" The veteran invites the new person back and makes sure he or she is coming to the next meeting. By teaming people, you say, "We welcome you."

A second aid is to alert new people right at the meeting that some of what goes on may be off-putting and enlist their help. "We have realized that we have problems with this. Sometimes we're exclusive in our language. If we're referring to something you don't know, stop us. If you're feeling like we're going over your head, put a halt to that discussion and ask us to explain. We want you here, so we really welcome your help."

A third way to combat Founders' Disease is to be clear about what your meetings are about. If a meeting is for business, let new people know that this is simply a business meeting where you are going to discuss the budget or programming strategy. If it is an educational forum, invite new people specifically to come. Be sure to review the agenda early on to make sure the meeting is what newcomers expected.

Fourth, empower new people by giving them meaningful tasks early on. Several years ago I joined a social change group that had been formed about a year earlier. When I first got there, they were talking about events that had happened a year before, what had worked, and what had not worked, and the information all went past me. Not until I had been to about four meetings did someone notice I had not said much. At the end of that fourth meeting this person asked if I would appear on a call-in radio program with another member of the group in three weeks. She helped me prepare for it and, although I still felt quite green about the issues and did not say very much on the show, I was buoyed up by her confidence in me. After the show, having publicly represented the group, I felt that I had done something important. Giving newcomers that kind of meaningful task early on is what groups need to do to keep new people.

Fifth, pay attention to the social dynamics of the group. Groups meet a lot of unnamed needs for people that are somewhat extraneous to their social change work, but no less significant: feelings of belonging and importance, feelings that the work brings together a strong community of people. We do, in fact, become family to each other in a real way. People take care of each other's kids and worry about who's sick when they don't show up. Those social ties bring people back to meetings. Of course, they care about the issues, and they want to be informed and involved, but the people-to-people connections bring people back time and time again.

People in the group who want to be more social than others can do so. Members of one group started having supper together before their meetings. You could come if you wanted or opt not to. A block away from the regular meeting place was an inexpensive restaurant, and people knew that there would probably be others from the meeting there beforehand and then they would wander over to the meeting together. (But be careful not to start the agenda over supper, thereby excluding those who do not come to the restaurant.)

Sixth, be open to new ideas and new ways of doing the work. Old-timers have to recognize that even if you did something three years ago, somebody new in the group may have a new take on it or a new idea, or may want to head it up differently. It does not help to respond automatically with "We did that." Treated in this manner, new people feel both they and their ideas are dismissed. Another approach to a familiar idea is to explore it again, point out what may have been tried that did or did not work, and why. Evaluate the idea with the new person, "This is not a good community for Christmas balls, *we think.*" But try to resist making absolute responses.

Another discouragement to new people is that those who have been part of the group for a while always seem to have more information. If a lot of group veterans will be giving reports — on finances or actions, for example — then ask a person who has been there only four or five times to co-facilitate. Make up the agenda with that person's help and then put her or him up front. This puts somebody else in charge. Longtime members have to raise their hands. (That will humble them.)

Also watch for jargon. There are two kinds of jargon:

alphabet soup and "insider lingo." Alphabet soup jargon is easier to avoid — watch for those initials and explain them (in a non-condescending way) *without* having to be asked. Being alert to "insider lingo" takes concentration. Even words like "empowerment" can alienate some people who may appreciate the idea a great deal but are put off by formula words.

Finally, don't simply involve new people in your group; involve your group in them. Making them feel welcome goes beyond offering them the chance to participate in the work of the organization; it means finding out how they chose to come to your group, what their past experiences have been, and what they hope to accomplish by working with you. Listen to them. Given them a chance to talk. Let the "new blood" flow through your organization and give it new life.

2. LIMITED SUCCESS WITH STRATEGIC PLANNING

People working in the social change movement seem to be very good at knowing what they are doing next month; when it comes to next year, however, they are less clear. We seem to be able to envision a peaceful, just world (the very long view), and we are able to conceive next month's event. It's the in-between — the crafting each event as a step toward reaching our vision — that is often missing. Groups do event after event, or action after action, it seems, without a sense of building toward one theme or long-range goal and without building on the last success or learning from the last failure. There is a sense of each thing being done in isolation from the others. An event is done, then the organization regroups and sort of picks up from the fatigue and goes on.

The challenge is to funnel ideas into goals and long-range plans and know what we can realistically accomplish in a specific amount of time.

Also, we need to focus on doing one or two things well. Too often we are merely responding to whatever is out there — prison reform *and* human rights violations *and* environmental degradation *and* environmental racism. As a result, we end up doing a little of many things poorly. By doing a piece of everything, groups remain *reactive* .

We need to do less and do it better. Then, when people think of your group, they think of the work you are doing on one particular issue that is making a difference. We have a big agenda and a big task, and we cannot do every piece of it. There are other groups, there are other ways — we need to do a few things well and go in-depth on them, so people really are moved along on the issue you choose. Use a series of programs instead of one evening or one week to focus on a whole issue. Have some continuity in your programs.

Activists also need to spend time in retreat looking ahead, one year, two, and even five. You have to decide what the agenda is for your group and pursue it. One of the greatest weaknesses and one of the greatest strengths of the social change movement right now is that we do not have one major leader. In fact, it is up to each of us to become the leaders and to get our agendas noticed. What does your group want to be remembered for? Think about what you want people to say about your group one year from now. Pretend that somebody will have a commemorative dinner to honor your group and they will say: "This is the group that in the last twelve months…" — you finish the sentence. If you can say three things that you did well, you are accomplishing something in your community.

3. BURNOUT

I am seeing a lot of weary faces in groups I visit now. We are tiring people out. Activists are working too long and too hard. People paid for quarter-time are working half-time, those paid for half-time work are working full-time. And there are those who are paid for full-time work who are putting in 50 and 60 hours a week. It shows in their work when they are carrying on fatigued, ill tempered, and at their limits.

As a movement, we cannot afford to have people drop out after four or five years and finally get the MBA they think they should have had and get a job that pays them adequately. We cannot afford to lose good people. It is a net loss for all of us working for change. When a good organizer leaves Iowa City, there is a ripple effect all around the state. I know, because I tried to track one down last year whom no one could find. We need to take time for ourselves and our families and our loved ones and dancing and singing and joyful, nonwork-related activity. It matters. It pays off. What shines through in people's work is less often *what* they're talking about than *the way* they are talking about it.

Understanding our own limits in social change is a big challenge. My mentor, Frances Crowe, is in her 80s and has been doing peace work since she was in her 30s. Frances can and will carry on, I am sure, to her dying day. She has touched and changed many, many lives. If Frances had tired and dropped out at 40, after 10 years of doing this work, the whole peace movement in western Massachusetts — and I think nationwide — would have been harmed. The fact that she has stayed with it over time has been a profound example to many of us. We need to see ourselves doing this work for decades, which means taking care of ourselves and each other today.

We all know the signs of burnout. We know them and we ignore them. When you have not done your favorite hobby or sport or some favorite thing in your life for months; when you are starting to feel that you give the same kinds of answers because it is easier than to think creatively about your work; when there is the sense of disengagement or not caring; when you just sit through meetings — there in body but not there in mind — you are exhibiting signs of burnout.

When people burn out, they leave the movement permanently and they leave with bitterness and some sense of guilt. Taking care now so that we can do this work over time means giving ourselves and the people with whom we work permission and support to set realistic limits. And to do things in our lives that bring us joy and nurture us.

One path to burnout is to elevate our own sense of importance, dragging ourselves to dozens of meetings and events and volunteering for too much. We do not need to be the people who take on every task. Sit in a meeting for awhile with your hands crossed. If you are quiet long enough, someone in the back might say, "I'll do that." And then maybe you could help them.

When we think about issues around burnout, we must remember that we are the professionals in social change work today. We all have "PhDs" in organizing on political issues by now. If we don't, who does? We need to start treating ourselves that way. Start knowing that there are limits. Let's all recognize and value the fact that we are the professional speakers and organizers and trainers in the movement and we need to keep going for a lifetime.

4. GROWTH WITH NO PLANS

I once worked with a group whose only goal for the year was to double their membership in six months. There was no sense of how they would involve the new people or what would be useful for them to do. Bigger is not better if you do not know what you are mobilizing people for. There seems to be a mad drive for national groups to have chapters, affiliates, and regional offices — with no vision of what they are going to do, how much autonomy each will have, and who answers to whom. Growth in any social movement is most effective if it is done with a road map that helps people know where they are heading.

A group I visit in South Carolina started with a vision that they wanted to be a center for nonviolence and justice — they wanted to have resources and organize events in their city. As they grew, they decided to spawn chapters in different neighborhood communities around the city —

chapters that they would oversee and nurture. As a member of the group explained to me, "Like a spider plant that has a mother plant and then shoots." That was the extent of their plan — to spawn chapters. And they did, getting subgroups started in churches around the community. When I went there to consult and asked what they were doing, half the group said, "We're a local peace center, doing local actions," and the other half said, "We're just a resource center, nurturing all our satellite groups." That day, each half looked at the other and said, "That's what you think we're doing?"

If you are going to grow in numbers or affiliates or chapters, know why and know what purpose the growth will serve, how autonomous each group will be, and what you will do with them in the future.

5. NO CLEAR LINES OF ACCOUNTABILITY

In some cases we have become so alternative — we want to do everything differently — that we have thrown out all trappings of hierarchy for good or for bad. Sometimes when we lack structure we are doing ourselves a disservice, because often people do not know what they are responsible for and to whom they are accountable. Not, that is, until something has gone wrong. When a disaster hits, everybody turns around and says, "You didn't do what?" and you realize that the project was in your lap.

We need not be so afraid of hierarchy. It can be a relief for people to know whom they answer to and what they are responsible for. When you delegate responsibility, say, "This is what we're counting on you to do, from start to finish," give the task away, and let the person be totally responsible for its completion and success. If people are only going to find out what was expected of them when they err, they will be less likely to take risks. People do not want to risk being wrong, so they don't risk anything at all. When you know you have some power in a certain area, your creativity can flow.

6. POOR OR NONEXISTENT OFFICE SYSTEMS

Inadequate record keeping and poor internal communication contribute to frustration and inefficiency. I once asked to see a group's financial files and records, and they pulled out an entire file simply titled "1992." Nothing was subdivided. Every receipt was in there — a bulging file of receipts and notes and scrawls. That is an extreme example, but it is one of several on a continuum of ineffectiveness. For every event, you need to write down what happened, the key things you learned, and the evaluation. You need files on donors. You need samples of your past work so you can reuse graphics and see what ideas worked well. The list goes on and on. In short, document your work and keep detailed files. It is also your group's history in that cabinet or computer file.

Documentation of our work helps us as individuals, too — it combats our feeling of being indispensable. If you could say, "Pull the file on Mr. Brewster. Read over my notes from last week's conversation and please make the follow-up call," then you can let that task go to someone else because it is all written down. The more you carry in your head, the more you are making yourself indispensable and minimizing the work of others. You are doing the group a disservice and leading yourself to burnout. Make notes. It makes life easier. It is time well spent.

7. HORRENDOUS MEETINGS

We have to accept the fact that the work we are doing gets done in meetings. We do not sit isolated in offices, we are not academicians, most of us, who write things and send them off to the publisher, we are not corporate executives making unilateral decisions. We do our work in meetings. We strategize, we socialize — we meet. But too many of our meetings are long and boring, with overly packed agendas or no agendas at all.

Stop exhausting yourselves and the people who come to your meetings by allowing packed agendas and poor facilitation. Stop attending horrendous meetings and stop running them. The keys to stop running horrendous meetings are 1) make some piece of it fun, 2) have agendas that are realistic, and 3) attempt to do fewer things better. Have committees that really get work done on the committee level and report back to the larger group: "We checked out this, this, we still are nowhere on this." "Thank you. Can you tell us more about it next time?"

Have fewer meetings. Have some meetings that go for a longer time, perhaps a day. Get out of the office or out of the home and take a picnic or a potluck lunch. Start and end your meetings with fun things.

If you can send out an agenda prior to the meeting, you start light-years ahead. People know what to expect when they arrive. They may even have talked to each other about some of the items. That can be very useful. An agenda created on the spot at the meeting, tends to be huge. People don't stop — they just add item after item and then spend forever prioritizing the list. Just creating the agenda consumes the bulk of the meeting. I always want to go home feeling, "That was a good meeting. We accomplished a great deal and had a good time doing it." You can have a subcommittee that creates the agenda. Leave time at the end for items that did not get in — five minutes per item at the most.

End on time. It feels good to know that a 7:30 meeting will end at 9:30 and you will be home by 10:00. Now, when meetings go longer than they are supposed to, I leave. That is living up to my responsibility to take good care of myself. I will not stay if I'm getting tired, my input is only going to be rote, and I'm going to be resentful.

CONCLUSION

Organizational development is perfecting the means by which we reach our goals. It means getting serious about our work — wanting to do this work more effectively and more efficiently. We must pay attention to these internal issues. We also must honor the fact that beyond the obstacles, the glue holding us to our work is not only the commitments to our beliefs but also the dedication we feel toward each other.

1986

Building Multiracial Organizations

By ROBIN FERGUSON and STEPHANIE ROTH

We begin with three examples:

End Hunger Today, a 25-year-old advocacy organization, hired its first African-American staff person as part of efforts to expand its work in the African-American community. Three months later she quit, citing the organization's unfair expectation that she single-handedly recruit people of color to the organization.

Alternatives for Youth, a small social service organization, hired two consultants to conduct an antiracism workshop for the entire staff. The (white) executive director did not attend, but came into the office to do other work.

About 15% of the membership of Action for the Environment were people of color. Because the predominantly white leadership believed in the importance of a multiracial movement, they often encouraged these members to represent the organization at public events. However, the people of color felt pressured by these "special invitations," claiming they felt responsible for demonstrating that the organization was racially diverse.

Those who follow trends in the nonprofit sector are well aware of the rising interest in issues of racial, cultural, and other kinds of diversity in community organizations. The reality, of course, is that people of color, women, lesbians and gay men, and others, have been confronting institutions about these issues for decades, if not centuries. And there is much to learn from the history of these struggles in different social change movements in this country.

As consultants to a wide variety of community organizations, we believe that building more equitable and diverse organizations is critical to their survival and success in working for social change. We also believe that you cannot separate becoming more diverse from addressing issues of power and oppression. There are plenty of examples of racially diverse organizations where the white people in the organization hold the positions of power. It is not enough to simply have a diverse group of people involved. Shared leadership and control are key elements in our definition of a truly multiracial organization.

This article is directed primarily at organizations that are predominantly white and struggling with how to begin (or continue) a process of becoming multiracial. Although we will not address other areas of diversity in this article, including gender, class, sexual orientation, age, or disability, we believe that the various forms of oppression based on these characteristics are interconnected and that ultimately it is necessary to work on all of them.

WHY BUILD MULTIRACIAL ORGANIZATIONS?

Considering a few questions within your organization can open up important discussion that needs to occur if your efforts to build a multiracial organization are to be successful. The answers will ground you in your values and prepare you for the organizational and personal upheaval that can result from any serious commitment to change. Some of the questions you might look at are the following: What has led you to look more carefully at issues of racial diversity and racism? Why is it important to you at this time? What is the need as experienced and perceived by those most involved and/or affected by your organization? Are you being driven by a funder's concerns about this issue and not by your own belief in the need for change?

A Beginning Exercise

Groups have found it useful to use the following exercise to clarify their motivation and commitment to becoming a multiracial organization.

In one large group, participants brainstorm their reasons for wanting to build a multiracial organization and the challenges they will face in the process. Some of the reasons and challenges that have come from groups that we've worked with include the following:

REASONS

- We will expand the number and kinds of people who want to participate in the organization.
- We will learn from the different perspectives brought by a diverse group of people.
- We will be more effective in reaching our goals for social change.
- We will be better able to respond to the needs of the community we serve.
- We will satisfy our funders' requirements.

CHALLENGES

- It takes time and resources, and we already feel overextended and underfunded.
- It may require changes in organizational structure or leadership that will make some people uncomfortable.
- We might have more conflict.
- We'll lose members who disagree with what we're trying to accomplish.
- We may lose donors.

Identifying why you're working toward the goal of a multiracial organization will remind you of what is important to you about increasing diversity, even as the process gets bogged down, or people start fighting, or funders lose interest. Identifying the challenges will prepare you for conflicts and upheaval; if prepared, you will be less likely to let them keep you from continuing the work.

After you make these lists, it is critical that your entire organization have a discussion about your responses and whether your reasons for seeking change will sustain you throughout the process. For example, if one of the key reasons you have listed is that you'll satisfy requirements of your funders, you will probably have less success over the long haul than if your motivation is more core to your mission and values.

MOVING FORWARD

There is no predictable set of foolproof steps to developing a truly multiracial organization. If there were, we think more organizations would have figured out how to become more diverse. The complexities of racism in the United States, combined with the difficulties in multiracial organizing, lead to much confusion and sometimes keep organizations from moving forward through the rough times. Although we can't give you a formula for success, the following are some lessons we've learned through our work that might be useful to consider as you navigate the journey. We discuss each of them below.

1. Change *is* possible.
2. The process is lifelong. There are no quick fixes.
3. You will make mistakes.
4. Effect may be different from intent.
5. Issues of power must be addressed.
6. All of the oppressions must be addressed.
7. Change must take place on both individual and organizational levels
8. Tokenism is a common pitfall.
9. Antiracism work does not require the presence of people of color.

1. Change is possible. If we didn't believe this, we wouldn't keep doing this work. Your organization will ultimately be stronger and more effective as a result of working on issues of oppression and diversity.

2. The process is lifelong. We get many calls from groups that want us to conduct a few hours of training for members of the organization, hoping that a "quick fix" will solve their problems. Because racism and other forms of oppression are pervasive in our society, we cannot escape its effects on us as individuals (of all races and ethnicities), or on the (even progressive) organizations we build. Even with a lot of work, a long-range plan, well-meaning people, and a willingness to struggle, building a truly multiracial organization that is also committed to fighting racism is an ongoing process. You must be prepared to be engaged in the work for the life of your organization.

Often, a group will begin working on issues of racism only to lose focus and momentum after a particularly difficult time. This usually happens after some positive change has occurred and a new problem arises. Action for the Environment, in the example above, had made significant progress in growing from an all-white organization to one with people of color as 15% of its members. They knew they had much more work to do to become truly multiracial, but they were not prepared for some of the conflicts that were related to race that arose between members. The questions raised by people of color in the organization about shared leadership and decision making gave the organization a new understanding that each stage of their development would bring different challenges.

3. You will make mistakes. The fear of making a mistake

and being thought to be racist often keeps white people from taking action on issues of racism and diversity. Because we live in a culture where racism is pervasive, we must realize that individuals and organizations struggling to become more racially diverse will encounter stumbling blocks along the way.

End Hunger Today, for example, eventually realized that it was a mistake to hire one person of color without a broader organizational commitment to change. After much discussion, some of it painful, they decided they needed to look at all the ways their organizational structure and functioning had led to the exclusion of people of color, however unconsciously. They also decided to develop strategies in addition to hiring that would spread the responsibility of the work beyond a small group of people of color who were involved at any given time. When the board realized that they had not thought through their expectations and assumptions about their new staff person, they were able to acknowledge the mistakes they had made. By not blaming themselves unduly or using the staff person's resignation as an excuse to stop doing the work, they learned some important lessons. If you assume that mistakes will be made, and that people may even be offended, you will be able to take the risks necessary to make real institutional change.

4. Intent and effect are different. Organizations that are criticized as racist are not always conscious of how their actions have produced this criticism. It is important to recognize that although white people don't necessarily *intend* their actions to be racist, they may in fact be offensive to people of color. While it is difficult to hear that one's words and actions are racist, openness to these comments about an individual's or organization's action is essential. Only by fully exploring the impact of an organization's policies, program, and structures on communities and individuals of color will an organization be able to make meaningful change.

The leadership of Action for the Environment believed that encouraging their members who were people of color to be involved in various projects and events was consistent with their agenda to do antiracism work. However, because not very many people of color were actively involved in the organization, they felt a greater burden than the white members to be present and visible. In addition, the leadership's expectations of the people of color were never articulated directly. Although the *intent* of the leadership was to become a multiracial organization and strengthen the role of people of color, the *effect* of their actions was often overwhelming and, ultimately, alienating to those very members.

5. Issues of power must be addressed. Changing the composition of an organization is an important part of the process of becoming multiracial. However, we have seen too many organizations in which the leadership and management are primarily white people and the administrative and "line workers" are people of color. The decision makers of an organization have the greatest ownership, influence, and control, and only when this group is truly diverse can a multiracial organization be a reality.

In addition to creating a racially diverse board of directors and management-level staff, you will need to address the dynamics of how the board and staff function and the organizational culture into which new people are coming. When people of color are invited onto a previously all-white (or mostly white) board, look out for the development of different levels of access to information and the tendency to expect new people to assimilate into the status quo. The organization must be willing to change as new perspectives and approaches emerge from a more diverse group.

Many organizations have an invisible power base made up of people with a long history with the organization, or a familiarity with the organization's way of functioning, or a connection to funding. Those outside this group often feel confused, overwhelmed, or "out of the loop." If people of color are new to an organization and don't come in with the same kinds of access to resources, it is important to be aware of the dynamics they will encounter and to be open to challenging the way you do business.

6. All of the oppressions must be addressed. Although the focus of this article is on racial diversity, we believe that true multiculturalism must encompass empowerment of all disenfranchised communities, including women, gays and lesbians, people with disabilities, older people, etc., as well as people of color. When organizations begin to diversify, exploring the effects of racism on the organization, questions arise as to the role of women in the organization or the extent to which homophobia and heterosexism are present or taken seriously. Your organization may have struggled with issues of sexism, heterosexism/homophobia, or other "isms." It can be useful to identify lessons you have learned that you can apply to your work on racism and racial diversity.

7. Change must take place on both individual and organizational levels. Organizations are made up of individuals. If those individuals have not had the opportunity to explore their own personal histories, identities, and relationships to issues of oppression and diversity, they will be less effective in implementing strategies for organizational change. Groups often want to move quickly to the step of identifying the structural solution that will change the composition of their organization without taking the time to explore the personal experiences, cultural differences, and interpersonal dynamics that contribute to the obstacles to true multiculturalism. Talking openly about race and racism is still taboo in our society, and people's fear of raising these topics can keep them from moving forward.

At the same time, it is obviously not enough to focus exclusively on individual feelings and relationships if organizational change is a goal. The leadership of an organization must be willing to examine the structural, institutional barriers to making organizational change.

When Alternatives for Youth hired consultants to work with the staff on issues of racism without a commitment from the executive director or board to participate in the process, the rest of the organization got the message that issues of racism and diversity were not being taken seriously. Because neither the executive director nor any board members attended the workshop, the staff could only focus on their individual experiences and attitudes. No processes for organizational change could be considered because the organization's leadership was not part of the process.

8. Tokenism is a common pitfall. In its more obvious manifestations, tokenism is something most people find offensive. When a corporation "allows" one person of color to enter the ranks of management, but never more than one, or when a board of directors has one position available for a representative of a particular ethnic group, the tokenism is clear. Unfortunately, many nonprofit organizations are also guilty of tokenism, even if it is not conscious. One effect of such tokenism is to set up unrealistic expectations for the role of people of color in the organization.

In the case of End Hunger Today, not only was the new staff person expected to bring other African Americans into the organization, but there was an unspoken expectation that she would represent the interests of all black people in any discussion or decision-making process. This creates tokenism because it assumes that all people of a particular ethnicity have the same experiences and perspectives.

9. Antiracism work does not require the presence of people of color. We believe that actively working on racism even if there are only white people in your organization is still an important step in overcoming it. If your community has very few people of color in it or your group hasn't yet been successful in diversifying your membership, you can still have a strong commitment to antiracist work. There are many communities in the U. S. that have very few people of color; at the same time, many previously all-white communities are experiencing growing numbers of various racial and ethnic groups. You do not need to have leadership from people of color to take on the challenge to fight against racism and all forms of oppression.

1992

Building Cultural Diversity into Fundraising

By KIM KLEIN

Many years ago, when I was living in Brooklyn, New York, I was asked to do a fundraising training for a coalition that had formed in the wake of a beating of a Korean merchant. The alleged attackers were Haitians who were responding to the merchant's accusation that he had caught a Haitian woman shoplifting. Whatever was true specifically about that incident never became known, but in the days that followed the attack there was a great deal of anger and hostility vented verbally and physically. Korean merchants operating in primarily Caribbean neighborhoods were accused of price gouging, of not hiring local people to work in their stores, and of controlling businesses in neighborhoods they did not live in. In turn, merchants accused the neighborhood residents of thievery, vandalism, and an unwillingness to work.

In this welter of race and class dynamics, cultural misunderstanding, and frustration, a Korean minister and two Haitian neighborhood activists called a meeting to try to diffuse the anger and violence. A group formed and, several meetings later, I was asked to help develop a fundraising strategy.

The meeting I went to had about 25 people in attendance. The first part of the meeting was to review work that had been done by various committees, then the group was to break up into their committees. I would meet with the fundraising committee. Of the 25 people, eight were from Haiti or Jamaica. Five were African Americans, seven were Korean, including three merchants, and the remaining five were white, of Italian or Irish descent. Thirteen of those present had been born in the United States, including four of the white people.

The strategy of the group was simple, even if its implementation wasn't: Get people talking to each other.

Through encouraging church exchanges, going into schools, and organizing town meetings, they hoped that a lot of frustration would naturally dissolve as people understood each other better. None of the organizers thought their work would actually solve the problems the community was having, but all felt it couldn't hurt.

The early part of the meeting proceeded smoothly and the chair called for the group to break into committees. He introduced me as a fundraising expert and asked the fundraising committee to meet in Room One down the hall. I walked down there and waited for the fundraising committee to join me.

I was taken aback when the only people who came to the meeting were the five white people. When I asked how the committees had been chosen, a woman responded that the chair had made assignments. She went on to say that since she had only been in America a few months (she was from Italy), she really knew nothing about fundraising and had never done anything like it in her country. She thought she might have been better on the education committee, since she was a schoolteacher.

After some discussion of how much money needed to be raised ($10,000), in what time period (over the next six months of the school year), for what (books, videos, and speaker fees), three other committee people chimed in that they had also never done any fundraising. I decided to find the coalition chair and suggest we reconvene the whole group and ask for volunteers for the fundraising committee.

To raise a small amount of money for a short-term project like this seemed a good opportunity to also use fundraising to further the goals of the group. I could envision some block parties, door-to-door canvassing inside some of the big apartment buildings, and possibly a raffle to involve merchants in donating prizes and in selling tickets.

The chair called the group back together and I explained what I had in mind and asked for volunteers. One person from the original committee raised her hand, followed by one Haitian, two African Americans, and the chair, who was Korean. The chair then asked if anyone else wanted to switch committees. There was minimal shuffling — the original fundraising committee members fanned out among the education, relations with police, and church outreach committees.

We went back to meeting. I now had people on the committee who had done a lot of fundraising. My ideas were rejected in favor of two events, which ultimately raised more than $13,000. The first was a barbecue contest. Those entering paid $5 to bring their entry, which had to be enough to feed 30. People paid $15 to eat. Given that barbecue is a favorite food of all the ethnic groups involved, it was a great event. People brought all kinds of food and set up booths. It was a multiblock party that lasted all afternoon and into the late evening. The second event was a second collection at a number of churches.

WHY DIVERSITY MATTERS IN FUNDRAISING

Although this group's situation was more dramatic than many because the group was so diverse to begin with, the tendency for people to see fundraising as the prerogative or talent or job of a certain group of people, usually defined by race, age, and class, is not uncommon. This organization defined it by race. Sometimes, people assume not that a certain group cannot do any fundraising, but that there is a particular kind of fundraising they would be good at. People under 25 are often given the task of organizing a special event or selling a product to make money. Upper-class or wealthy people are always thought to be better at face-to-face solicitation, even though having money does not give anyone skill at raising it. Planned giving is often directed at older people, even though none of us knows when we are going to die, and some planned giving strategies can benefit a wider age margin than is often realized.

There are two reasons to pay attention to cultural diversity when planning for fundraising. First, the world, and the United States as one country in the world, is culturally diverse. Second, you will raise more money if you take the fact of this diversity into account.

Though it is nearly a cliché these days to say that the world is diverse, I see evidence every day of people's beliefs otherwise. I work almost entirely with organizations that are defined as "out of the mainstream." They are working on a broad span of issues, including environ-ment, public education, health, rent control, peace, foreign policy, accessible mass transit, and so on. Why these issues are "out of the mainstream" has led many of us to ask, "Where is the mainstream, anyway?"

The types of organizations I work with cover the gamut of rights and liberation struggles, including those for the poor, the physically or mentally challenged, gays and lesbians, seniors, youth, women, and people of color. Any sharp-eyed reader will have noticed something about this list, which is that it includes the majority of people. Most people in the world are people of color; in several states, including the one I live in (California), so-called minorities are the majority of the population. More than half the people in the world are women and the vast majority of people live in poverty. What we call the "Third World" would be more appropriately called "the majority world."

Even in cities and towns that are racially homogeneous, there are vast age spreads, there are cultural differences between neighborhoods, there are gay people and straight people, and so on. The point is obvious: To be a viable nonprofit with more than a handful of members requires attracting people of all types because that's how the world is. For many of us, understanding this fact requires a shift in what we think, often involuntarily, is the norm.

For example, a board member of a group I was working with recently announced, "We have recruited four new board members — one is a woman and one is Asian." Another board member said, "What are the other two, chopped liver?" This remark made people realize how we often think of people — albeit unconsciously: The norm is white, straight, and male, and everyone is defined against that norm. As another board member pointed out, "You probably wouldn't announce that you had four new board members and two were white men."

Assumptions about what is the norm are pervasive is our society. School curricula talk about "authors" and "black authors." A newspaper recently announced a conference for journalists, with a special panel by "disabled journalists."

WE GIVE AWAY MONEY

Shifting our core assumptions about the world will not only put us in closer touch with reality, it will also enable us to raise more money! If the majority of us are actually demographically members of various "minority" groups, then we will want to tailor our message accordingly. The evidence about who gives away money follows closely the pattern of who makes up the majority of people. It helps to know that, of the three nongovernment sources of funding — individuals, foundations and corporations — individuals give away the lion's share of charitable dollars. For all the time that the fundraising field has been keeping records, which is now more than 60 years, 85–90% of money given away each year is given by individuals. Only about 10–12% of funding comes from foundations and corporations, and of course, the source of most foundation assets is the accumulated wealth of an individual or family.

Who are the individuals giving away money — in 1999, more than $190 billion? Most of us. Seven out of ten adults give away money. When we look closely at who these people are, we see that last year, as in most years, about 82% of donors were from households with incomes of less than $60,000. These donors are fairly evenly divided by education, with a little more than one-third of them (37%) being high school graduates, 22% having some college education, and 25% being college graduates. The remaining 16% have less than a high school education. Most donors were employed full-time (54%), though some worked part-time (11%), and about one-third were unemployed. Slightly more women than men made contributions, and all races were represented as givers. (These statistics are taken from *Giving USA,* published by the American Association of Fund Raising Counsel and *Giving and Volunteering in the United States,* Vol. 2, published by the Independent Sector.)

PLANNING WITH DIVERSITY

Here are some examples of what fundraising looks like in organizations that plan around the diversity present in their board, staff, volunteers, and constituents.

• *An Oakland, CA group organizing on issues of police accountability, lead paint in schools, and toxic dumping — all issues affecting poor neighborhoods in the city — has a fundraising dinner every year.* The members of the organization make the food and people pay $15 to attend. Because the membership is quite multicultural, the food always includes barbecued ribs, potato salad, roasted chicken, egg rolls, tamales, rice and beans, lasagna, and several kinds of dessert. The group puts together an adbook for the dinner and sells ads not only to merchants in the neighborhoods in which they work, but also to other nonprofits, unions, and a wide circle of friends who have started coming to the dinner because of the food. With 200 to 300 people attending the dinner, plus the proceeds from the adbook, this group nets from $5,000 to $10,000 from the dinner annually. More than 50 people work on the dinner every year.

• *A program for battered women in a rural community started a major donor program by creating categories of donors based on what people had in common.* When someone became a major donor with a minimum gift of $100, they were invited to join one or more of various clubs. The clubs included Local Merchants, Vacation Homeowners, Hikers, Gardeners, Retirees, Fisher People, High School Jocks, and Odd Ducks. The latter was a self-identified group of writers, artists, musicians, and other people who felt that they didn't fit in anywhere. Only three people were needed to start a club, and each club member got a certificate produced by a computer graphics program that one of the Odd Ducks owned. There were no other benefits for being part of these clubs, except a certain camaraderie. Sometimes the organization invited people from all the clubs to get-togethers. Of course the money from these major donations was important to the group, but so was the feeling that all kinds of people are committed to stopping violence against women.

• *An environmental organization working in very-low-income and primarily immigrant neighborhoods had a lot of trouble getting their membership drive off the ground.* Membership dues were set at $15. They were able to raise money from a large number of people, but they raised almost no money from the neighborhoods they served. Thinking that the dues were too high, they lowered them to $10 and later to $5. Neither move helped generate more local membership. Finally, they brought two current members onto the membership committee; they explained that people didn't need membership dues to be lower, but they needed a way to pay them without having to use a check, since few had checking accounts. The organization set up a system where one of the members who owns a store agreed to take in the contributions and give receipts every Saturday. People brought cash and got a membership card and a receipt. Most people paid $15, and soon a high percentage of those living in the neighborhoods had joined.

• *A health clinic focusing on primary care and family planning and delivering more than half of their service to uninsured people does an annual phone-a-thon to their lapsed donors and to a list of people they think would be interested in their work.* One year, the teenage daughter of a board member showed up to volunteer and ended up being the highest income-generator of the evening. When the coordinator asked what her secret was, she explained that she and her friends have raised so much money to be able to do the things they want to do — including going to Cuba on a student exchange, taking the school choir to a competition in New York City, and her Sunday School class to Greece — that she feels very comfortable asking for money. The coordinator asked if she would come to the second night of the phone-a-thon and bring some friends. She and six friends came the next night and raised more money than this phone-a-thon had ever raised before.

WHAT HAVE WE LEARNED?

Are these stories about diversity? Yes and no. They are actually a lot about common sense, which I believe is fundamental to building a diverse fundraising base. Based on these and other stories, I suggest the following template for working with cultural diversity in raising money.

1. Remember that there are two groups of people to consider in using cultural diversity in fundraising: those you work with to raise money and those you raise money from. There is clearly an interrelationship here — the more diverse the group that raises the money, the more diverse the donor base will be; and the more diverse the donor base, the more people you will be able to ask to help you raise the money.

2. Be careful about your assumptions. After 22 years in fundraising, I can testify that there are two kinds of people: havers and givers. As I said above, 70% of adults are givers. Givers give and havers have. Some poor people are havers: What little they have, they hang on to. Some rich people are havers, and the fact that they have more than they can spend in several lifetimes doesn't cause them to give any of it away. Givers come in all types. Some are more generous than others, but one cannot predict generosity based on age, education, income, gender, or any other variable. If you make it a habit to look at every person who comes through your organization as a giver, and then as a person who might be willing to help raise money, you will never overlook any possible helpers or gifts. Of course, you may be wrong, but far better to be wrong because you thought the person might give when he or she wasn't going to than to lose a gift because you assumed the person couldn't give.

3. Figure out what people like to do and feel comfortable doing, then use those talents in fundraising. Few people of any cultural background feel comfortable "raising money," which they imagine is asking people in person for donations. As in the Oakland group, most people love to eat and some people love to cook. Put those together and you have the basis of an event. It can be helpful to create a list of activities that are needed for fundraising and ask people to check off what they are willing to do. Items would include making phone calls, cooking for a crowd, going door-to-door in your own neighborhood/in a neighborhood where you don't know anyone, addressing envelopes, writing fundraising letters, and so on. Sometimes people

are not sure what they are good at or are embarrassed to volunteer for big tasks, even if they think they could do them. You may need to let people know that you have confidence in their ability to do a specific task, or even ask them directly if they are willing to do something you think they could do. Sometimes people assume that to be a fundraiser you have to be well educated or comfortable around affluence or a salesperson. Of course, these things are helpful, but not required.

4. Don't rush to conclusions in solving problems. The group that kept lowering its dues because it thought the membership fee was too high did not allow for any other issue to be the barrier. The real problem in this group was that no neighborhood people were on the membership committee, so the committee members were trying to figure out what to do for a group of people they knew only slightly. Once they invited people from the neighborhood they were organizing in onto the committee, the problem became clear.

5. Keep careful records of what people do well, and use those in future planning. The young people that were so successful in the phone-a-thon ought to be invited onto the major gifts committee. Their comfort in asking for money will be useful in many ways. People grow out of some strategies and into others. Many people start their fundraising efforts doing special events; as they become more comfortable with events, they are willing to go to other strategies. As you keep records, think about what a person has learned from a particular strategy and how that might be helpful in another strategy. For example, creating a script for a phone-a-thon requires some of the same skills as writing a press release or making a pitch at a house party.

6. Educate your volunteer force about who really gives away money and what is true about charities. I have seen many people burst into applause and laugh with relief when they learn that most money given away in the U.S. comes from individuals and that most of those people are of middle-class, working-class, and poor backgrounds. The news media give the impression that most giving is from corporations, wealthy people, and foundations. Grassroots groups in particular waste precious time trying to break into those worlds, trying to meet people whom they only imagine exist. When they find out that in fact most money is given away by most people, they are thrilled. They already know all the people they need to know to raise all the money they need to raise.

7. Think long term. Who is going to run the development office in five years? Ten years? Help the young people in your organization to see development as a career; if they show interest, help them get experience and knowledge. There are degree programs at several universities for people wishing to make the nonprofit sector their career. Unfortunately, these programs are not well advertised, and the idea of a nonprofit career is still not one to be found at job fairs and career-day expositions. We need to change that.

REWARDS IN AND BEYOND OUR TIME

Building a fundraising base that reflects the diversity of the organization and the community requires a constant and unflinching commitment. There are struggles involved. There are bound to be misunderstandings, resentments, and confrontations. Sadly, in our society people do not fluidly cross race or age lines, women and men rarely work together as equal partners, and class remains a primary barrier.

Sometimes groups make a commitment to honoring diversity in its programs and its fundraising in response to a demand from funders, or because it's something the group thinks it "should" do, even if it would rather not.

Commitments made in order to get funding or to relieve guilt will not last long and the results will not be satisfying. At the same time, if a group makes a sincere commitment to incorporate diversity into its fundraising program, it cannot expect immediate results. The work required may be long and sometimes tedious, with the feeling of going in circles as often as making true progress.

Groups that have made this commitment and keep working on building diversity into their organization and into their fundraising, however, do find that they can raise more money. Along the way, they form friendships and alliances that extend even outside of the work and, most important, they see how rich and complex life can be.

Reinhold Niebuhr, the great Protestant theologian, has said, "Nothing that is worth doing can be achieved in our lifetime, therefore we must be saved by hope. Nothing which is true or beautiful or good makes complete sense in any immediate context of history; therefore we must be saved by faith. Nothing we do, however virtuous, can be accomplished alone; therefore we are saved by love.

2000

Fundraising as a Profession

Make Fundraising Your Career

By KIM KLEIN

What would you say if you could have a career that paid you a salary from $10,000–$150,000? Where your work had fairly measurable outcomes? Where talking about your values and writing about what you believe are part of the job? Where all the people you work with agree that what you do is really important?

Sounds like a great career, doesn't it? It is; it's a career in fundraising.

I have had many goals in my life, but my new goal is to have more people make fundraising their career. I have several reasons for wanting this:

- I have too much work, much more than I can handle. In another 10 or 15 years, I want to retire knowing that there are many other people able to do the work I was doing.

- I want fewer phone calls from headhunters, desperate executive directors, friends who sit on boards of directors, all saying, "Do you know anyone who can take our development job? We've looked everywhere. We've extended the deadline for applications indefinitely."

- I want to see good organizations succeed in their fundraising, and one thing many groups need in order to succeed is someone who is paid to coordinate the organization's fundraising efforts.

Of course, my goal is more specific than simply bringing new people into fundraising. What I really want is to bring a new generation into fundraising for progressive social change, which is at the lower end of the salary scale I mentioned above.

"But fundraising isn't a cool career," I hear you say. "Not like actually doing advocacy or service, or maybe even being a public interest attorney — being on the front lines of changing society."

A woman I worked with in the past recently wrote to tell me that she had just left her fundraising position to take a job as an advocate in an agency serving homeless mentally ill adults. "I'm glad to have had this fundraising experience," she wrote, "but it will be good to be out on the front lines again." Her letter came on the same day as a phone call from another colleague who said, "I just have to get back into doing the real work. I can't do this fundraising anymore."

I know that we need organizers and attorneys and social workers. But none of these positions needs to be exempt from fundraising, and someone needs to be the main person in charge of that fundraising.

Before you dismiss a fundraising career as for nerds only, consider the following facts. Fundraising allows you — in fact, requires you — to talk to people whom you would probably never otherwise meet about what you believe in and the difference their money will make in translating those beliefs into actions. Fundraising gives you the chance to experiment with strategies. Will this letter work? Can you raise money on the Internet? Would people pay to come to this kind of event? While some strategies are formulaic — you follow a recipe and you can predict the result (comforting, but often boring), others are a combination of good luck, timing, and creativity.

Of course, fundraising does have its drawbacks. As with any difficult job, you have to be able to handle lots of tasks at the same time. In most organizations the fundraising staff has a lot of responsibility with very little authority. People tend to blame the fundraising department for everything that goes wrong in the organization. People who have no knowledge of fundraising have unrealistic ideas of how much money can be raised in short periods of time. And worse, they tend to believe that all the organization's problems can be solved by finding previously unknown, but very large foundations to get grants from, or by meeting lonely, generous, and previously unsolicited rich people.

WHY FUNDRAISING IS COOL

Now I'm going to tell you why people think fundraising isn't cool, and why they're wrong. Let's admit it, fundraisers are regarded with the same mixture of admiration, loathing, suspicion, and awe with which we in America regard money itself. And this explains some of the problems in attracting people to fundraising positions. Money is one of the great taboos of our culture. We are taught not to talk about it or ask about it, except to a very limited number of people in a very limited number of circumstances. As with the subjects of sex, death, mental illness, religion, politics, and other taboos, people say little about their experiences with money. If people are so carefully taught that it is rude to talk about money, it's certainly not going to be easy to ask for it.

Yet, as George Pillsbury points out, "Although money cannot buy social change, no significant change can happen without it." Organizations cannot do their work without money. An organization that does not have enough money to accomplish its goals winds up wasting the time of its volunteers and staff, and possibly hurting the constituency it claims to be working for.

When I decided to make fundraising my career 20 years ago, it wasn't because I liked fundraising. In fact, like most people drawn to working for social change, I had wanted to do advocacy work. But I found that the advocacy work was not going to happen unless someone brought in money, and if I wanted to do work that was important and useful for the groups and movements that I cared about, fundraising was one of the most useful things I could do.

I also chose fundraising because it meant that I would have to talk about money, which, in a small way, could begin to break down the taboo that surrounds it. This taboo, I believe, helps promote both racism and sexism. If you can't ask others at your workplace what they are earning, you will never know if minorities there are being paid less than whites or women less than men. That way, management has no fear that workers will seek more equitable salaries. The taboo supports the class structure in other ways as well. If only a tiny handful of ruling-class people understand how the stock market or other forms of investing work, they need not fear any threats to the economic system they control.

In fact, people who cannot talk about money, who will not learn to ask for it and deal with it, actually collaborate with a system that the rest of social change work seeks to dismantle. That alone makes fundraising not only a way cool profession, but also a dangerous one.

Here are some other reasons fundraising is exciting, sexy, and cool.

1. Although there are technical aspects to fundraising, it does not require years of education. In fact, the three main requirements for success in fundraising can be found in people of all educational backgrounds: common sense, a basic affection for other people, and a passionate belief in a cause.

2. Fundraising requires you to learn new things all the time, while perfecting the set of basic skills you bring.

3. Fundraising connects donors to an organization. Many donors have little relationship to the organizations they support aside from giving money. They don't have time to volunteer, or they are not part of the constituency. A fundraiser helps them continue to feel connected and useful so that they will want to continue to give.

4. Fundraising is organizing. Good fundraisers organize teams of volunteers to help with fundraising, and they should be teaching organizers how to ask for money, too. Organizers usually ask people only for time — go to a meeting, plan a strategy, come to a demonstration. Good fundraisers teach people fundraising skills and give them confidence that they actually can raise money. With a combined strategy of fundraising and organizing, people are asked for time and money — as much of either or both as they can give. A much wider range of gifts and talents and abilities can be brought out in our constituents by adding fundraising strategies to the mix.

5. Fundraising will allow you, perhaps even force you, to confront basic issues of class in yourself, in your organization, and in the people you raise money for and from.

BECOMING A FUNDRAISER

You can get into fundraising in a variety of ways. One of the best ways to learn fundraising is to volunteer to help with fundraising tasks at one of your favorite organizations. Fundraising is in fact one of the few jobs for which volunteer experience qualifies you. Being on the fundraising committee of a board of directors or helping put on a special event has launched many a fundraising career. Interning with the fundraising department or staff person at an organization is another form of volunteering that can be very instructive.

You can also learn about fundraising in college classes

and courses, but they only have merit if you have a way to apply what you have learned in a real-life setting. Working in a large organization as an assistant to the development director will give you a range of experience without requiring you to take on a lot of responsibility.

If you are serious about fundraising as a career, find a mentor. Many development directors enjoy mentoring people new to the field and can help you find your way through the difficult times.

And don't hesitate to jump in at the deep end. Take a job that you are not totally qualified for, then read, take classes, use your mentor, and wing it. I have often encouraged organizations to stop looking for the person with perfect skills who may not exist, and instead to find a bright, hardworking, quick learner. Give that person a solid team of volunteers to work with and watch what happens. With enough support and a little latitude, this person is likely to be successful.

JOIN THE FRONT LINES

As you can see, when I say I want people to make fundraising their career, what I really mean is that I want people to say, "My role in working for social justice will be to help generate money." Fundraising cannot be separated from its context. It is a necessary and central part of developing an organization and fulfilling its mission. It is real work, and though it takes place on slightly different set of front lines, they are front lines all the same. The more fundraising is integrated into the rest of the organization, the more successful it will be, and the more fundraisers we can hope to have in the future. The sooner that happens, the sooner I can retire.

1998

Why People of Color Need to Be Good Fundraisers

By MIKE ROQUE

When I started out in fundraising ten years ago, I was usually the only person of color in the room. Today, the situation is much the same. Whether it is a meeting with a potential donor to my organization or a training I am giving to the fundraising committee of a nonprofit organization, the people in the room are usually white, except for me.

Even within people-of-color organizations or multiracial organizations, often the people who do the bulk of the fundraising are white. I could give a long diatribe on how society oppresses people of color and wants to keep them from controlling money or talk about how people of color's internalized oppression keeps them from taking control of money. But instead, I want to challenge progressive nonprofits to be more aware of the power dynamics of who raises money for them, and I want to challenge people of color to train themselves and others to be good fundraisers.

The one thing I remember most from the first fundraising training I went to taught by Kim Klein is her saying, "Those who control the money, control the organization." I was then a community organizer with a small, mostly Chicano community organization in southern Colorado. The board of the organization was 70% Chicano, mostly low-income members, yet the fundraising committee was made up of three white people. It was much the same with other organizations with which I worked over the years. Now, after fundraising for both small community organizing groups and large foundations, I still find truth in Kim's statement: Those who control the money, control the organization.

I believe that people of color have been systematically excluded from fundraising for nonprofit organizations. I do not believe that it has been a malicious exclusion or a conspiracy that needs to be investigated by Mulder and Scully. But many organizations have simply not examined the power dynamics of their fundraising work. In this article I put forth six reasons that people of color have been excluded from fundraising and offer ways for organizations to recruit, develop and maintain people of color as fundraisers.

WHY PEOPLE OF COLOR ARE EXCLUDED FROM FUNDRAISING

There are a number of reasons that people of color are not asked to participate in an organization's fundraising.

• *Program Work Only.* The first board I joined promptly put me on the program committee, even though my interest was with finance. This being my first board membership, I just did what they told me. Often when people of color are brought onto boards, the organization restricts them to programmatic work or, worse, uses them in public relations efforts to give the appearance of being diverse.

• *Banker Boards.* We've all been through a Junior League–type training in which the first thing they say is that you need to fill your board with bankers, company presidents, and other prominent (i.e., rich) people. This often leaves people of color out.

• *It's Who You Know.* Unlike the previous reason for the lack of people of color on a board, in this model the board members themselves don't have to be rich, just know rich people. Even well-intentioned organizations buy into this trap of only putting people on the finance/fundraising committee who already know potential funders — both individual donors and foundations. This usually means people with connections to well-off people. Again, assuming that they would not have such contacts, organizations mistakenly leave people of color off.

• **Lack of Training.** Organizations want people on board and staff who can come in and fundraise from day one. In addition, they want them to understand often unnecessarily complicated financial statements. If organizations are not willing to put the time and money into training new fundraisers, they run the risk of burning out existing fundraisers and not having anyone to take their place.

• **"We Are So Glad Just to Have You."** Often organizations are just so happy to have people of color (especially their first) on their boards that they do not hold them to the same standards as other board members. If giving a personal gift and fundraising are responsibilities of other board members (which they should be for every organization) then they should be for people of color too.

• **Fear of Losing Control.** When organizations begin to recruit board members outside of the original founders — whether it's people of color, gays and lesbians, rural folks, etc. — the very nature of the organization changes. This change happens most dramatically when new people begin to raise money from different constituencies. The organization becomes accountable to a new group of people and the original members of the organization can feel threatened or left out. If you want people of color to share in the ownership of the organization, you need to give up some control.

CHALLENGE TO ORGANIZATIONS

In order to overcome these reasons for people of color being excluded from fundraising, organizations are going to have to look at themselves more closely and change some of their behaviors.

• **Be Aware of Power Dynamics.** Organizations should examine the makeup of their fundraising committee and fundraising staff. This fundraising team tends to have little turnover, indicating its importance within the organization. Even when people of color join a fundraising committee, they're often not made to feel included or productive. They will serve for one or two years but then rotate off, often feeling that they did not make a difference or were not wanted. This can lead to stagnation and complacency on behalf of the organization and eventually burnout of the members. Even within the most progressive organizations, I have noticed that much of their fundraising team is

white. Organizations need to make a point of examining their fundraising team every year and recruiting people of color specifically to serve on the fundraising team.

• **Invest in Training.** Organizations need to make a commitment to invest in fundraising training for new committee and staff members. Even experienced staff and committee members will benefit from training. Or, the experienced folks can provide the training for newer members. Training does not have to be expensive. Look around for low-cost training opportunities and get as many of your members to them as possible. Or, try to pull together other nonprofits and share the cost of bringing in a trainer or, better yet, get a foundation to underwrite a training workshop.

• **Seek Money from Communities of Color.** When bringing people of color to the fundraising team, trust them to know how to approach fundraising in their community. If this is something the organization has not tried before, don't automatically assume it will not be effective or appropriate for your group. Communities of color have been supporting their own issues in informal ways for years. Use fundraising basics (you have to ask), but don't be afraid of trying new fundraising methods. I have seen successful pig ear sales, church appeals, and salsa dances (obviously not everything is appropriate for every group). By reaching out to communities of color to raise funds, your organization will tap into another source of money and make contact with other people of color who may one day become board members.

• **Plan for Transitions.** Organizations need to plan carefully for leadership transitions, especially when a person of color is replacing a white (oftentimes founding) executive director or development director. Progressive organizations often try to recruit people of color when hiring new staff people. This is an important effort and needs to be encouraged, but don't overlook the organizational dynamics of that transition. Without transition activities built into the move from one staff person to the next, the person of color is put into a position where no one can succeed. Organizations need to consider that, if the previous executive or development director has done their job well, funders (individuals and foundations) will have a strong relationship with him or her. The organization must take the time for a systematic transition of these relationships from the outgoing to the new director. Also, the organization should ensure that the rest of the fundraising team will stay on to facilitate a transfer of organizational memory.

CHALLENGE TO PEOPLE OF COLOR

People of color also need to meet the challenges of becoming more involved in fundraising. Here are some things we can do to increase our visibility and effectiveness as fundraisers.

• *Join Boards, Join Fundraising Committees.* When asked to join a board, do a thorough investigation of the organizational and board dynamics. Don't join the board unless you have the time and commitment to give it your full effort. Once you join, demand to be put onto the fundraising or finance committee and learn where the real power lies. Even if "numbers" are not your strong point, join. If you're not clear on the fundraising strategy or an item on the financial statements, ask questions. Number geeks (which I consider myself to be) love people who are interested in learning more about what financial statements say. Once you've mastered the basics, the rest is easy.

• *Go to Any and All Trainings You Can.* Training, training, and more training. You can never get enough training. Be on the lookout for training opportunities. Ask the organization you work with to pay for you to attend.

• *Raise Our Own Money and Create Our Own Organizations.* As people of color, we need to be good fundraisers. We need to raise our own money from our own communities and create and sustain our own organizations. If we are to see substantial change within our communities we need to be able to control our destiny. Remember, those who control the money, control the organization. If we hope to truly develop self-determination in our communities, we must be able to sustain institutions within our communities financially, whether nonprofit organizations or businesses. Being a good fundraiser is a strong step in that direction.

This does not mean we should not work with each other or with white organizations; we all need to support each other's struggle for justice and equality.

1998

Why Good Fundraisers Are Never Paid on Commission

By KIM KLEIN

An organization that worked with abused children desperately needed a new facility. However, they could barely meet their annual operating costs, so taking on higher rent or purchasing a building seemed impossible. Nevertheless, because their program was seriously suffering from lack of adequate space, they shopped around. Whether they rented or bought, they would have to remodel any building for safety and accessibility and to make it pleasant for the children.

The group found a building that the owner was eager to sell, and she offered them a good deal. They saw that, with a little work, this could be the ideal space. The obstacle was the cost: They would need $500,000 to cover everything. This amount seemed completely unattainable and then, as if in answer to a prayer, a handsome stranger showed up and offered to raise the $500,000 for a 20% commission. If he didn't succeed, he explained, they would not be out anything; however, they would pay him 20% of any money he did raise. He proposed to raise $700,000, which would cover his costs and the costs of the campaign, as well as the $500,000 needed for the building. He could finish the campaign in a year, he said, but he might complete it in six months. He would earn $70,000–$140,000, depending on how long he took.

However, the group knew that paying on commission is highly frowned on in fundraising and all the trade associations of fundraisers, including the Association of Fundraising Professionals (AFP, formerly the National Society of Fundraising Executives), the National Association of Hospital Developers, and the Council for the Advancement and Support of Education (CASE), have issued statements decrying the practice of commission-based fundraising.

Why is this an absolute no-no? There are several reasons. First, no one else in nonprofit organizations is paid on commission. In this particular group, the counselors are not paid more for every child that shows improvement nor are the social workers paid for each child whose abuse they report. Everyone is paid a salary in recognition that their work is a process and that they may be very good counselors or social workers and still not show a lot of progress with every child.

Second, a commission tends to distort salaries. In this case, this fundraiser would be paid $140,000 per year, about three times as much as the executive director who earned $45,000.

Third, this person would not bring his own list of contacts. He would be working with the organization's donors. He said he has some contacts from previous jobs, but would you want him to use them? And would you want him taking your donor information to his next job? Further, his whole livelihood depends on donors saying yes to his requests. Even a totally honest fundraiser working under these conditions would be tempted to distort information, seeing his rent check in the eyes of each prospect. Also, many big gifts take cultivation and several visits. He may be willing to settle for a small gift in order to get it quickly rather than take the time a larger gift would require in proper cultivation.

Fourth, what would the donors think if and when they found out that 20% of their gift, designated for a new building, went to this temporary staff person? Donors know that it costs money to raise money, but few things make donors angrier than seeing that too large a part of their designated gift was used for expenses, and 20% going to salary alone is too big.

Fifth, and most important, one person should not be in charge of actually raising money for an entire campaign. Suppose this fundraiser was both honest and successful. When he left, the group would be $500,000 richer, to be sure, but no wiser with regard to fundraising. The role of a fundraiser is to get the board and other volunteers to help raise the money. A good development person coordinates, researches, plans, and helps decide which volunteer should go with which other staff or board member to ask for the money, when each prospect should be solicited (should Sally Jones be asked right away, or not until her close friend Mabel Smith has given?), and other strategy issues.

Finally, the person coordinating the fundraising should absolutely believe in the cause and be a part of the team of people putting the campaign together.

For all these reasons, paying on commission is not an option for fundraising.

Some people in small organizations will say, "But we don't have the cash to hire someone outright and it's risky to hire a person when you can't afford it, both for the person and for us if they are not good." However, for all the reasons listed above, a small organization especially cannot afford the risk involved in hiring someone on commission.

Here are some other ways the children's group could raise the money they needed. They could go to the eager property owner and see if she would accept a lower down payment, then they could explore how to finance the building instead of trying to pay for it all at once. A committee composed of a couple of members of the board, a couple of volunteers, and the executive director would need to make a list of ten people who could give the money for the down payment and the costs of moving and fixing the space up. Then they would need to go and ask these prospects for the money. These slow, thoughtful, and group-generated steps will provide the needed money, build support from the constituency, and, by the way, save the commission fees of the handsome stranger.

No matter how strapped for cash you are, you should never consider doing something unethical to raise the money you need, and commission fundraising is unethical.

1992

About the Authors

Kim Klein is an internationally known fundraising trainer, speaker, and consultant. She is best known for adapting traditional fundraising techniques — particularly major gift campaigns — for use by grassroots organizations. She has provided training and consultation in all fifty states and in sixteen countries. Kim is the founder and co-publisher of the *Grassroots Fundraising Journal* and the author of *Fundraising for Social Change* (Chardon Press), *Fundraising for the Long Haul* (Chardon Press), and *Ask and You Shall Receive: A Fundraising Training Program for Religious Organizations and Projects* (Jossey Bass). Kim lives in Berkeley, California.

Stephanie Roth has been a trainer and consultant in fundraising and board development since 1988. She is co-owner of Chardon Press and the *Grassroots Fundraising Journal*. Her articles on fundraising and building better boards have appeared in a number of periodicals. Stephanie was a founder of the Grassroots Institute for Fundraising Training (GIFT), which offers a fundraising internship program for people of color and provides fundraising training and technical assistance to social justice organizations. In her prior life on the East Coast, she was co-founder and director of the Long Island Technical Assistance Center and co-director of New York Women Against Rape. She lives in Berkeley, California.

Nancy Adess, a freelance editor of books, articles, reports, and proposals, works with nonprofit groups throughout the country, particularly in the fields of health, environment, and nonprofit fundraising and organizing. She has been the editor of the *Grassroots Fundraising Journal* since its inception and of Chardon Press since she and Kim Klein founded the publishing house in 1983. In the 1980s, Nancy, a health educator, was executive director of DES Action, a health advocacy organization for people exposed to the prenatal drug DES. In the 1990s, she was publications editor for The Nature Conservancy of California. Nancy's service on boards of directors includes the Coalition for the Medical Rights of Women, DES Action, and numerous local health and environmental organizations in her home town of Point Reyes Station, California.

Andrea Ayvazian cut her activist teeth while organizing for reproductive rights in the women's movement in the early 1970s. She was active in the anti-Vietnam War movement in the 1970s and the anti-nuclear weapons and Nuclear Freeze movements of the 1980s. She has been a war-tax resister since 1982. In the mid-1980s she became an anti-racism educator and for a dozen years provided anti-racism training and consultation throughout the country. An ordained minister in the United Church of Christ, Andrea is currently Dean of Religious Life at Mount Holyoke College in Hadley, Massachusetts. Her work with grassroots movements for peace, social justice, and gay and lesbian civil rights over the last thirty years inform her writing about the needs and challenges of grassroots organizations.

Carol Blanton is Special Projects Director for the Membership and Interactive Marketing Department of The Nature Conservancy. She was previously Director of Membership for The Nature Conservancy of California. She lives in San Francisco.

Lincoln Cushing is a graphic artist who has worked in the printing trade since 1976. He is a collective member of Inkworks Press in Berkeley, California, a worker-owned union shop that has helped hundreds of community and nonprofit organizations print their materials at affordable rates. With a Master's Degree in Information Management from U.C. Berkeley, he is pursuing the documentation, cataloging, and publication of political graphic artwork that might otherwise be lost in the digital tidal wave. His work can be viewed at *www.sims.berkeley.edu/~lcush*.

Robin Ferguson has worked in a broad range of nonprofit organizations in New York City over the past 20 years, including a shelter for victims of domestic violence, a community foundation, and most recently a health education and theater program for young people. She has been a nonprofit management consultant and grantwriter for more than 10 years. Robin is also an activist, singer and writer. She lives in Brooklyn, New York.

Lucy Grugett worked for 15 years at The Center for Anti-Violence Education, a community-based nonprofit in Brooklyn, NY, that educates and organizes women, teen women, and children. As the Center's Associate Director, she experienced firsthand the pleasures and challenges of donor, event, and foundation fundraising. Lucy now works at Bailey House, Inc., one of the nation's first AIDS housing providers, where, among other things, she helps others learn the fundraising ropes through the Technical Assistance Clearinghouse (*www.taclearinghouse.org*). She is also a member of the North Star Fund's Community Advisory Board and a grateful student of karate and aikido.

A victim of an overly active social conscience, **Sue Merrilees** has always worked in nonprofit organizations and has been fundraising for a variety of them — large and small — for more than 13 years. She has worked to promote women's rights, end homelessness, assist environmental efforts, and extend opportunities in higher education, among other causes. Most recently, she left Stanford University's reunion campaign program to serve as Director of Development for the Institute for Neurodegenerative Diseases at the University of California, San Francisco.

Sara Mersha is Executive Director of DARE (Direct Action for Rights and Equality) in Providence, Rhode Island. Sara entered the organizing world in 1997, when she attended the Movement Activist Apprenticeship Program of the Center for Third World Organizing (CTWO). As a field organizer through CTWO's Winning Action for Gender Equity project, she organized home daycare providers in Providence and food service and temporary workers through the Carolina Alliance for Fair Employment. Sara became Lead Organizer at DARE in 1999. With members, she launched DARE's Jobs with Dignity campaign for living wages and community access to jobs. Sara is also on the National Planning Committee of Jobs with Justice, a national coalition with local chapters that brings together unions, community organizations, and religious and student groups to fight for workers' rights.

Octavia Morgan has more than ten years of experience in social change organizations, including five years serving as the development director for the San Francisco-based International Gay and Lesbian Human Rights Commission. She has worked in human rights, youth services, domestic violence, and the environment, and spent a year consulting for nonprofits in Zimbabwe. She is currently deputy director of the Independent Media Institute in San Francisco. Octavia is committed to creating nonprofit work cultures that support and sustain staff and that prevent burnout within the social justice movement. She also works to enact her belief that professionalizing financial, personnel, and programmatic management enables nonprofits to better pursue their missions. Octavia is an avid outdoor enthusiast, a novice mountaineer, and a devoted student of Iyengar Yoga.

Pat Munoz has been involved in nonprofit fundraising for more than 20 years. She is currently a Watershed Program Manager for River Network, a national organization whose mission is to help people understand, protect, and restore rivers and watersheds. Previously, Pat worked for another national river organization, American Rivers, where she focused on building that organization's membership base, major donor program, foundation base, and workplace giving program. Pat has served on the boards of various small nonprofits, including the Coalition for the Capitol Crescent Trail, the West Virginia Rivers Coalition, and the Cacapon Institute. Pat is an avid whitewater canoeist and kayaker.

Amy O'Connor is a development consultant and trainer who helps nonprofits build successful organizations through planning, communication, and membership and board development. Amy's passion for wilderness protection led her to become an activist; previously she worked for the Southern Utah Wilderness Alliance. Amy brings 15 years of experience with nonprofits to her work and has consulted with dozens of organizations through her business, Integrated Development Consulting, based in Salt Lake City, Utah.

Vicki Quatmann spent 14 years fundraising and organizing with SOCM (Save Our Cumberland Mountains) in Tennessee. She helped develop and has taught the five-day Fundraising and Organizing School for the Southern Empowerment Project and now teaches fundraising all over the eastern and southern United States. She is an avid bicyclist, hiker and canoer. Vicki lives in Lake City, Tennessee.

Liz Raisbeck is Vice President for Regional Operations of the National Parks Conservation Association. Her career spans twenty years of environmental lobbying and campaign organizing. As a senior vice president for the National Audubon Society, she headed up the Washington government affairs office and the regional division, and led the Platte River campaign to protect the wildlife of the Platte. At River Network she helped river protection organizations build organizational capacity and develop programs. Her career in environmental politics included a stint as staff director to former Congresswoman Claudine Schneider of Rhode Island. She has served as a board member for a number of organizations, including the Keystone Center, Friends of the Earth, the Global Tomorrow Coalition, and the Institute for Conservation Leadership. Liz's favorite pastime is kayaking or rowing among the Thousand Islands of her favorite river, the St. Lawrence.

Sheldon Rampton is co-editor of *PR Watch,* published by the Center for Media and Democracy. He has a diverse background as newspaper reporter, activist, and author. Sheldon has co-authored three books with *PR Watch* co-editor, John Stauber: *Toxic Sludge Is Good For You: Lies, Damn Lies and the Public Relations Industry* (1995); *Mad Cow U.S.A.: Could the Nightmare Happen Here?* (1997); and *Trust Us, We're Experts: How Industry Manipulates Science and Gambles With Your Future* (2001). He is also co-author with Liz Chilsen of the 1998 book, *Friends In Deed: the Story of US-Nicaragua Sister Cities.* Sheldon has worked closely with the Wisconsin Coordinating Council on Nicaragua on a project that has channeled more than $5 million in loans from socially responsible U.S. investors to support economic development efforts in low-income Central American communities. He lives in Madison, Wisconsin.

Andy Robinson is a fundraising consultant and trainer. He has been in fundraising for more than 20 years. He is the author of *Grassroots Grants: An Activists Guide to Proposal Writing* (Chardon Press) and is working on a book about nonprofits creating businesses and selling products to support their mission. Andy is a long time social justice activist. He got his start in fundraising as a canvasser for Oregon Fair Share. Previously he was the development director for Native Seeds/SEARCH. Andy lives in Tucson, Arizona.

Mike Roque is Executive Director of the Grassroots Institute for Fundraising Training (GIFT). He has been active in the social justice movement for more than 15 years. Mike was Executive Director of the Chinook Fund, a radical community foundation in Denver, Colorado, for eight years. He was also Director and Lead Organizer of HOPE Alive, a grassroots organization that organizes within the low-income and Chicano neighborhoods in southern Colorado. Mike lives in Denver with his daughter, Amandla.

A writer with more than 100 published stories and articles, **Shirley Wilcox** was for many years an active farm wife, driving the tractor, feeding chickens, chasing pigs, milking cows, and doing whatever else was needed. However, she considers her most important work raising five children who have grown up to become, in her words, "decent and honorable adults." Shirley and her husband, now retired, live near the town of North Manchester in northeastern Indiana.

Index

Authors' names are in bold, followed by the first page number of the article(s) they authored.

Resources for Social Change

★ 2000 Edition

Fundraising for Social Change, Fourth Edition
BY KIM KLEIN

A book no one can afford to be without! Hands-on, specific, and accessible fundraising techniques geared to nonprofits with budgets of less than $1 million that want to raise money from the biggest source of donations— individuals. Thoroughly updated and expanded since the 1996 edition.

Expanded chapters on how to: Ask for money; Use direct mail effectively; Produce successful special events; Get your board to raise money; Conduct capital and endowment campaigns for small groups.

New chapters on how to: Work effectively with your executive director; Use the Internet for fundraising; Make a career of social change fundraising.

$35 / 416 pages

Fundraising for the Long Haul
BY KIM KLEIN

How to survive and thrive through all your fundraising challenges. Klein shares her own most important lessons learned, then details the elements of a healthy organization and fundraising program. Includes advice on the common barriers to organizational health— founder's syndrome, searching for financial security, and taking donors for granted.

$20 / 160 pages

Grassroots Fundraising Journal

Bi-monthly journal that keeps you up-to-date on new fundraising techniques and issues. Learn how to increase your income and diversify your sources of funding using proven, practical strategies, including special events, direct mail, major donor programs, membership campaigns and more.

6 issues/year; $32

The Board of Directors & Getting Major Gifts

Two reprint collections from the *Grassroots Fundraising Journal* on issues central to successful fundraising: how to create a steady income through a Major Gifts Program and how to develop an effective — and fundraising — Board of Directors.

$12 each BD: 36 pages / GMG: 40 pages

Cómo Recaudar Fondos en su Comunidad

An introduction to the most common and successful fundraising strategies in 14 of the best articles from the *Grassroots Fundraising Journal*. Small organizations can put these strategies to use immediately. This reprint collection in Spanish only.

$12 / 40 pages

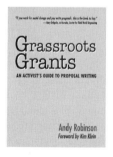

Grassroots Grants
BY ANDY ROBINSON

A guide on what it takes to win grants for social justice: the pros and cons of grant-seeking, building your proposal piece by piece, using your grant proposal as an organizing plan, and developing relationships with foundation staff.

$25 / 194 pages

Inspired Philanthropy
BY TRACY GARY & MELISSA KOHNER

A workbook on creating a personal giving plan to match your values with your giving. Clear text and substantive exercises create a giving plan that will make your charitable giving—large or small—catalytic.

$20 / 128 pages

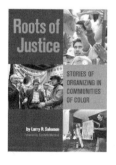

Roots of Justice: Stories of Organizing in Communities of Color
BY LARRY SALOMON

Recaptures some of the nearly forgotten histories of communities of color. These are the stories of people who fought back against exploitation and injustice— and won. Read how, through organizing, ordinary people have made extraordinary contributions to change society.

$15 / 160 pages

Making Policy / Making Change: How Communities are Taking Law into Their Own Hands
BY MAKANI N. THEMBA

Learn how activists are influencing policymaking to benefit their communities. Includes many examples of successful grassroots campaigns.

"This book has big concepts, insightful analysis, tested strategies and tactics."
—LAWRENCE WALLACK, UC BERKELEY

$19 / 160 pages

To order, call us toll free at (888) 458-8588 or use the order form on the next page

In the San Francisco Bay Area, please call (510) 596-8160

See all our publications at www.chardonpress.com

Bulk discounts available!

 CHARDON PRESS 3781 Broadway, Oakland, CA 94611 • FAX: (510) 596-8822 • E-MAIL: chardon@chardonpress.com

Hartford Public Library
500 Main Street
Hartford, CT 06103-3075

Order below or visit us online at www.chardonpress.com

ORDER HERE (Subscribe to the *Grassroots Fundraising Journal* separately in box below.)

TITLE	UNIT PRICE	QUANTITY	TOTAL
	SUBTOTAL		

TAKE A DISCOUNT: 5–9 copies of any one title: take **20%** off that title's total
10 or more copies of any one title: take **40%** off that title's total

less discount

TOTAL

SUBSCRIBE TO THE
GRASSROOTS FUNDRAISING JOURNAL

United States
☐ 1 year @ $32 _____
☐ 2 years @ $58 _____

Canada, Mexico and Overseas
☐ 1 year @ $39 _____
☐ 2 years @ $65 _____

Please allow 6 weeks for new subscriptions. There is no tax or shipping charges for subscriptions.

☐ Please send me a free Chardon Press Catalog.

CREDIT CARD ORDERS

☐ MasterCard ☐ Visa ☐ Discover ☐ Amex
Card #: _____
Exp. date: _____
Signature: _____

SHIPPING & HANDLING CHARGES

ORDER TOTALS	SHIPPING FEE
$ 5.00 – 10.00	$ 2.00
$ 10.01 – 25.00	$ 4.00
$ 25.01 – 50.00	$ 6.00
$ 50.01 – 75.00	$ 8.00
$ 75.01 –100.00	$10.00
$100.01 or more	**10% of order**

Books normally shipped book rate; large orders shipped UPS Ground. Please allow 2–4 weeks for delivery.

☐ 3 Day Select . . . . fee at left × 2
☐ 2nd Day Air . . . . fee at left × 3
☐ Overnight . . . . fee at left × 4
☐ Priority Mail flat
(single book order only) $5
☐ International Air Mail
(including Canada & Mexico) . . . . . fee at left × 2
Payment in U.S. dollars only.

TOTAL YOUR ORDER HERE

Subtotal from *ORDER HERE* box $ _____
In CA add 8.25% sales tax $ _____
Shipping & Handling (see chart above) $ _____
Grassroots Fundraising Journal Subscription $ _____
TOTAL AMOUNT ENCLOSED: $ _____

Name _____
Organization _____
Address _____
City/State/Zip _____
If we have questions about your order, should we reach you by:
☐ Phone _____ OR ☐ E-mail _____

PAYABLE TO CHARDON PRESS: 3781 Broadway • Oakland, CA 94611
PHONE: (888) 458-8588 • **IN SF BAY AREA:** (510) 596-8160 • **FAX:** (510) 596-8822 • **E-MAIL:** chardon@chardonpress.com